Career Discoveries
Career Planning Workbook
Second Edition

Rick Roberts
Vivian Senior
University of North Florida

Kendall Hunt
publishing company

Front and back cover designed by Jeremy Thomas.

Cover image © Shutterstock, Inc.

www.kendallhunt.com
Send all inquiries to:
4050 Westmark Drive
Dubuque, IA 52004-1840

Printed in the United States of America
10 9 8 7 6 5 4 3 2

CONTENTS

Chapter 10: You Don't Get a Second Chance to Make a Good First Impression: Interviewing 247

Chapter 11: Finding Your Dream Job: Job Search Strategies 277

Career Planning and You

CHAPTER

CHAPTER QUEST

At the end of this chapter you should be able to:

- Understand how various factors influence career planning

- State career planning factors specific to you

- Determine the information you are lacking

- Discover your starting point within the career planning process

CAREER

© Feng Yu, 2009. Used under license from Shutterstock, Inc.

Charting Your Course

The Career Planning Process

From the moment you enter college or a university, you are immediately and consistently asked, "What's your major?" or "What are your career goals?" You either respond with clear-cut ideas and aspirations or rattle off something so as to not appear unfocused or confused. Depending on where you feel you are in the career planning process, you may find certain aspects of this workbook to be more beneficial than others.

If your career goals are clear, you might feel that you will greatly benefit from many of the latter chapters of this book regarding career exploration, employability skills, and job hunting. However, remain tuned in, just to make sure you have made the best choice. Since you are using this workbook, it is quite possible that you are still discovering the best career path to pursue. Have you ever considered the underlying reason for your struggle?

Are you feeling pressure from your parents or significant other?
Are you putting pressure on yourself to choose a certain type of major or career?
Are you afraid of being stuck for life with the decisions you make now?
Are you concerned about not being able to live the type of lifestyle you desire?
Are your career options too broad?
Are your career options too narrow?
Are you concerned about how you will finance your education?
Are you skeptical about your ability to pass certain courses?
Are you concerned about being able to find a job when you graduate?

This list of legitimate concerns could go on and on. Having a list of concerns is normal, and what's most important are the steps you take to resolve your concerns by engaging in effective career planning. Career planning is an intricate process of discovery and activities that lead to meaningful educational and career goals. The career planning process typically looks like the following:

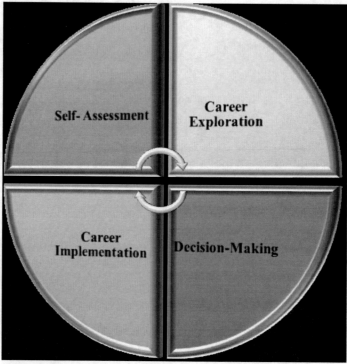

Diagram 1.1 The Career Planning Process

© ImageTeam, 2009. Used under license from Shutterstock, Inc.

Phase 1: Self-Assessment

Explore your interests, personality, skills, and values in relation to suitable majors and careers. Career Counselors are available to assist you in clarifying those factors significant to you. In some cases, supplemental tools such as career assessments are used. These tools are not magical in terms of pinpointing your career, and they are not always necessary. However, career assessments have proven to be a quick and easy way to organize information about you. Learn more about yourself by discovering key factors about your background, interests, personality, skills, and values. It is important to remember that all of these factors are equally important, so take the necessary time to fully evaluate each area. At some point during this phase, it may become necessary to prioritize as a strategy for narrowing your options to a workable list of tangible career options. Your Career Counselor will help you decide between various self-assessment activities and resources. Discovering your passion, feeling connected, and looking forward to class projects or job tasks are good indications that you know yourself well in relation to majors and careers. The desired end result of this phase is discovering a target list of majors and careers to further explore.

EXERCISE 1.1
Self-Evaluation

What do you already know about yourself in relation to the significant factors of the self-assessment phase? List your thoughts and ideas for each of the areas listed below.

TASK 1: INTERESTS
What do you like or enjoy? Which academic subjects do you enjoy the most and the least?

_____

_____

_____

_____

_____

TASK 2: PERSONALITY
How would you or other people typically describe you?

_____

_____

_____

_____

_____

TASK 3: VALUES
What do you think will make and keep you happy and satisfied personally and professionally?

_____

_____

_____

_____

_____

TASK 4: ABILITIES/SKILLS
What are you good at doing? What are your challenges or areas for improvement?

_____

_____

_____

_____

© Yuri Arcurs, 2009. Used under license from Shutterstock, Inc.

Phase 2: Career Exploration

Research majors, career options, and job market data using various career resources and activities.   When entering this phase, you should have a pretty good idea of majors and careers that may be a good fit for you. However, your list may be broad and diverse. Use the process of elimination and narrow your options further by taking the time to research careers. Engaging in different exploration activities will help you discover the wide variety of career options available, while learning the specifics about job responsibilities and qualifications. UNF Career Services houses a Career Library that provides a wide variety of books and resources to help you discover pertinent facts and details about careers and majors. A comprehensive website is also available at www.unf.edu/dept/cdc.

© Pinon Road, 2009. Used under license from Shutterstock, Inc.

Phase 3: Decision-Making

Learn and apply the necessary skills for information integration and smart, informed decision-making.   During this phase, you are now better able to process information gained from the first two phases. Processing this type of knowledge allows you to eliminate options that conflict with your needs and preferences, while focusing on options that are a good fit. Remember, your career "fit" must also fit into the realities of the world of work. The information and trends you discover in the self-assessment and career exploration phases will work to your advantage in determining where you are most compatible and competitive with employment demands. This allows you to discover and target key skill areas to develop in order to acquire the qualifications future employers desire in job applicants. Make sure that you have fully researched all potential options, because decisions based solely on initial perceptions could result in prematurely eliminating good opportunities or selecting unrealistic options. Even after all of the discovering and processing, you may still wonder if you are making the right choice. While there is never a 100% guarantee, you can emerge from this process with a smart choice.

Phase 4: Career Implementation

Develop and carry out an action plan for ensuring career planning success.   During your college career, you should engage in active knowledge and skill building through various career planning and work experience programs and activities. Work experi-

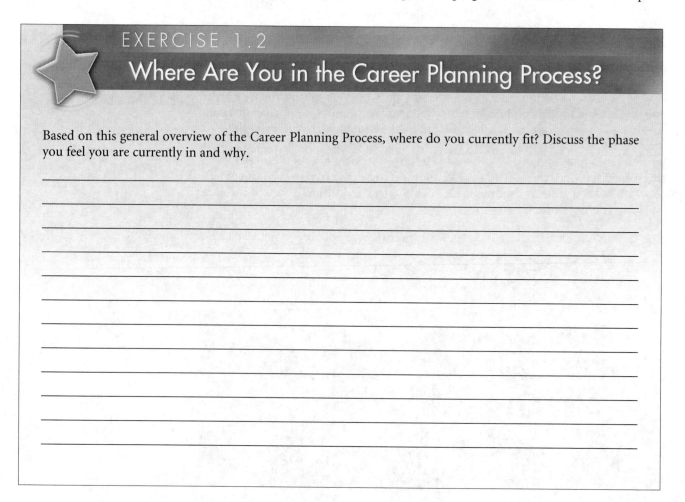

EXERCISE 1.2

Where Are You in the Career Planning Process?

Based on this general overview of the Career Planning Process, where do you currently fit? Discuss the phase you feel you are currently in and why.

_____

_____

_____

_____

_____

_____

_____

_____

_____

_____

_____

ences allow you to "test the water" and explore careers from a hands-on perspective. You are then better able to confirm career interests and clarify your work values while building valuable skills (i.e., gaining work experience and building skills and knowledge for resume writing, networking, and job interviewing).

As you may notice in Diagram 1.1, activities in the implementation process may lead back to self-assessment if you discover that your initial choice was not the best fit for you. This reengagement in the self-assessment phase does not necessarily mean that you must change your major or return to college if you have already graduated: it may simply mean that you need to discover other career options available to you. Remember, career planning is a process of discovering information about yourself, careers, and the world of work. Chapters 2 and 3 will introduce you to career planning theories that influence and supplement this process. The theories presented will help you establish critical self-awareness factors resulting in an increased sense of competence and confidence. Starting this process now will help you at the various points throughout life where you will have to make and evaluate decisions concerning your career goals.

Some final points to remember regarding the career planning process:

- The world of work is constantly changing, so stay abreast of employment trends.
- You need to be proactive and take charge of your career future.
- You are the best person to determine which major or career path is best for you.

The career planning process may seem tedious. This is normal, as it takes time to evaluate and make important life decisions. However, you should remember that while career planning is a lifelong process, your current career goals are not lifelong decisions. Your journey through life will expose you to many different experiences in college and in employment settings that will help you continuously revaluate your career goals.

DID YOU KNOW?

UNF Career Services offers the **Career Discoveries Program**. This series of programs and services is targeted to students needing assistance with exploring career options or choosing a major. The following activities and events are designed to help you discover your career path:

Career Counseling   Explore-A-Major Fair
Career Assessments   Career Myths & Urban Legends
Choosing a Major Workshop   Peer Advising
Career Planning Tips & Strategies   Career Library

Visit the Career Services website for more information at www.unf.edu/dept/cdc.

© Damla AYZEREN., 2009. Used under license from Shutterstock, Inc.

Your Career Quest

This practical guide is designed to help you discover the best path to career planning success. This success is contingent on many factors, including self-motivation, available resources, and job market trends. A good starting point is to reflect on where you are in the career planning process and then develop a good plan of action. At this stage, it is not necessary to map out the entire plan; instead, keep your focus on the next best step. Compiling a comprehensive list of questions, concerns, and issues is a great starting point for establishing your Career Quest, your personal journey toward career success.

One of the most common reasons students struggle with career planning is lack of information. Students typically identify three main areas where they lack information: college awareness, career awareness, and self-awareness. It is important to evaluate and clarify your information needs. What do you already know? What do you need to discover? All three topics are the driving force of this workbook, as introduced in the career planning process. It is important to address them now as a means to discover the best starting point for you.

College Awareness

Do you find that much of your confusion regarding career planning revolves around educational topics? During career counseling sessions, students often clearly state their career goals, but are not sure which major is the best route to pursue. Students are also often confused by the terminology used in colleges and universities (i.e., undergraduate studies vs. graduate studies, majors vs. minors, tracks vs. core curriculum). Many of these concerns are best addressed by a visit to an Academic Advisor.

Career Awareness

Are you clear about the major you wish to pursue, but concerned about the availability of career options? This is a very common concern among students. Another common concern is whether you will enjoy the career you will eventually select.

EXERCISE 1.3
What Concerns You the Most?

What are your current questions and concerns regarding careers and the world of work? What concerns you the most?

_____
_____
_____
_____
_____
_____
_____
_____
_____
_____
_____

Self-Awareness

The self-assessment phase of career planning and all of its significant factors will be addressed throughout this workbook. The aim is to help you become more self-aware in relation to careers and the world of work. However, another key element of self-awareness is to identify how past and current life factors might influence how you make decisions.

© Monkey Business Images, 2009. Used under license from Shutterstock, Inc.

Personal and External Influences

As you continue on your journey to discover your career path, you will encounter opportunities and obstacles. The opportunities include positive experiences that allow you to become more self-aware in relation to viable career options and to increase your college and career awareness. However, you should also consider potential personal and external influences that may interfere with a successful career planning process. These hurdles or obstacles appear in many forms, and identifying their presence allows you to develop strategies to overcome them.

Personal Influences

Opportunities
Supportive family and friends
Self-motivation
High academic ability
Coping skills
Positive outlook on life

Obstacles
Anxiety about making the wrong choice
Low self-esteem
Low confidence regarding academic ability
Poor study habits
Procrastination

External Influences

Opportunities
Career Counseling
Networking
Information interviews
Work experience while in college
Prior educational or work experience

Obstacles
Personal finances for college education
Economic trends
Job market trends and outlook
Family priorities/Competing life roles
Societal expectations

What are some thoughts or factors that automatically come to mind as important considerations? Who or what influences your decisions? List potential barriers and positive contributions to your career planning process.

EXERCISE 1.4
Your Personal and External Influences

PERSONAL INFLUENCES

Opportunities   Obstacles

_____

_____

_____

_____

_____

_____

_____

_____

EXTERNAL INFLUENCES

Opportunities   Obstacles

_____

_____

_____

_____

_____

_____

_____

_____

© Yuganov Konstantin, 2009. Used under license from Shutterstock, Inc.

Develop the Right Mindset for Success

Your success within the career planning process is contingent on your attitude and belief system. Elements of the career planning process are designed to increase your level of competence regarding self-awareness, college awareness, and career awareness. This process should give you an increased sense of competence. However, negative thinking or a passive approach could thwart your efforts. A key consideration is exploring whether you are undecided or indecisive. Feeling undecided could simply mean that you have not started the process and lack critical information. However, indecisiveness relates to the inability to decide even with adequate information and maturity. The inability to select a career path or make other key life decisions may stem from many factors. How committed are you to this process? What did you discover in Exercise 1.4 that may impact your beliefs about your ability to be successful? You will only be as successful as you think you will be.

Throughout the career planning process and life in general, you will be faced with making many decisions. It is important to learn how to integrate and process information by determining which resources to use, weighing pros and cons, calculating risks and consequences, and problem-solving for potential obstacles.

Allow the contents of this workbook to guide you through this journey of discovering the best path for you.

EXERCISE 1.5

Your Career Quest

Considering all of the topics covered in this chapter, provide a summary of the factors you discovered to be most significant for you. Do you feel you have a dilemma, or major issues, or simply a detailed list of questions and concerns? Did you notice any patterns? Be honest with yourself and be as specific as possible. At the end of your summary, describe what you feel to be the best starting point for your Career Quest.

_____

_____

_____

_____

_____

_____

_____

_____

_____

_____

Exercise 1.6: How Do Career Development Theories Relate To You?

Name _____   Date _____

Theories provide plausible explanations for observed facts or concepts and guide our understanding of complex issues. Just as there are many theories about weight loss, student learning styles, and evolution, several researchers have also proposed theories to explain the selection of a career. The contributions of these theorists relate to the Career Planning Process. Brief descriptions of the views of three theorists are given below. React to each and how you think it applies to your life.

Anne Roe believed career choice was heavily influenced by factors related to childhood and home environment. For example, if your childhood home life encouraged creativity and ingenuity, then you might be more likely to choose a career in the arts field. Her theory influenced the inclusion of personality as a significant self-assessment factor.

_____

_____

_____

_____

_____

Eli Ginzberg focused on advancement through developmental stages, seeing career development as a long-term process. As you learn more about yourself and the world of work, you will make the necessary adjustments between your initial ideal preferences and what's actually realistic or practical.

_____

_____

_____

_____

_____

Donald Super emphasized focusing on how you view yourself and your belief system in regard to interests and abilities. Over time, internal and external factors will influence the development of your self-knowledge, which will eventually reveal a characteristic pattern that allows you to connect with viable career options.

_____

_____

_____

_____

_____

Chapter 1: Key Discoveries

- Career planning is a process of discoveries that include self-assessment, career exploration, decision-making, and career implementation.
- Career assessments are supplemental tools for career counseling that are quick and easy ways to organize information about you.
- The self-assessment phase of career planning involves an in-depth exploration of your interests, values, skills, personality traits, and internal and external influences.
- Students often lack information regarding three main areas: college awareness, career awareness, and self-awareness.
- Personal and external influences on career planning include both opportunities and obstacles.
- Your career planning success is contingent on your attitude and belief system.

Career Connections: Internet Links

- http://www.unf.edu/dept/cdc/ (*UNF Career Services*)
- http://www.facts.org (*Florida Choices Planner*)
- http://www.myplan.com (*My Plan*)
- http://careerplanning.about.com/cs/choosingacareer/a/cp_process.htm (*About.com: Career Planning*)

Getting to Know You . . .

Name _____   Date _____

Group Discussion

- Break into groups of two or three with people you don't already know or are not well acquainted with.

- Talk about yourselves (i.e., name, major or career interests, class level, general interests, hobbies, unique info).

- Write at least three facts that are unique about someone else in the blue circle—*take a few notes as each person talks.*

- Decide on ways that you are all alike and write those things in the intersecting area of the diagram.

- Write things you would like us to know to understand you better as a class member in the red circle.

Class Discussion (15–20 minutes)

- Introduce each other to the class with the unique facts.

- What did you have in common with your group?

- What helps us understand you better as a class member?

- What did you relate to from other groups?

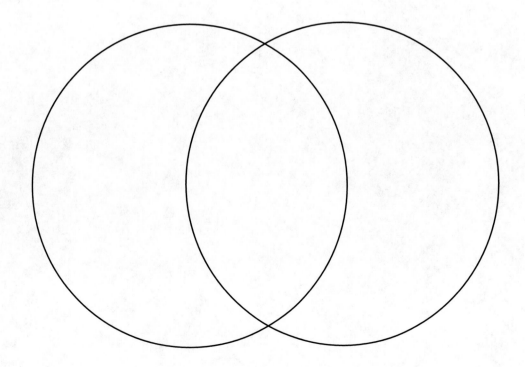

Name _____ Date _____

Your Father's Father
(Your Grandfather)

Highest Degree _____

Major: _____

Occupation: _____

Employer: _____

Your Father's Mother
(Your Grandmother)

Highest Degree _____

Major: _____

Occupation: _____

Employer: _____

Your Father

Highest Degree: _____

Major: _____

Occupation: _____

Employer: _____

Your Mother's Father
(Your Grandfather)

Highest Degree: _____

Major: _____

Occupation: _____

Employer: _____

Your Mother's Mother
(Your Grandmother)

Highest Degree: _____

Major: _____

Occupation: _____

Employer: _____

Your Mother

Highest Degree: _____

Major: _____

Occupation: _____

Employer: _____

Your Name: _____ Your Interests:

CHAPTER

2

CHAPTER QUEST

Read to answer these key questions:

• What are my interests?

• What lifestyle do I prefer?

• How do my interests relate to possible careers?

• What are my values?

• How do I put my values into action?

© Kurhan, 2009. Used under license from Shutterstock, Inc.

Exploring Interests and Values

From *College and Career Success*, Fourth Edition by Marsha Fralick. Copyright © 2008 Kendall Hunt Publishing Company. Reprinted by permission.

Holland's Basic Categories of Career Interests

- Realistic
- Investigative
- Artistic
- Social
- Enterprising
- Conventional

Becoming aware of your interests and values will increase self-understanding and help you to make good decisions about your college major and future career. Interests and values are also important considerations in thinking about your preferred lifestyle.

© Robyn Mackenzie, 2009. Used under license from Shutterstock, Inc.

Using Interests to Choose a Career

Interests are simply what a person likes to do. Interests are a result of many factors, including personality, family life, values, and the environment. Knowing about your interests is helpful in planning a satisfying career. By studying people who are satisfied with their careers, psychologists have been able to help people choose careers based on their interests. John L. Holland proposed one of the most widely used theories of career development. He described six basic categories of occupational interests that are widely used today in career counseling: realistic, investigative, artistic, social, enterprising, and conventional.[1] As you read the descriptions below, think about which occupational areas you prefer.

Realistic Persons

- Enjoy working with tools, machines, and equipment
- Work outdoors with animals, machines, or nature
- Prefer active and adventurous activities
- Like jobs that produce concrete results, such as fixing, building, and repairing
- Have good mechanical abilities
- Are employed in manufacturing, construction, transportation, and engineering

Investigative Persons

- Have a strong interest in science
- Work with abstract theories, analyze data, and solve problems
- Work independently doing research and analysis
- Are analytical, curious, original, and creative
- Have good skills in mathematics and science
- Are employed in science or laboratory work

Artistic Persons

- Enjoy visual arts, music, drama, or writing
- Are creative and value self-expression
- Appreciate beauty and aesthetic qualities
- Work in unstructured and flexible environments
- Have artistic talent
- Work in museums, theaters, concert halls, advertising, and other artistic careers

Social Persons

*   Like to work with people
*   Enjoy helping, nurturing, and caring for others
*   Have social, communication, and teaching skills
*   Work with people through leading, directing, or persuading
*   Are often humanistic, idealistic, kind, and understanding
*   Work in schools, social services, religious occupations, health care, and mental health facilities

Enterprising Persons

*   Like to persuade, lead, or supervise others
*   Have skills in selling and communication
*   Work to enhance organizational goals and economic success
*   Seek positions of leadership, status, and power
*   Are often ambitious, sociable, adventuresome, energetic, and risk-taking
*   Are employed in business, government, retail, and wholesale firms and in politics

Conventional Persons

*   Enjoy activities involving organization, data systems, detail, and accuracy
*   Like mathematics, accounting, and finance
*   Are efficient, organized, and patient
*   Do work involving financial analysis, operating office machines, keeping financial and office records, and writing business reports
*   Prefer structured organizations
*   Work in business, large corporations, accounting, quality control, and financial institutions

Holland arranged these interests on a hexagon that shows the relationship of the interests to one another. He notes that most people are not just one type but rather a combination of types. Types that are close to each other on the hexagon are likely to have interests in common. For example, a person who is social is likely to have some artistic interests and some enterprising interests. Interests on opposite points of the hexagon are very different. For example, artistic and conventional types are opposites. Artistic types prefer freedom to be creative; conventional types prefer structure and order.

ACTIVITY 2.1
Learn about Your Interests

Place a checkmark next to the items in each list that are interesting to you. Keep a positive attitude when thinking about your interests. You do not need to know how to do these activities or even have the opportunity to do them to select items that are interesting to you. When you are finished with each section, tally the number of checkmarks in each area. Sample job titles for each area of interest are included.[2] Underline any jobs that appeal to you.

REALISTIC (R)

I am interested in

_____ Operating or designing heavy equipment

_____ Fixing, building, or repairing

_____ Seeing the concrete results of my work

_____ Using tools on the job

_____ Mechanical, construction, or repair occupations

_____ Nature and the outdoors

_____ Doing physical activities

_____ Adventurous activities (skydiving, auto racing, mountain climbing)

_____ Hunting, fishing, camping, or rock climbing

_____ Action rather than thought

_____ Having a job where I can dress casually

_____ Reading magazines about cars, airplanes, boats, or sports

© maga, 2009. Used under license from Shutterstock, Inc.

R =

MATCHING JOB TITLES

Auto mechanic
Gardener/groundskeeper
Plumber
Police officer

Rancher
Electrician
Engineer
Forester
Machinist
Radiologic technologist

Vocational agriculture teacher
Industrial arts teacher
Building contractor
Horticultural worker
Military officer
Cabinetmaker

INVESTIGATIVE (I)

I am interested in

_____ Science and mathematics

_____ Exploring new facts and theories

_____ Academic and research environments

_____ Getting an advanced degree

_____ Solving problems through thinking

_____ Doing scientific or research work

_____ Computers

_____ Activities that require learning complex principles (skiing, sailing, scuba diving, chess)

_____ Working with abstract tasks, analyzing and interpreting data

_____ Working independently on a scientific or technical project

_____ Conducting research

_____ Original and creative ways to use technology to solve problems

© Tomasz Trojanowski, 2009. Used under license from Shutterstock, Inc.

I =

MATCHING JOB TITLES

College professor	Dentist	Veterinarian
Physician	Medical technician	Geologist
Psychologist	Optometrist	Physicist
Pharmacist	Research and development	Science teacher
Chemist	manager	Medical technologist
Chiropractor	Respiratory therapist	

ARTISTIC (A)

I am interested in

_____ Art, music, drama, or writing

_____ Creating art (painting, sculpture, photography), or music

_____ Acting, performing, dancing, playing a musical instrument, designing or decorating

_____ Creative or imaginative work

_____ Going to concerts, theaters, museums, or libraries

_____ Collecting artwork or books

_____ Working independently on a creative project

_____ Beauty and aesthetic qualities

_____ Working in a studio, theater, or concert hall

_____ Doing creative work as a hobby

© AYAKOVLEVdotCOM, 2009. Used under license from Shutterstock, Inc.

_____ Reading magazines about art, music, drama, or writing

_____ Trying creative new ideas

A =

MATCHING JOB TITLES

Commercial artist
Fine artist
Musician
Reporter
Art teacher

Advertisement executive
Broadcaster
Technical writer
English teacher
Lawyer

Librarian
Architect
Photographer
Medical illustrator
Corporate trainer

SOCIAL (S)

I am interested in

_____ Working with people

_____ Helping or caring for others

_____ Talking about feelings and sharing personal concerns

_____ Teaching and explaining

_____ Guiding and facilitating

_____ Selecting and training

_____ Informing and organizing

_____ Relationships with people

_____ Solving people problems

_____ Listening to personal concerns

_____ Improving the welfare of others

_____ Working in a school, mental health, or social services environment

© Lisa F. Young, 2009. Used under license from Shutterstock, Inc.

S =

MATCHING JOB TITLES

Child care provider
Elementary school teacher
Public health nurse
Community service director
High school counselor

Home economics teacher
Parks and recreation coordinator
Physical education teacher
Student personnel worker
Occupational therapist
Social worker

Speech pathologist
Social science teacher
Nurse
Agricultural extension agent
Physical therapist

ENTERPRISING (E)

I am interested in

_____ Selling and purchasing

_____ Positions of leadership, power, and status

_____ Being financially successful

_____ Finances and money

_____ Politics and political activities

_____ Managing people and projects

_____ Fund-raising

_____ Setting goals and achieving them

_____ Entertaining and socializing

_____ Attending conventions

_____ Investing money to make a profit

_____ Working in a business or financial environment

E =

© R. Gino Santa Maria, 2009. Used under license from Shutterstock, Inc.

MATCHING JOB TITLES

Life insurance agent
Realtor
Salesperson
Buyer
Store manager

Marketing executive
Sales manager
Purchasing agent
Restaurant manager
Travel agent

Dental hygienist
Flight attendant
Florist

CONVENTIONAL (C)

I am interested in

_____ Working with data

_____ Doing work that is detailed and accurate

_____ Accounting or investment management

_____ Working in an organized environment

_____ Doing a financial analysis

_____ Mathematics

_____ Operation of office machines

_____ Money and finances

_____ Organizing an office

_____ Keeping records and bookkeeping

© Seonphoto, 2009. Used under license from Shutterstock, Inc.

_____ Writing business reports

_____ Efficiency and organization

C = [   ]

MATCHING JOB TITLES

Bookkeeper	Administrative assistant	Dental assistant
Medical records technician	Banker	Business education teacher
Clerical worker	Certified public accountant	Food service manager
Proofreader	Credit manager	Nursing home administrator
Accountant	Store salesperson	Secretary

JOURNAL ENTRY #1

What are your top three interest areas (realistic, investigative, artistic, social, enterprising, conventional)? List some careers that match each interest area.

© Gelpi, 2009. Used under license from Shutterstock, Inc.

Interests and Lifestyle

Our occupational interests determine what we study and the kind of occupations we choose. While study and work form the basis of our lifestyle, there are other important components. What we choose to do for fun and relaxation helps us to be refreshed and keeps life interesting. Another component of a balanced lifestyle is time spent with friends and family. It is important to choose work that allows you to have the resources and time to lead a balanced lifestyle with all of these components. A balanced lifestyle has been described as a triangle with work and study forming the base, leisure and recreation forming one side and kinship and friendship forming the other side.

Give some thought to the kind of lifestyle you prefer. Think about balancing your work, leisure, and social activities.

JOURNAL ENTRY #2

Visualize your ideal lifestyle. How would you balance work, study, leisure, and social life?

QUIZ
Interests

Test what you have learned by selecting the correct answer to the following questions.

1. Realistic people are likely to choose a career in

   a. construction or engineering
   b. accounting or real estate
   c. financial investments or banking

2. Investigative people are likely to choose a career in

   a. art or music
   b. teaching or social work
   c. science or laboratory work

3. Enterprising people are likely to choose a career in

   a. computer programming or accounting
   b. business management or government
   c. health care or social services

4. Conventional people are likely to choose a career in

   a. health care or social services
   b. financial investments or banking
   c. manufacturing or transportation

5. Social types generally

   a. enjoy working with tools and machines
   b. are humanistic and idealistic
   c. have skills in selling and communication

How did you do on the quiz? Check your answers: 1. a, 2. c, 3. b, 4. b, 5. b

Using Values to Make Important Life Decisions

Values are what we think is important and what we feel is right and good. Values come from many sources, including our parents, friends, the media, our religious background, our culture, our society, and the historical time in which we live. Our values make us different and unique individuals. Knowing our values helps us to make good decisions about work and life. For example, consider a situation in which a person is offered a high-paying job that involves a high degree of responsibility and a lot of stress. If the person values challenge and excitement and views stress as a motiva-

© Glenda M. Powers, 2009. Used under license from Shutterstock, Inc.

© Stephen Coburn, 2009. Used under license from Shutterstock, Inc.

tor, the chances are that it would be a good decision to take the job. If the person values peace of mind and has a difficult time coping with stress, it might be better to forgo the higher income and maintain quality of life. Making decisions consistent with our values is one of the keys to happiness and success.

Values and needs are closely related. Humanistic psychologist Abraham Maslow[4] theorized that we adopt certain values to fulfill psychological or physical needs. He described needs and values in terms of a pyramid in which needs are organized in a hierarchy arranged from the most basic to the most complex and personal. We cannot move to the next higher level until lower-level needs are met. These needs, listed in order from most basic to most complex can be defined as follows:

Biological needs. Basic needs for survival including food, water, air, and clothing

Safety needs. Basic needs for shelter and a safe and predictable environment

Love and belongingness. Includes love, respect, and caring from our family and friends

Self-esteem. Feeling good about yourself and having confidence in your abilities

Intellectual. Having the knowledge and understanding needed for survival

Aesthetic. Having an appreciation of beauty

Self-actualization. Developing and reaching your fullest potential, enabling you to contribute to society

An example of a practical application of this theory is finding a solution for homeless people in society. It is easy to say that they should just go get a job. Applying Maslow's hierarchy of needs, we would say that the first step in helping the homeless is to meet their biological needs. Before they can worry about employment, they need food, water, and clothing. Next they need shelter so they have a safe and predictable environment. They need to know that people care about them so they can develop self-esteem. Once people have self-esteem and confidence, they can begin to be trained and educated. Once they have skills, they can become employed and enjoy the good life, appreciate beauty, and reach their potential. A person who is employed pays taxes and may do volunteer work to contribute to society.

Self-actualization is another word for success. It means knowing about and using your talents to fulfill your potential. It means being healthy and creative. It is being the best that you can be. Abraham Maslow said, "We may still often (if not always) expect that a new discontent and restlessness will soon develop, unless the individual is doing what he's fitted for. A musician must make music, an artist must paint, a poet must write, if he's to be ultimately at peace. What a person can be, he must be. This need we call self-actualization."[5]

We are all ultimately aiming for self-actualization. Here are some characteristics of the self-actualized person:

- Feels secure, loved, respected, and makes a connection with others
- Values self and others
- Is independent
- Can make decisions and accept responsibility
- Appreciates other people and cares for the world
- Is open to new ideas

- Resists conformity
- Has little need for status symbols
- Is emotionally balanced
- Is not burdened with anxiety, guilt, or shame
- Treats others with respect
- Feels at one with humankind
- Has deep and caring relationships
- Can look at life with a sense of humor
- Is creative, passionate, and enjoys life
- Takes time for self-renewal and relaxation
- Has strong values and a philosophy of life

© Cheryl Casey, 2009. Used under license from Shutterstock, Inc.

This sounds great, but may be difficult. Remember that we are always on the road to self-actualization. Life is about growing and changing. If we do not grow and change, life becomes boring. It all begins with basic needs for survival. Once we have the basic needs for survival, we can focus on wants or desires (the possibilities). We can't have everything, so we determine what is important or what we value the most. Knowing what we value helps us to make good decisions about life goals. In setting our goals, we put values into practice. Meeting the challenges of our lives and accomplishing our goals leads to satisfaction and happiness. The process looks like this:

Needs ⟶ Wants ⟶ Values ⟶
Meet basic survival needs. What is possible? What is important?

Decisions ⟶ Goals ⟶ Accomplish goals
Make choices based on values. Decide on life goals. Become self-actualized.

JOURNAL ENTRY #3
Picture yourself as a self-actualized person. Describe what life would be like.

ACTIVITY 2.2
Values Checklist

Assessing Your Personal Values

Use the following checklist to begin to think about what values are important to you.
Place a checkmark next to any value that is important to you. There are no right or wrong answers. If you think of other values that are important to you, add them to the bottom of the list.

_____ Having financial security
_____ Making a contribution to humankind
_____ Being a good parent
_____ Being honest
_____ Acquiring wealth
_____ Being a wise person
_____ Becoming an educated person
_____ Believing in a higher power (God)
_____ Preserving civil rights
_____ Never being bored
_____ Enjoying life and having fun
_____ Making something out of my life
_____ Being an ethical person
_____ Feeling safe and secure
_____ Having a good marriage
_____ Having good friends
_____ Having social status
_____ Being patriotic
_____ Having power
_____ Having good morals
_____ Being creative
_____ Having control over my life
_____ Growing and developing
_____ Feeling competent
_____ Feeling relaxed
_____ Having prestige
_____ Improving society
_____ Having good mental health
_____ Being a good athlete
_____ Enjoying the present moment
_____ Maintaining peace of mind

_____ Having good family relationships
_____ Preserving the environment
_____ Having the respect of others
_____ Becoming famous
_____ Happiness
_____ Freedom and independence
_____ Common sense
_____ Having pride in my culture
_____ Doing community service
_____ Achieving my goals in life
_____ Having adventures
_____ Having leisure time
_____ Having good health
_____ Being loyal
_____ Having a sense of accomplishment
_____ Participating in church activities
_____ Being physically fit
_____ Helping others
_____ Being a good person
_____ Having time to myself
_____ Loving and being loved
_____ Being physically attractive
_____ Achieving something important
_____ Accepting who I am
_____ Appreciating natural beauty
_____ Using my artistic talents
_____ Feeling good about myself
_____ Making a difference
_____ Other: _____
_____ Other: _____
_____ Other: _____

JOURNAL ENTRY #4
What is your most important value? Why is it important to you?

Act on Your Values

Values are what are most important to you; they are your highest principles. They provide the road map to your success and happiness. You will face important turning points along life's journey. Should I go to college? What will be my major? What career will I have? Who should I marry? What job should I take? Where shall I live? You can find good answers to these questions by being aware of your values and using them to make decisions and guide your actions. If your decisions follow your values, you can get what you want out of life.

The first step is knowing your values. You may need some time to think about your values and change them if they are not right for you. What values were you taught as a child? What values do you want to keep as an adult? Look around at people that you admire. What are their values? What values have you learned from your religion? Are these values important to you? Ask your friends about their values and share yours. Revise and rethink your values periodically. Make sure your values are your own and not necessarily values that someone has told you were important. When you begin to think about values, you can come up with many things that are important. The key is to find out which values are most important. In this way, when you are faced with a choice, you will not be confused. You will know what is most important to you.

Knowing about values is not enough. It is important to act consistently with your values and to follow them. For example, if people value health but continue to smoke, they are saying one thing but doing another. If they value family but spend all of their time at work, they are not acting consistently with their values. As a result, they might find that their family is gone and they have lost something that is really valuable.

Use your actions to question or reaffirm your values. Do you really value your health and family? If so, take action to preserve your good health and spend time with your family. It is necessary to periodically look at your patterns of behavior. Do you act out of habit or do you act according to what is important to you? Habits might need to be changed to get what you value most out of life.

© gabor2100, 2009. Used under license from Shutterstock, Inc.

In times of doubt and difficulty, your values can keep you going. If you truly value getting a college education, you can put in the effort to accomplish your goal. When you have doubts about whether you can be successful, examine your values again and remind yourself of why you are doing what you are doing. For example, if you value being an independent business entrepreneur, you will put in the effort to be successful. If you value being a good parent, you will find the patience and develop the skill to succeed. Reminding yourself of your values can help you to continue your commitment to accomplishing your goals.

By knowing your values and following them, you have a powerful tool for making decisions, taking action, and motivating yourself to be successful.

JOURNAL ENTRY #5

Write down your most important value. Write an intention statement about how you plan to act on this value. For example, my most important value is to maintain my good health. I intend to act on this value by eating right and exercising.

QUIZ
Values

Test what you have learned by selecting the correct answer to the following questions.

1. Values are

   a. What we find interesting
   b. What we find important
   c. What we find entertaining

2. Abraham Maslow described values as a

   a. Circle
   b. Pyramid
   c. Square

3. According to Maslow, our most basic needs are

   a. Social
   b. Biological
   c. Intellectual

4. According to Maslow, we are all aiming for

   a. Independence
   b. Wealth
   c. Self-actualization

5. Knowing what we value helps us to make good

   a. Wages
   b. Decisions
   c. Expenditures

How did you do on the quiz? Check your answers: 1. b, 2. b, 3. b, 4. c, 5. b

JOURNAL ENTRIES

Exploring Interests and Values

Go to http://www.collegesuccess1.com/ for Word files of the Journal Entries

Success over the Internet

Visit the *College Success website* at
http://www.collegesuccess1.com/

The *College Success Website* is continually updated with new topics and links to the material presented in this chapter. Topics include

- Occupations for realistic, investigative, artistic, social, enterprising, and conventional interests

- Holland's self-directed search
- Various self-assessments
- Being a self-actualized person

Contact your instructor if you have any problems in accessing the *College Success Website*.

Notes

1. John L. Holland, *Making Vocational Choices: A Theory of Careers* (Englewood Cliffs, NJ: Prentice-Hall, 1973).
2. Lenore W. Harmon, Jo-Ida C. Hansen, Fred H. Borgen, and Allen L. Hammer, *Strong Interest Inventory Applications and Technical Guide* (Stanford, CA: Stanford University Press, 1994).
3. The Lifestyle Triangle adapted with permission from NTL Institute, "Urban Middle-Class Lifestyles in Transition," by Paula Jean Miller and Gideon Sjoberg, p. 149, *Journal of Applied Behavioral Science*, Vol. 9, Nos. 2/3, copyright 1973.
4. Abraham Maslow, *Motivation and Personality* (New York: Harper and Row, 1970).
5. Maslow, *Motivation and Personality*, 91.

Name _____ Date _____

Knowing your values is important to making good decisions. Read the following scenarios and think about the values of the person described. Make a recommendation to answer the question posed in each case. You may want to do this exercise in a group with other students.

Scenario 1: What should be my major?

Shawn is 20 years old and has completed two years of college. He has been trying to decide whether to major in engineering or music. He has completed all of his general education requirements as well as several courses in music, math, and physics. As a child, Shawn was interested in science and dreamed of making new inventions. He always took things apart to see how they worked. Math was always easy for Shawn, and he received awards for achievement in science.

He also took part in band throughout his school years and learned to play several instruments. As a teenager, he had a garage band and became so interested in playing the piano that he spent two hours a day practicing. Shawn's dilemma was that he was becoming stressed out trying to do both majors and no longer had time to do well in both music and engineering. He also wanted to have time to get a part-time job in order to become more independent. Shawn's top five values are being independent and living on his own, having a secure future, doing interesting work, achieving something important, and being able to relax.

What are Shawn's values?

What major should Shawn consider? Why?

Scenario 2: Should I continue my education?

Maria is a married mother of two young boys ages five and seven and a part-time college student. Maria and her husband, Juan, are very proud of their Mexican heritage and value their marriage and family. They both think that it is important for Maria to spend time with the children. Maria learned to speak English as a second language and has made sure that her children speak both English and Spanish. While the children are in school, Maria has been attending college part-time with the goal of becoming a teacher's aide in a class for bilingual children. She has some experience as a teacher's aide and gets a great deal of satisfaction from helping the children.

Juan works in construction, and the family has sacrificed to come up with the money to pay for Maria to attend college. Maria has struggled to earn her associate's degree and is proud of her accomplishments. She values her education and wants her children to do well in school. Now Maria is considering continuing her education to earn the bachelor's degree so that she can become a teacher. She would enjoy having her own classroom, loves working with children, and would have a higher income as a teacher than she would as a teacher's aide. Maria's husband is concerned that she will spend too much time at college and will not be home for the children. He is also relieved that Maria has finished college and plans to work part-time to supplement the family income while the children are in school.

What are Maria's values? Should Maria continue her education?

Name _____ Date _____

Your instructor may ask you to do this exercise in class. In five minutes, see if you can make a list of twenty things that you like to do. To help you with this list, think about the following questions:

- What do you like to do for fun in the summer? fall? winter? spring?
- What do you like to do with your family? friends?
- What do you like to do on vacation?
- What do you like to do on a rainy day when you are home alone?
- What do you like to do to relax?
- What kinds of physical activities do you like?
- What are your hobbies?
- What do you like to do at school? at work?

_____ 1. _____
_____ 2. _____
_____ 3. _____
_____ 4. _____
_____ 5. _____
_____ 6. _____
_____ 7. _____
_____ 8. _____
_____ 9. _____
_____ 10. _____
_____ 11. _____
_____ 12. _____
_____ 13. _____
_____ 14. _____
_____ 15. _____
_____ 16. _____
_____ 17. _____
_____ 18. _____
_____ 19. _____
_____ 20. _____

Write one or more of these symbols to the left of each item.

$\quad$ **\$** $\qquad$ For activities that cost more than \$20 each time you do them

$\quad$ **P** $\qquad$ For things that you do with people

$\quad$ **I** $\qquad$ For things that you do by yourself

$\quad$ **T** $\qquad$ For activities that involve working with things (e.g., gardening, crafts, working on your car)

$\quad$ **D** $\qquad$ For activities that involve working with data (e.g., working with your computer, doing budgeting, filing, organizing)

$\quad$ **A** $\qquad$ For activities that involve some physical activity

$\quad$ **R** $\qquad$ For activities that involve risk or adventure (e.g., car racing, skydiving, skiing)

$\quad$ **MT** $\qquad$ For activities that you would like to have more time to do

$\quad$ **1–5** $\qquad$ For the five most important activities, with 1 being most important

After labeling the items in your list, answer the following lifestyle questions.

1. Look at the number of items with a \$. How important is money to your lifestyle? Do you need a high-paying occupation or could you take a job that pays less but offers great personal satisfaction?

2. Do you like to do things with people, things, or data? Can you see a pattern? Would you prefer to work with people or alone? Do you have the same preference for your leisure time?

3. Are you physically active? Do you enjoy risk and adventure?

4. Which items do you wish you had more time to do?

5. Look at the top five items that you selected. Why are they important to your lifestyle?

Name _____ Date _____

Look at the items you selected in the exercise, "Twenty Things You Like to Do." Separate them into the following categories and list them below

Leisure/Recreation	Study/Work	Kinship/Friendship

How balanced is your lifestyle? Do you need to add more activities in any of the categories?

In the future, my lifestyle will be . . .

Name _____   Date _____

Look back at your scores from the activity in this chapter titled "Learn about Your Interests." Rank the interest areas from 1 to 6 based on your scores, with 1 being the area you are most interested in.

_____ Realistic

_____ Investigative

_____ Artistic

_____ Social

_____ Enterprising

_____ Conventional

The areas that you ranked 1, 2, and 3 form a code that you can use to look up occupations that match your interests. For example, if A, R, and E are your first three choices, you can look up the code ARE in a career resource such as the *Occupations Finder** to find careers matching the artistic, realistic, and enterprising interests. Under this code, you would find occupations such as merchandise displayer, floral designer, pastry chef, and architect.

Write your interest code here:

The *Occupations Finder* is available in most college career centers. You can learn more about your interests and recommended occupations by taking the Strong Interest Inventory or other assessments, also available in most college career centers.

Using the *Occupations Finder*, or pages 258–262 in this chapter, the results of the Strong Interest Inventory or other assessments, list some careers that match your interest code above.

*John L. Holland, *The Occupations Finder* (Odessa, FL: Psychological Assessment Resources, 1996).

Name _____   Date _____

Look at the "Values Checklist" you completed on page 266 of this chapter. Choose the ten values most important to you and list them here.

_____   _____

_____   _____

_____   _____

_____   _____

_____   _____

Next, pick out the value that is most important and label it 1. Label your second most important value 2, and so on until you have picked out your top five values.

1. My most important value is_____. Why?

2. My second most important value is_____. Why?

3. My third most important value is _____. Why?

4. My fourth most important value is _____. Why?

5. My fifth most important value is _____. Why?

CHAPTER QUEST

At the end of this chapter you should be able to:

- Understand the different types of skills

- Realize the connection between skills and careers

- Understand how skills identification impacts career decisions

© Pete Saloutos, 2009. Used under license from Shutterstock, Inc.

Clarify Your Skills

Skills and Career Choice

In addition to interests and values, it is also important to appropriately assess your skills and abilities. Understanding your academic strengths and weaknesses are critical to determining a suitable major. Likewise, developing a keen awareness of your skills will assist you in determining the best career path. In the previous chapter, you were presented with assessments to assist in clarifying and prioritizing interests and values. This chapter will offer different ways to understand and assess skills. You may discover that your current skills match well with your career interests, or it may be necessary to develop a new set of skills through your major and work experiences during your college career.

Let's first establish a good working definition of skills. A skill is a natural or learned ability to perform a particular task with minimal time or energy. Unlike other factors of the self-assessment phase that may be relatively stable, the skills dimension can expand and increase with time, experience, and concentrated efforts in particular areas. A good starting point is to determine your natural or inborn abilities. What are some tasks you naturally perform well and automatically? Do people tend to provide positive feedback regarding a particular strength you possess? Compiling an inventory of your skills with supporting detail and information is an important activity for career planning and decision-making. This type of inventory will also prove extremely valuable when developing a resume and presenting yourself effectively in job interviews.

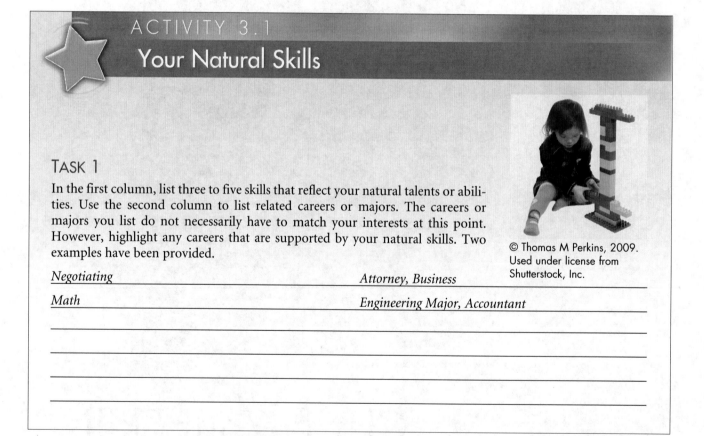

ACTIVITY 3.1
Your Natural Skills

TASK 1

In the first column, list three to five skills that reflect your natural talents or abilities. Use the second column to list related careers or majors. The careers or majors you list do not necessarily have to match your interests at this point. However, highlight any careers that are supported by your natural skills. Two examples have been provided.

© Thomas M Perkins, 2009. Used under license from Shutterstock, Inc.

Negotiating   *Attorney, Business*

Math   *Engineering Major, Accountant*

TASK 2

It is also helpful to inventory academic weaknesses or general areas for improvement. Some students actually find this task much easier to complete. List your weaknesses or areas where your performance is currently lacking. It is important to carefully consider majors or careers that appear difficult. However, based on the career interests you will confirm, some of the items in your list may be later identified as areas you wish to develop.

_____

_____

_____

_____

_____

_____

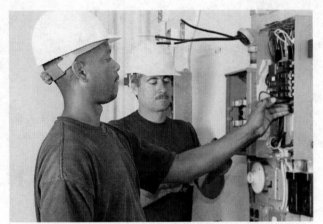

© Lisa F. Young, 2009. Used under license from Shutterstock, Inc.

Types of Skills

Effective engagement in the career planning process allows time to assess skills in connection to your interests as well as in relation to the demands of the world of work. These demands typically require that you are able to contribute a broad range of skills to ensure you add value to the company or organization. Assessing your skills and abilities now will not only help you with your more immediate decisions, such as choosing which major is the best fit, but will also help with your other planning tasks. Planning tasks include determining the skills necessary for the career interests you confirm and then determining how to best acquire any skills you may be lacking. Each potential career you discover will require a particular skill set desired by employers. This skill set can typically be categorized into three broad categories: work-related, transferable, and personal traits.

Work-Related Skills

Work-related skills reflect specific knowledge, abilities, and experience directly required to complete job tasks. Evidence of these skills is typically gained from prior work experience in the target area or from majors designed to teach job-specific skills.

This category of skill is highly preferable, as it allows you to demonstrate to the employer that you already possess the exact requirements they desire.

Transferable Skills

Transferable skills are qualities considered valuable across many careers and work environments. As indicated by the title, these skills can be easily transferred from one job to the next. See Table 3.1 for examples. These skills may be acquired through prior work experience, coursework activities, and extracurricular activities.

Personal Traits

Similar to transferable skills, personal traits are easily transported from one job to the next. However, in this case, these traits reveal the personal characteristics of job applicants. These traits provide insight into how you handle work situations and people, particularly in the midst of a major change or when a problem or conflict arises. In addition to core job requirements and skills, employers make hiring decisions based on your work ethic or work style. See Table 3.2 for examples.

Table 3.1 Transferable Skills

Written communication	Foreign language
Verbal communication	Sign language
Public speaking	Coordination/Planning
Analytical	Instructional/Training
Critical thinking	Negotiation
Problem-solving	Proofreading/Editing
Research	Interpersonal/Human relations
Organizational	Interviewing
Planning	Decision-making
Management	Creative thinking
Leadership	Financial management
Computer literacy	

ACTIVITY 3.2
Your Transferable Skills

Using the content in Table 3.2, list your current transferable skills. Include any additional skills you possess that are not represented in this list. Provide an example or supporting information in the second column.

1. _____   _____

2. _____   _____

3. _____   _____

4. _____   _____

5. _____   _____

Table 3.2 Personal Traits

Adaptability	Flexibility
Work well under pressure	Motivational
Team player	Delegate responsibility
Decision-making	Relate well to others
Willingness to learn	Assess and evaluate work
Attention to detail	Deal with obstacles and crises
Time management	Think outside of the box

ACTIVITY 3.3
Your Personal Traits

Using the content in Table 3.2, list your current personal traits. Include any additional skills you possess that are not represented in this list. Provide an example or supporting information in the second column.

1. _____   _____

2. _____   _____

3. _____   _____

4. _____   _____

5. _____   _____

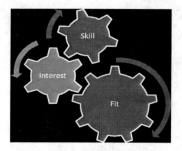

Phillip's Dilemma

Phillip is a 19-year-old freshman student with a common dilemma. He came to career counseling to sort through career interests in order to make a decision about his career path. Phillip's parents own a successful plumbing company where he has been an employee for several years. His parents would love for him to eventually take over the business. Phillip is currently a management major, well on his way to realizing his parents' dream of continuing the family business. However, he's conflicted because he finds his job and the services industry boring. Additionally, he dislikes managing conflicts between customers and contractors and begrudges his time sitting behind a desk all day at his computer. Phillip dreams of a career where he can be outside on occasion enjoying the sunshine. He seems to revel in his biweekly mystery/detective show and wonders how some of the roles in that show translate to real life. He's considered law

© Laser222, 2009. Used under license from Shutterstock, Inc.

enforcement, but has a few concerns about that choice. Recently, one of his friends has been sharing his thoughts about his major in criminal justice, a major Phillip finds very interesting. Additionally, Phillip finds his current management major difficult, and recently his grades have been declining.

After three years working in customer service for his parents' business, Phillip has developed exceptional problem-solving skills in this area. His parents regularly comment on how well he is able to resolve issues that arise with their customers and uncover potential problems before they arise. Phillip enjoys this positive feedback, and even though he finds the work boring, he wonders if running the family business one day is indeed the right choice. After all, he is very talented at his current job and it happens to come with promises of future wealth. However, his gut instinct tells him that there has to be more to a career than the current direction he's heading. Although his parents want him to take over the family business, they are supportive of any direction he chooses. It's important to Phillip to pursue a career that he's good at. Achievement and a sense of accomplishment are important values in his future career, and he's unsure about his talents in areas he's not currently familiar with. Phillip is weighing the choice to step outside of the family business by changing his major and pursuing opportunities in a very different area or to follow his current familiar path.

Discussion Points

1. Do you have areas of high talent/skill that you are also considering pursuing as a career?
2. Outside of skills/abilities, what are other important considerations before choosing a career path?
3. How would you go about sorting through career options if you have many areas you're skilled in?
4. Do you think Phillip could be happy if he pursued his current path of business ownership? Why or why not?
5. Find clues in the story to explain how Phillip's skills are supported (or not) by his interests.

© Kurhan, 2009. Used under license from Shutterstock, Inc.

Connecting Skills to Careers

Career Counselors often recommend that students complete skills or aptitude assessments to assist in the career planning process. In some cases, simple self-analysis, as in the previous activities, generates an appropriate amount of information. Self-analysis provides quick and easy brainstorming activities designed to help you identify what's already known. In other cases, in-depth assessments are recommended to provide a rank-ordered listing of your abilities followed by a connection to career opportunities. Remember, career assessments are supplemental to career counseling. Speak with a Career Counselor to determine the best course of action for you. Both informal self-assessment and formal assessments can help validate skills you currently possess or identify new skills you have yet to realize or were unable to put into words. Many tools and activities are available to supplement your understanding of the connection between skills and relevant careers. The U.S. Department of Labor developed the Occupational Information Network, or O*NET, which is a comprehensive source of occupational information. The Skills Search aspect of this system provides a list of 10 basic skills. See Table 3.1.

Table 3.3 O*Net Basic Skills

Active Learning	Engaging new information to understand its implications for current and future use
Active Listening	Taking the time to understand what other people are saying and asking appropriate questions
Critical Thinking	Applying logical analysis to identify the pros and cons of alternative solutions to problems or work situations
Learning Strategies	Using multiple instructional and learning strategies when teaching or learning new concepts or material
Mathematics	Using mathematics to solve problems
Monitoring	Assessing your performance and that of others and organizations to determine areas for improvement
Reading Comprehension	Understanding written content in work-related documents
Science	Using scientific methods to solve problems
Speaking	Talking to others to convey information effectively
Writing	Communicating effectively in writing in relation to the needs of the audience

O*NET Online: http://online.onetcenter.org/skills/ U.S. Department of Labor, Employment & Training Administration: http://www.doleta.gov/programs/ONet/

O*NET Online also presents other key work-related skill areas. After you identify and select your skills, the system generates a list of related careers. You may also conduct a reverse search by first identifying and selecting your career interests to generate a list of required skills and abilities. Conducting this latter search allows you to determine if these careers are supported by your natural skills or if you are willing to invest the time necessary to develop those skills through appropriate coursework and activities during your college career.

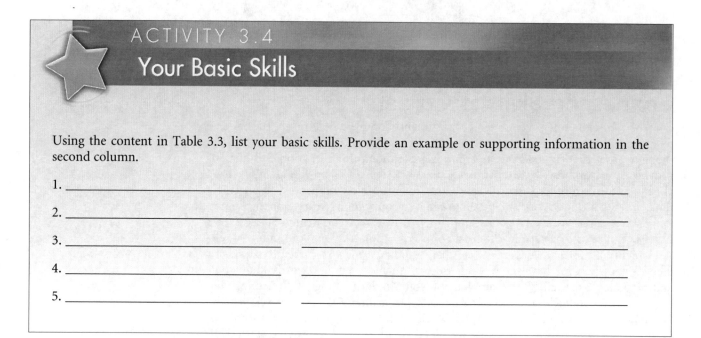

ACTIVITY 3.4
Your Basic Skills

Using the content in Table 3.3, list your basic skills. Provide an example or supporting information in the second column.

1. _____   _____

2. _____   _____

3. _____   _____

4. _____   _____

5. _____   _____

Key Discoveries

- Skills are natural or learned abilities that are an important dimension of the career planning process.
- The three main categories of skills are work-related, transferable, and personal traits.
- The U.S. Department of Labor developed O*NET Online as a resource for occupational information.
- O*NET Online provides 10 basic skills and related occupational information.
- It is important to make sure that your career interests are balanced with your skill level.
- As you progress in the career planning process, you will discover skill areas to target for further development.

Career Connections: Internet Links

- http://mymajors.com/index.html (*My Major Quiz: College Planning*)
- http://online.onetcenter.org (*O*NET*)
- http://www.facts.org (*Florida Choices Planner*)
- http://www.bls.gov/oco/ (*Occupational Outlook Handbook*)
- http://www.vault.com/cb/careerlib/careerlib_main.jsp?parrefer=1023 (*Vault Online Career Library*)
- http://www.myplan.com (*My Plan*)

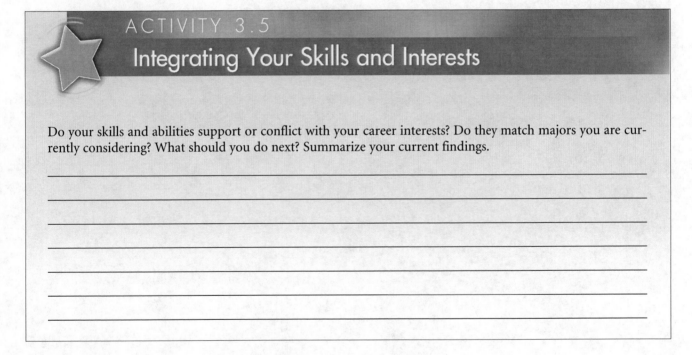

ACTIVITY 3.5

Integrating Your Skills and Interests

Do your skills and abilities support or conflict with your career interests? Do they match majors you are currently considering? What should you do next? Summarize your current findings.

_____

_____

_____

_____

_____

_____

CHAPTER QUEST

Read to answer these key questions:

- What are the different personality types?

- What is my personality type?

- How is personality type related to choice of a major and career?

- What are the characteristics of my ideal career?

- What careers and majors should I consider based on my personality type?

- What are some other factors in choosing a major?

© James Steidl, 2009. Used under license from Shutterstock, Inc.

Exploring Your Personality and Major

To assure your success in college, it is important to choose the major that is best for you. If you choose a major and career that matches your personality, interests, aptitudes and values, you will enjoy your studies and excel in your work. It was Picasso who said that you know you enjoy your work when you do not notice the time passing by. If you can become interested in your work and studies, you are on your way to developing passion and joy in your life. If you can get up each morning and enjoy the work that you do (at least on most days), you will surely have one of the keys to happiness.

Choose a Major That Matches Your Gifts and Talents

The first step in choosing the major that is right for you is to understand your personality type. Psychologists have developed useful theories of personality that can help you understand how personality type relates to the choice of major and career. The personality theory used in this textbook is derived from the work of Swiss psychologist Carl Jung (1875–1961). Jung believed that we are born with a predisposition for certain personality preferences and that healthy development is based on the lifelong nurturing of inborn preferences rather than trying to change a person to become something different. Each personality type has gifts and talents that can be nurtured over a lifetime.

The theories of Carl Jung were further developed by American psychologists Katherine Briggs and her daughter Isabel Myers, who created the Myers-Briggs Type Indicator (MBTI) to measure different personality types. The connection between personality type and career choice was established through statistical analysis. The "Do What You Are" online personality assessment is based on the practical application of the theories of these psychologists.

While assessments are not exact predictors of your future major and career, they provide useful information that will get you started on the path of career exploration and finding the college major that is best suited to you. Knowledge of your personality and an understanding of the personality of others are not only valuable in understanding yourself, but are also valuable in appreciating how others are different. This understanding of self and others will empower you to communicate and work effectively with others. Complete the "Do What You Are" personality assessment that is included with this textbook before you begin this chapter.

Understanding Personality Types

Just as no two fingerprints or snowflakes are exactly alike, each person is a different and unique individual. Even with this uniqueness, however, we can make some general statements about personality. When we make generalizations, we are talking about averages. These averages can provide useful information about ourselves and other people, but it is important to remember that no individual is exactly described by the average. As you read through the following descriptions of personality types, keep in mind that we are talking about generalizations or beginning points for discussion and thoughtful analysis. Based on the work of Carl Jung, Katherine Briggs, and Isabel Myers, personality has four dimensions:

1. Extraversion or Introversion
2. Sensing or Intuitive
3. Thinking or Feeling
4. Judging or Perceptive

These dimensions of personality will be defined and examined more in depth in the sections that follow.

Extraversion or Introversion

The dimension of extraversion or introversion defines how we interact with the world and how our energy flows. In the general school population, 75 percent of students are usually extraverts and 25 percent are introverts.

Extraverts (E) focus their energy on the world outside themselves. They enjoy interaction with others and get to know a lot of different people. They enjoy and are usually good at communication. They are energized by social interaction and prefer being active. These types are often described as talkative and social.

Introverts (I) focus their energy on the world inside of themselves. They enjoy spending time alone to think about the world in order to understand it. Introverts prefer more limited social contacts, choosing smaller groups or one-on-one relationships. These types are often described as quiet or reserved.

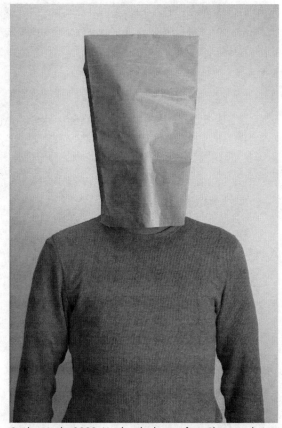

© Alex Hinds, 2009. Used under license from Shutterstock, Inc.

We all use the introvert and extravert modes while functioning in our daily lives. Whether a person is an extravert or an introvert is a matter of preference, like being left- or right-handed. We can use our nondominant hand, but it is not as comfortable as using our dominant hand. We are usually more skillful in using the dominant hand. For example, introverts can learn to function well in social situations, but later may need some peace and quiet to recharge. On the other hand, social contact energizes the extravert.

One personality type is not better than the other; it is just different. Being an extravert is not better than being an introvert. Each type has unique gifts and talents that can be used in different occupations. An extravert might enjoy working in an occupation with lots of public contact such as being a receptionist or handling public relations. An introvert might enjoy being an accountant or writer. However, as with all of the personality dimensions, a person may have traits of both types.

© Yuri Arcurs, 2009. Used under license from Shutterstock, Inc.

ACTIVITY 4.1

The list below describes some qualities of introverts and extraverts. For **each pair of items**, choose the phrase that describes you best and place a checkmark next to the item that usually describes yourself. Remember that one type is not better than another. You may also find that you are a combination type and act like an introvert in some situations and an extravert in others. Each type has gifts and talents that can be used in choosing the best major and career for you. To get an estimate of your preference, notice which column has the most checkmarks.

Introvert (I)

_____ Energized by having quiet time alone

_____ Tend to think first and talk later

_____ Tend to think things through quietly

_____ Tend to respond slowly, after thinking

_____ Avoid being the center of attention

_____ Difficult to get to know, private

_____ Have a few close friends

_____ Prefer quiet for concentration

_____ Listen more than talk

_____ View telephone calls as a distraction

_____ Talk to a few people at parties

_____ Share special occasions with one or a few people

_____ Prefer to study alone

_____ Prefer the library to be quiet

_____ Described as quiet or reserved

_____ Work systematically

Extravert (E)

_____ Energized by social interaction

_____ Tend to talk first and think later

_____ Tend to think out loud

_____ Tend to respond quickly, before thinking

_____ Like to be the center of attention

_____ Easy to get to know, outgoing

_____ Have many friends, know lots of people

_____ Can read or talk with background noise

_____ Talk more than listen

_____ View telephone calls as a welcome break

_____ Talk to many different people at parties

_____ Share special occasions with large groups

_____ Prefer to study with others in a group

_____ Talk with others in the library

_____ Described as talkative or friendly

_____ Work through trial and error

Here are some qualities that describe the ideal work environment. Again, as you **read through each pair of items**, place a checkmark next to the work environment that you prefer.

Introvert (I)

_____ Work alone or with individuals

_____ Quiet for concentration

_____ Communication one on one

_____ Work in small groups

_____ Focus on one project until complete

_____ Work without interruption

_____ **Total** (from both charts above)

Extravert (E)

_____ Much public contact

_____ High-energy environment

_____ Present ideas to a group

_____ Work as part of a team

_____ Variety and action

_____ Talk to others

_____ **Total** (from both charts above)

Do these results agree with your personality assessment on the "Do What You Are"? If your results are the same, this is a good indication that your results are useful and accurate. Are there some differences with the results obtained from your personality assessment? If your results are different, this provides an opportunity for further reflection about your personality type. Here are a couple of reasons why your results may be different.

1. You may be a combination type with varying degrees of preference for each type.

2. You may have chosen your personality type on the "Do What You Are" based on what you think is best rather than what you truly are. Students sometimes do this because of the myth that there are good and bad personality types. It is important to remember that each personality type has strengths and weaknesses. By identifying strengths, you can build on them by choosing the right major and career. By being aware of weaknesses, you can come up with strategies to compensate for them to be successful.

Look at the total number of checkmarks for extravert and introvert on the two above charts. Do you lean toward being an introvert or an extravert? Remember that one type is not better than the other and each has unique gifts and talents. On the chart below, place an X on the line to indicate how much you prefer introversion or extraversion. If you selected most of the introvert traits, place your X somewhere on the left side. If you selected most of the extravert traits, place your X somewhere on the right side. If you are equally introverted and extraverted, place your X in the middle.

Introvert _____|_____ Extavert

Do you generally prefer introversion or extraversion? In the box below, write **I** for introversion or **E** for extraversion. If there is a tie between **E** and **I**, write **I**.

☐

Notice that it is possible to be a combination type. At times you might prefer to act like an introvert and at other times you might prefer to act like an extravert. It is beneficial to be able to balance these traits. However, for combination types, it is more difficult to select specific occupations that match this type.

JOURNAL ENTRY #1

Look at the results from "Do What You Are" and your own self-assessment above. Are you an introvert or an extravert or a combination of these two types? Can you give examples of how it affects your social life, school, or work? Write a paragraph about this preference.

© Lena Sergeeva, 2009. Used under license from Shutterstock, Inc.

Sensing or Intuitive

The dimension of sensing or intuition describes how we take in information. In the general school population, 70 percent of students are usually sensing types and 30 percent are intuitive types.

Sensing (S) persons prefer to use the senses to take in information (what they see, hear, taste, touch, smell). They focus on "what is" and trust information that is concrete and observable. They learn through experience.

Intuitive (N) persons rely on instincts and focus on "what could be." While we all use our five senses to perceive the world, intuitive people are interested in relationships, possibilities, meanings, and implications. They value inspiration and trust their "sixth sense" or hunches. (Intuitive is designated as **N** so it is not confused with **I** for Introvert.)

We all use both of these modes in our daily lives, but we usually have a preference for one mode or the other. Again, there is no best preference. Each type has special skills that can be applied to the job market. For example, you would probably want your tax preparer to be a sensing type who focuses on concrete information and fills out your tax form correctly. An inventor or artist would probably be an intuitive type.

ACTIVITY 4.2

Here are some qualities of sensing and intuitive persons. As you **read through each pair of items**, place a checkmark next to the item that usually describes yourself.

Sensing (S)	**INtuitive (N)**
_____ Trust what is certain and concrete	_____ Trust inspiration and inference
_____ Prefer specific answers to questions	_____ Prefer general answers which leave room for interpretation
_____ Like new ideas if they have practical applications (if you can use them)	_____ Like new ideas for their own sake (you don't need a practical use for them)
_____ Value realism and common sense	_____ Value imagination and innovation
_____ Think about things one at a time and step by step	_____ Think about many ideas at once as they come to you
_____ Like to improve and use skills learned before	_____ Like to learn new skills and get bored using the same skills
_____ More focused on the present	_____ More focused on the future
_____ Concentrate on what you are doing at the moment	_____ Wonder what is next
_____ Do something	_____ Think about doing something
_____ See tangible results	_____ Focus on possibilities
_____ If it isn't broken, don't fix it	_____ There is always a better way to do it

Sensing (S)		INtuitive (N)	
_____	Prefer working with facts and figures	_____	Prefer working with ideas and theories
_____	Focus on reality	_____	Use fantasy
_____	Seeing is believing	_____	Anything is possible
_____	Tend to be specific and literal (say what you mean)	_____	Tend to be general and figurative (use comparisons and analogies)
_____	See what is here and now	_____	See the big picture

Here are some qualities that describe the ideal work environment. Again, as you **read through each pair of items**, place a checkmark next to the work environment that you prefer.

Sensing (S)		INtuitive (N)	
_____	Use and practice skills	_____	Learn new skills
_____	Work with known facts	_____	Explore new ideas and approaches
_____	See measurable results	_____	Work with theories
_____	Focus on practical benefits	_____	Use imagination and be original
_____	Learn through experience	_____	Freedom to follow your inspiration
_____	Pleasant environment	_____	Challenging environment
_____	Use standard procedures	_____	Invent new products and procedures
_____	Work step-by-step	_____	Work in bursts of energy
_____	Do accurate work	_____	Find creative solutions
_____	**Total** (from both charts above)	_____	**Total** (from both charts above)

Look at the two charts above and see whether you tend to be more sensing or intuitive. One preference is not better than another; it is just different. On the chart below, place an X on the line to indicate your preference for sensing or intuitive. Again, notice that it is possible to be a combination type with both sensing and intuitive preferences.

Sensing _____|_____ Intuitive

Do you generally prefer sensing or intuition? In the box below, write **S** for sensing or **N** for intuitive. If there is a tie between **S** and **N**, write **N**.

[ ]

JOURNAL ENTRY #2

Look at the results from "Do What You Are" and your own self-assessment above. Are you a sensing, intuitive, or combination type? Can you give examples of how it affects your social life, school, or work? Write a paragraph about this preference.

Thinking or Feeling

© Suzanne Tucker, 2009. Used under license from Shutterstock, Inc.

The dimension of thinking or feeling defines how we prefer to make decisions. In the general school population, 60 percent of males are thinking types and 40 percent are feeling types. For females, 60 percent are feeling types and 40 percent are thinking types.

Thinking (T) individuals make decisions based on logic. They are objective and analytical. They look at all the evidence and reach an impersonal conclusion. They are concerned with *what they think is right*.

Feeling (F) individuals make decisions based on what is important to them and matches their personal values. They are concerned about *what they feel is right*.

We all use logic and have feelings and emotions that play a part in decision making. However, the thinking person prefers to make decisions based on logic, and the feeling person prefers to make decisions according to what is important to self and others. This is one category in which men and women differ. Most women are feeling types, and most men are logical types. When men and women are arguing, you might hear the following:

Man: "I think that . . ."

Woman: "I feel that . . ."

By understanding these differences, it is possible to improve communication and understanding. Be careful with generalizations since 40 percent of men and women would not fit this pattern.

When thinking about careers, a thinking type would make a good judge or computer programmer. A feeling type would probably make a good social worker or kindergarten teacher.

ACTIVITY 4.3

The following chart shows *some qualities of thinking and feeling types*. As you **read through each pair of items**, place a checkmark next to the items that usually describe yourself.

Thinking (T)	Feeling (F)
_____ Apply impersonal analysis to problems	_____ Consider the effect on others
_____ Value logic and justice	_____ Value empathy and harmony
_____ Fairness is important	_____ There are exceptions to every rule
_____ Truth is more important than tact	_____ Tact is more important than truth
_____ Motivated by achievement and accomplishment	_____ Motivated by being appreciated by others
_____ Feelings are valid if they are logical	_____ Feelings are valid whether they make sense or not
_____ Good decisions are logical	_____ Good decisions take others' feelings into account

Thinking (T)	Feeling (F)
_____ Described as cool, calm, and objective	_____ Described as caring and emotional
_____ Love can be analyzed	_____ Love cannot be analyzed
_____ Firm-minded	_____ Gentle-hearted
_____ More important to be right	_____ More important to be liked
_____ Remember numbers and figures	_____ Remember faces and names
_____ Prefer clarity	_____ Prefer harmony
_____ Find flaws and critique	_____ Look for the good and compliment
_____ Prefer firmness	_____ Prefer persuasion

Here are some qualities that describe the ideal work environment. As you **read through each pair of items**, place a checkmark next to the items that usually describe the work environment that you prefer.

Thinking (T)	Feeling (F)
_____ Maintain business environment	_____ Maintain close personal relationships
_____ Work with people I respect	_____ Work in a friendly, relaxed environment
_____ Be treated fairly	_____ Be able to express personal values
_____ Fair evaluations	_____ Appreciation for good work
_____ Solve problems	_____ Make a personal contribution
_____ Challenging work	_____ Harmonious work situation
_____ Use logic and analysis	_____ Help others
_____ **Total** (from both charts above)	_____ **Total** (from both charts above)

While we all use thinking and feeling, what is your preferred type? Look at the charts above and notice whether you are more the thinking or feeling type. One is not better than the other. On the chart below, place an X on the line to indicate how much you prefer thinking or feeling.

Thinking _____|_____Feeling

Do you generally prefer thinking or feeling? In the box below, write **T** for thinking or **F** for feeling. If there is a tie between **T** and **F**, write **F**.

☐

JOURNAL ENTRY #3

Look at the results from "Do What You Are" and your own self-assessment above. Are you a thinking, feeling, or combination type? Can you give examples of how it affects your social life, school, or work? Write a paragraph about this preference.

Judging or Perceptive

The dimension of judging or perceptive refers to how we deal with the external world. In other words, do we prefer the world to be structured or unstructured? In the general school population, the percentage of each of these types is approximately equal.

© Dmitriy Shironosov, 2009. Used under license from Shutterstock, Inc.

Judging (J) types like to live in a structured, orderly, and planned way. They are happy when their lives are structured and matters are settled. They like to have control over their lives. **Judging does not mean to judge others.** Think of this type as being orderly and organized.

Perceptive (P) types like to live in a spontaneous and flexible way. They are happy when their lives are open to possibilities. They try to understand life rather than control it. **Think of this type as spontaneous and flexible.**

Since these types have very opposite ways of looking at the world, there is a great deal of potential for conflict between them unless there is an appreciation for the gifts and talents of both. In any situation, we can benefit from people who represent these very different points of view. For example, in a business situation, the judging type would be good at managing the money, while the perceptive type would be good at helping the business to adapt to a changing marketplace. It is good to be open to all the possibilities and to be flexible, as well as to have some structure and organization.

ACTIVITY 4.4

As you **read through each pair of items,** place a checkmark next to the items that generally describe yourself.

Judging (J)	Perceptive (P)
_____ Happy when the decisions are made and finished	_____ Happy when the options are left open; something better may come along
_____ Work first, play later	_____ Play first, do the work later
_____ It is important to be on time	_____ Time is relative
_____ Time flies	_____ Time is elastic
_____ Feel comfortable with routine	_____ Dislike routine
_____ Generally keep things in order	_____ Prefer creative disorder
_____ Set goals and work toward them	_____ Change goals as new opportunities arise
_____ Emphasize completing the task	_____ Emphasize how the task is done
_____ Like to finish projects	_____ Like to start projects
_____ Meet deadlines	_____ What deadline?
_____ Like to know what I am getting into	_____ Like new possibilities and situations
_____ Relax when things are organized	_____ Relax when necessary
_____ Follow a routine	_____ Explore the unknown
_____ Focused	_____ Easily distracted
_____ Work steadily	_____ Work in spurts of energy

Here are some qualities that describe the ideal work environment. Again, as you **read through each pair of items**, place a checkmark next to the work environment that you prefer.

Judging (J)

_____ Follow a schedule

_____ Clear directions

_____ Organized work

_____ Logical order

_____ Control my job

_____ Stability and security

_____ Work on one project until done

_____ Steady work

_____ Satisfying work

_____ Like having high responsibility

_____ Accomplish goals on time

_____ Clear and concrete assignments

_____ **Total** (from both charts above)

Perceptive (P)

_____ Be spontaneous

_____ Minimal rules and structure

_____ Flexibility

_____ Many changes

_____ Respond to emergencies

_____ Take risks and be adventurous

_____ Juggle many projects

_____ Variety and action

_____ Fun and excitement

_____ Like having interesting work

_____ Work at my own pace

_____ Minimal supervision

_____ **Total** (from both charts above)

Look at the charts above and notice whether you are more the judging type (orderly and organized) or the perceptive type (spontaneous and flexible). We need the qualities of both types to be successful and deal with the rapid changes in today's world. On the chart below, place an X on the line to indicate how much you prefer judging or perceiving.

Judging _____|_____Perceptive

Do you generally have judging or perceptive traits? In the box below, write **J** for judging or **P** for perceptive. If there is a tie between **J** and **P**, write **P**.

☐

JOURNAL ENTRY #4

Look at the results from "Do What You Are" and your own self-assessment above. Are you a judging, perceptive, or combination type? Can you give examples of how it affects your social life, school, or work? Write a paragraph about this preference.

SUMMARIZE YOUR RESULTS

Look at your results above and summarize them on this composite chart. Notice that we are all unique, according to where the Xs fall on the scale.

Extravert (E) _____|_____		Introvert (I)
Sensing (S) _____|_____		Intuitive (N)
Thinking (T)_____|_____		Feeling (F)
Judging (J) _____|_____		Perceptive (P)

Write the letters representing each of your preferences.

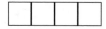

The above letters represent your estimated personality type based on your understanding and knowledge of self. It is a good idea to confirm that this type is correct for you by completing the online personality assessment, "Do What You Are."

JOURNAL ENTRY #5

What is your personality type? What is your evaluation of the personality assessment?

QUIZ
Personality Types

Test what you have learned by selecting the correct answer to the following questions.

1. A person who is energized by social interaction is a/an:

   a. introvert
   b. extravert
   c. feeling type

2. A person who is quiet and reserved is a/an:

   a. introvert
   b. extravert
   c. perceptive type

3. A person who relies on experience and trusts information that is concrete and observable is a/an:

   a. judging type
   b. sensing type
   c. perceptive type

4. A person who focuses on "what could be" is a/an:

   a. perceptive type
   b. thinking type
   c. intuitive type

5. A person who makes decisions based on logic is a/an:

    a. thinker
    b. perceiver
    c. sensor

6. A person who makes decisions based on their personal values is a/an:

    a. feeling type
    b. thinking type
    c. judging type

7. The perceptive type:

    a. has extrasensory perception
    b. likes to live life in a spontaneous and flexible way
    c. always considers feelings before making a decision

8. The judging type likes to:

    a. judge others
    b. use logic
    c. live in a structured and orderly way

9. Personality assessments are an exact predictor of your best major and career.

    a. true
    b. false

10. Some personality types are better than others.

    a. true
    b. false

How did you do on the quiz? Check your answers: 1. b, 2. a, 3. b, 4. c, 5. a, 6. a, 7. b, 8. c, 9. b, 10. b

Personality and Preferred Work Environment

Knowing your personality type will help you to understand your preferred work environment and provide some insights into selecting the major and career that you would enjoy. Understanding other types will help you to work effectively with co-workers.

© Andresr, 2009. Used under license from Shutterstock, Inc.

Since the **extravert** likes variety, action and talking to others, this type enjoys a work environment that provides the opportunity for social interaction. Extraverts communicate well and meet people easily. They like to talk while working and are interested in other people and what they are doing. They enjoy variety on the job and like to perform their work in different settings. They learn new tasks by talking with others and trying out new ideas. They are career generalists who like to use their skills in a variety of ways.

The **introvert** likes quiet for concentration and likes to focus on a work task until it is completed. They need time to think before taking action. This type often chooses to work alone or with one other person and prefers written communication such as emails to oral communication or presentations. They learn new tasks by reading and reflecting and using mental practice. They are career specialists who develop in depth skills.

The **sensing** type is realistic and practical and likes to develop standard ways of doing the job and following a routine. They are observant and interested in facts and finding the truth. They keep accurate track of details, make lists and are good at doing precise work. This type learns from personal experience and the experience of others. They use their experience to move up the job ladder.

The **intuitive** type likes to follow their inspirations and enjoys working on challenging and complex problems. They like change and finding new ways of doing work. This type focuses on the whole picture rather than the details. The intuitive type is an initiator, promoter and inventor of ideas. They enjoy learning a new skill more than using it. They often change careers to follow their creative inspirations.

The **thinking** type likes to use logical analysis in making decisions. They are objective and rational and treat others fairly. They want logical reasons before accepting any new ideas. They follow policy and are often firm-minded and critical, especially when dealing with illogic in others. They easily learn facts, theories and principles. They are interested in careers with money, prestige or influence.

The **feeling** type likes harmony and the support of co-workers. They are personal, enjoy warm relationships and relate well to most people. Feeling types know their personal values and apply them consistently. They enjoy doing work that provides a service to people and often do work that requires them to understand and analyze their own emotions and those of others. They prefer a friendly work environment and like to learn with others. They enjoy careers in which they can make a contribution to humanity.

The **judging** type likes a work environment that is structured, settled and organized. They prefer work assignments that are clear and definite. The judging type makes lists and plans to get the job done on time. They make quick decisions and like to have the work finished. They are good at doing purposeful and exacting work. They prefer to learn only the essentials that are necessary to do the job. This type carefully plans their career path.

The **perceptive** type likes to be spontaneous and go with the flow. They are comfortable in handling the unplanned or unexpected in the work environment. They prefer to be flexible in their work and feel restricted by structures and schedules. They are good at handling work which requires change and adaptation. They are tolerant and have a "live and let live" attitude toward others. Decisions are often postponed because this type wants to know all there is to know and explore all the options before making a decision. This type is often a career changer who takes advantage of new job openings and opportunities for change.

> ## JOURNAL ENTRY #6
>
> Describe your ideal working environment.

Personality and Decision Making

Your personality type affects how you think and how you make decisions. Knowing how you make decisions will help with self-understanding and working with others in decision making or creative problem solving. Each personality type views the decision making process in a different way. Ideally it would be good to have a variety of types involved in making a decision so that the strengths of each type could be utilized.

The **introvert** thinks up ideas and reflects on the problem before acting. The **extravert** acts as the communicator in the decision making process. Once the decision is made, they take action and implement the decision. The **intuitive** type develops theories and uses intuition to come up with ingenious solutions to the problem. The **sensing type** applies personal experience to the decision making process and focuses on solutions that are practical and realistic.

The thinking and feeling dimensions of personality determine how a decision is made. Of course people use both thinking in feeling in the decision making process, but tend to prefer or trust either thinking or feeling. Those who prefer **thinking** use cause and effect reasoning and solve problems with logic. They use objective and impersonal criteria and include all the consequences of alternative solutions in the decision making process. They are interested in finding out what is true and what is false. They use laws and principles to treat everyone fairly. Once a decision is made, they are firm minded, since the decision was based on logic. This type is often critical of those who do not use logic in the decision making process. The **feeling** type considers human values and motives in the decision making process (whether they are logical or not) and values harmony and maintaining good relationships. They consider carefully how much they care about each of the alternatives and how they will affect other people. They are interested in making a decision that is agreeable to all parties. Feeling types are tactful and skillful in dealing with people.

It is often asked if thinking types have feelings. They do have feelings, but use them as a criterion to be factored into the decision making process. Thinking types are more comfortable when feelings are controlled and often think that feeling types are too emotional. Thinking types may have difficulties when they apply logic in a situation where a feeling response is needed, such as in dealing with a spouse. Thinking types need to know that people are important in making decisions. Feeling types need to know that behavior will have logical consequences and that they may need to keep emotions more controlled to work effectively with thinking types.

Judging and perceptive types have opposite decision making strategies. The judging type is very methodical and cautious in making decisions. Once they have gone through the decision making steps, they like to make decisions quickly so that they can have closure and finish the project. The perceptive type is an adventurer who wants to look at all the possibilities before making a decision. They are open-minded and curious and often resist closure to look at more options.

If a combination of types collaborates on a decision, it is more likely that the decision will be a good one which takes into account creative possibilities, practicality, logical consequences and human values.

JOURNAL ENTRY #7

Describe your decision-making process.

Personality and Time Management

How we manage our time is not just a result of personal habits; it is also a reflection of our personality type. Probably the dimension of personality type most connected to time management is the judging or perceptive trait. **Judging types** like to have their lives planned, orderly, and under control. **Perceptive types** prefer more spontaneity. Understanding the differences between these two types will help you to better understand yourself and others.

© Vadim Balantsev, 2009. Used under license from Shutterstock, Inc.

Judging types are naturally good at time management. They often use schedules as a tool for time management and organization. Judging types plan their time and work steadily to accomplish goals. They are good at meeting deadlines and often put off relaxation, recreation, and fun. They relax after projects are completed. If they have too many projects, they find it difficult to find time for recreation. Since judging types like to have projects under control, there is a danger that projects will be completed too quickly and that quality will suffer. Judging types may need to slow down and take the time to do quality work. They may also need to make relaxation and recreation a priority.

Perceptive types are more open-ended and prefer to be spontaneous. They take time to relax, have fun, and participate in recreation. In working on a project, perceptive types want to brainstorm all the possibilities and are not too concerned about finishing projects. This type procrastinates when the time comes to make a final decision and finish a project. There is always more information to gather and more possibilities to explore. Perceptive types are easily distracted and may move from project to project. They may have several jobs going at once. These types need to try to focus on a few projects at a time in order to complete them. Perceptive types need to work on becoming more organized so that projects can be completed on time.

Research has shown that students who are judging types are more likely to have a higher grade point average in the first semester.[1] It has also been found that the greater the preference for intuition, introversion, and judgment, the better the grade point average.[2] Why is this true? Many college professors are intuitive types that use intuitive and creative ideas. The college environment requires quiet time for reading and studying, which is one of the preferences of introverts. Academic environments require structure, organization, and completion of assignments. To be successful in an academic environment requires adaptation by some personality types. Extroverts need to spend more quiet time reading and studying. Sensing types need to gain an understanding of intuitive types. Perceptive types need to use organization to complete assignments on time.

JOURNAL ENTRY #8

How does being a judging or a perceptive type explain how you manage your time? In other words, are you usually orderly and organized or do you prefer to be more spontaneous and flexible with how you manage your time? Judging types are generally good with time management, whereas perceptive types need to place greater importance on meeting deadlines. How can you use this information to complete assignments necessary to be successful in college?

Personality and Money

Does your personality type affect how you deal with money? Otto Kroeger and Janet Thuesen make some interesting observations about how different personality types deal with money.

- **Judging types (orderly and organized).**
  These types excel at financial planning and money management. They file their tax forms early and pay their bills on time.

- **Perceptive types (spontaneous).**
  These types adapt to change and are more creative. Perceivers, especially intuitive perceivers, tend to freak out as the April 15 tax deadline approaches and as bills become due.

- **Feeling types (make decisions based on feelings).**
  These types are not very money conscious. They believe that money should be used to serve humanity. They are often attracted to low-paying jobs that serve others.[3]

© Jason Stitt, 2009. Used under license from Shutterstock, Inc.

In studying stockbrokers, these same authors note that ISTJs (introvert, sensing, thinking, and judging types) are the most conservative investors, earning a small but reliable return on investments. The ESTPs (extravert, sensing, thinking, perceptive types) and ENTPs (extravert, intuitive, thinking, perceptive types) take the biggest risks and earn the greatest returns.[4]

JOURNAL ENTRY #9

How does **your** personality affect how you spend money?

Personality and Career Choice

While it is not possible to predict exactly your career and college major by knowing your personality type, it can be helpful in providing opportunities for exploration. Suggestions about career selections are based on the general characteristics of each type, and research that correlates personality type with choice of satisfying career. Here are some general descriptions of personality types and preferred careers. Included are general occupational fields, frequently chosen occupations, and suggested majors. These suggestions about career selections are based on the general characteristics of each type and research that correlates personality type with choice of a satisfying career.[5] Continue your career exploration with the online career database included with the "Do What You Are" personality assessment included with your textbook.

ISTJ

ISTJs are responsible, loyal, stable, practical, down-to-earth, hardworking, and reliable. They can be depended upon to follow through with tasks. They value tradition, family and security. They are natural leaders who prefer to work alone but can adapt to working with teams if needed. They like to be independent and have time to think things through. They are able to remember and use concrete facts and information. They make decisions by applying logic and rational thinking. They appreciate structured and orderly environments and deliver products and services in an efficient and orderly way.

General occupations to consider

business	education	health care
service	technical	military
law and law enforcement		

Specific job titles

business executive	lawyer	electronic technician
administrator	judge	computer occupations
manager	police officer	dentist
real estate agent	detective	pharmacist
accountant	corrections officer	primary care physician
bank employee	teacher (math, trade,	nursing administrator
stockbroker	technical)	respiratory therapist
auditor	educational administrator	physical therapist
hairdresser	coach	optometrist
cosmetologist	engineer	chemist
legal secretary	electrician	military officer or enlistee

College majors

business	engineering	chemistry
education	computers	biology
mathematics	health occupations	vocational training
law		

ISTP

ISTPs are independent, practical, and easygoing. They prefer to work individually and frequently like to work outdoors. These types like working with objects and often are good at working with their hands and mastering tools. They are interested in how and why things work and are able to apply technical knowledge to solving practical problems. Their logical thinking makes them good troubleshooters and problem solvers. They enjoy variety, new experiences, and taking risks. They prefer environments with little structure and have a talent for managing crises. The ISTP is happy with occupations that involve challenge, change, and variety.

General occupations to consider

sales	technical	business and finance
service	health care	vocational training
corrections		

Specific job titles

sales manager	engineer	office manager
insurance agent	electronics technician	small business manager
cook	software developer	banker
fire fighter	computer programmer	economist
pilot	radiologic technician	legal secretary
race car driver	exercise physiologist	paralegal
police officer	coach	computer repair
corrections officer	athlete	airline mechanic
judge	dental assistant/hygienist	carpenter
attorney	physician	construction worker
intelligence agent	optometrist	farmer
detective	physical therapist	military officer or enlistee

College majors

business	computers	health occupations
vocational training	biology	physical education
law		

ISFJ

ISFJs are quiet, friendly, responsible, hardworking, productive, devoted, accurate, thorough, and careful. They value security, stability, and harmony. They like to focus on one person or project at a time. ISFJs prefer to work with individuals and are very skillful in understanding people and their needs. They often provide service to others in a very structured way. They are careful observers, remember facts, and work on projects requiring accuracy and attention to detail. They have a sense of space and function that leads to artistic endeavors such as interior decorating or landscaping. ISFJs are most comfortable working in environments that are orderly, structured, and traditional. While they often work quietly behind the scenes, they like their contributions to be recognized and appreciated.

General occupations to consider

health care	education	artistic
social service	business	religious occupations
corrections	technical	vocational training

Specific job titles

nurse	social worker	counselor
physician	social services	secretary
medical technologist	administrator	cashier
dental hygienist	child care worker	accountant
health education	speech pathologist	personnel administrator
practitioner	librarian	credit counselor
dietitian	curator	business manager
physical therapist	genealogist	paralegal
nursing educator	corrections worker	computer occupations
health administrator	probation officer	engineer
medical secretary	teacher (preschool, grades	interior decorator
dentist	1–12)	home economist
medical assistant	guidance counselor	religious educator
optometrist	educational administrator	clergy
occupational therapist		

College majors

health occupations	education	graphics
biology	business	religious studies
psychology	engineering	vocational training
sociology	art	

ISFP

ISFPs are quiet, reserved, trusting, loyal, committed, sensitive, kind, creative, and artistic. They have an appreciation for life and value serenity and aesthetic beauty. These types are individualistic and generally have no desire to lead or follow; they prefer to work independently. They have a keen awareness of their environment and often have a special bond with children and animals. ISFPs are service-oriented and like to help others. They like to be original and unconventional. They dislike rules and structure and need space and freedom to do things in their own way.

General occupations to consider

artists	technical	business
health care	service	vocational training

Specific job titles

artist	recreation services	forester
designer	physical therapist	botanist
fashion designer	radiologic technician	geologist
jeweler	medical assistant	mechanic
gardener	dental assistant/hygienist	marine biologist
potter	veterinary assistant	teacher (science, art)
painter	veterinarian	police officer
dancer	animal groomer/trainer	beautician
landscape designer	dietician	merchandise planner
carpenter	optician/optometrist	stock clerk
electrician	exercise physiologist	store keeper
engineer	occupational therapist	counselor
chef	art therapist	social worker
nurse	pharmacy technician	legal secretary
counselor	respiratory therapist	paralegal

College majors

art	forestry	psychology
health occupations	geology	counseling
engineering	education	social work
physical education	business	vocational training
biology		

INFJ

INFJs are idealistic, complex, compassionate, authentic, creative, and visionary. They have strong value systems and search for meaning and purpose to life. Because of their strong value systems, INFJs are natural leaders or at least follow those with similar ideas. They intuitively understand people and ideas and come up with new ideas to provide service to others. These types like to organize their time and be in control of their work.

General occupations to consider

counseling	religious occupations	health care
education	creative occupations	social services
		business

Specific job titles

career counselor	director of religious education	dental hygienist
psychologist	fine artist	speech pathologist
teacher (high school or college English, art, music, social sciences, drama, foreign languages, health)	playwright	nursing educator
	novelist	medical secretary
	poet	pharmacist
	designer	occupational therapist
	architect	human resources manager
librarian	art director	marketer
home economist	health care administrator	employee assistance program
social worker	physician	merchandise planner
clergy	biologist	environmental lawyer

College majors

psychology	drama	architecture
counseling	foreign languages	biology
education	English	business
art	health occupations	law
music	social work	

INFP

INFPs are loyal, devoted, sensitive, creative, inspirational, flexible, easygoing, complex, and authentic. They are original and individualistic and prefer to work alone or with other caring and supportive individuals. These types are service-oriented and interested in personal growth. They develop deep relationships because they understand people and are genuinely interested in them. They dislike dealing with details and routine work. They prefer a flexible working environment with a minimum of rules and regulations.

General occupations to consider

creative arts	counseling	health care
education	religious occupations	organizational development

Specific job titles

artist	photographer	dietician
designer	carpenter	psychiatrist
writer	teacher (art, drama, music, English, foreign languages)	physical therapist
journalist		occupational therapist
entertainer		speech pathologist
architect	psychologist	laboratory technologist
actor	counselor	public health nurse
editor	social worker	dental hygienist
reporter	librarian	physician
journalist	clergy	human resources specialist
musician	religious educator	
graphic designer	missionary	social scientist
art director	church worker	consultant

College majors

art	foreign languages	medicine
music	architecture	health occupations
graphic design	education	social work
journalism	religious studies	counseling
English	psychology	business

INTJ

INTJs are reserved, detached, analytical, logical, rational, original, independent, creative, ingenious, innovative, and resourceful. They prefer to work alone and work best alone. They can work with others if their ideas and competence are respected. They value knowledge and efficiency. They enjoy creative and intellectual challenges and understand complex theories. They create order and structure. They prefer to work with autonomy and control over their work. They dislike factual and routine kinds of work.

General occupations to consider

business and finance	education	law
technical occupations	health care and medicine	creative occupations

Specific job titles

management consultant	astronomer	dentist
human resources planner	computer programmer	biomedical engineer
economist	biomedical researcher	attorney
international banker	software developer	manager
financial planner	network integration	judge
investment banker	specialist	electrical engineer
scientist	teacher (university)	writer
scientific researcher	school principal	journalist
chemist	mathematician	artist
biologist	psychiatrist	inventor
computer systems analyst	psychologist	architect
electronic technician	neurologist	actor
design engineer	physician	musician

College majors

business	physics	journalism
finance	education	art
chemistry	mathematics	architecture
biology	medicine	drama
computers	psychology	music
engineering	law	vocational training
astronomy	English	

INTP

INTPs are logical, analytical, independent, original, creative, and insightful. They are often brilliant and ingenious. They work best alone and need quiet time to concentrate. They focus their attention on ideas and are frequently detached from other people. They love theory and abstract ideas and value knowledge and competency. INTPs are creative thinkers who are not too interested in practical application. They dislike detail and routine and need freedom to develop, analyze, and critique new ideas. These types maintain high standards in their work.

General occupations to consider

planning and development	technical	academic
health care	professional	creative occupations

Specific job titles

computer software designer	pharmacist	historian
computer programmer	engineer	philosopher
research and development	electrician	college teacher
systems analyst	dentist	researcher
financial planner	veterinarian	logician
investment banker	lawyer	photographer
physicist	economist	creative writer
plastic surgeon	psychologist	artist
psychiatrist	architect	actor
chemist	psychiatrist	entertainer
biologist	mathematician	musician
pharmaceutical researcher	archaeologist	inventor

College majors

computers	philosophy	mathematics
business	music	archeology
physics	art	history
chemistry	drama	English
biology	engineering	drama
astronomy	psychology	music
medicine	architecture	vocational training

ESTP

ESTP's have great people skills, are action-oriented, fun, flexible, adaptable, and resourceful. They enjoy new experiences and dealing with people. They remember facts easily and have excellent powers of observation that they use to analyze other people. They are good problem solvers and can react quickly in an emergency. They like adventure and risk and are alert to new opportunities. They start new projects but do not necessarily follow through to completion. They prefer environments without too many rules and restrictions.

General occupations to consider

sales	entertainment	technical
service	sports	trade
active careers	health care	business
finance		

Specific job titles

marketing professional	insurance agent	dentist
fire fighter	sportscaster	carpenter
police officer	news reporter	farmer
corrections officer	journalist	construction worker
paramedic	tour agent	electrician
detective	dancer	teacher (trade, industrial, technical)
pilot	bartender	
investigator	auctioneer	chef
real estate agent	professional athlete or coach	engineer
exercise physiologist		surveyor
flight attendant	fitness instructor	radiologic technician
sports merchandise sales	recreation leader	entrepreneur
stockbroker	optometrist	land developer
financial planner	pharmacist	retail sales
investor	critical care nurse	car sales

College majors

business	vocational training	English
physical education	education	journalism
health occupations		

ESTJ

ESTJs are loyal, hardworking, dependable, thorough, practical, realistic, and energetic. They value security and tradition. Because they enjoy working with people and are orderly and organized, these types like to take charge and be the leader. This personality type is often found in administrative and management positions. ESTJs work systematically and efficiently to get the job done. These types are fair, logical, and consistent. They prefer a stable and predictable environment filled with action and a variety of people.

General occupations to consider

managerial	service	professional
sales	technical	military leaders

Specific job titles

retail store manager
fire department manager
small business manager
restaurant manager
financial or bank officer
school principal
sales manager
top-level manager in city/
    county/state
    government
management consultant
corporate executive

military officer or enlistee
office manager
purchasing agent
police officer
factory supervisor
corrections
insurance agent
detective
judge
accountant
nursing administrator
mechanical engineer

physician
chemical engineer
auditor
coach
public relations worker
cook
personnel or labor
    relations worker
teacher (trade, industrial,
    technical)
mortgage banker

College majors

business
business management
accounting
finance

small business
    management
engineering

law
education
vocational training

ESFP

ESFPs are practical, realistic, independent, fun, social, spontaneous, and flexible. They have great people skills and enjoy working in environments that are friendly, relaxed, and varied. They know how to have a good time and make an environment fun for others. ESFPs have a strong sense of aesthetics and are sometimes artistic and creative. They often have a special bond with people or animals. They dislike structure and routine. These types can handle many activities or projects at once.

General occupations to consider

education
social service

health care
entertainment

business and sales
service

Specific job titles

child care worker	medical assistant	promoter
teacher (preschool, elementary school, foreign languages, mathematics)	critical care nurse	special events coordinator
	dentist	editor or reporter
	dental assistant	retail merchandiser
	exercise physiologist	fund raiser
athletic coach	dog obedience trainer	receptionist
counselor	veterinary assistant	real estate agent
library assistant	travel or tour agent	insurance agent
police officer	recreation leader or amusement site worker	sporting equipment sales
public health nurse		retail sales
respiratory therapist	photographer	retail management
physical therapist	designer	waiter or waitress
physician	film producer	cashier
emergency medical technician	musician	cosmetologist
	performer	hairdresser
dental hygienist	actor	religious worker

College majors

education	health occupations	journalism
psychology	art	drama
foreign languages	design	music
mathematics	photography	business
physical education	English	vocational training

ESFJ

ESFJs are friendly, organized, hardworking, productive, conscientious, loyal, dependable, and practical. These types value harmony, stability, and security. They enjoy interacting with people and receive satisfaction from giving to others. ESFJs enjoy working in a cooperative environment in which people get along well with each other. They create order, structure, and schedules and can be depended on to complete the task at hand. They prefer to organize and control their work.

General occupations to consider

health care	social service	business
education	counseling	

Specific job titles

medical or dental assistant
nurse
radiologic technician
dental hygienist
speech pathologist
occupational therapist
dentist
optometrist
dietician
pharmacist
physician
physical therapist
health education
  practitioner
medical secretary
teacher (grades 1–12,
  foreign languages,
  reading)

coach
administrator of
  elementary
  or secondary school
administrator of student
  personnel
child care provider
home economist
social worker
administrator of social
  services
police officer
counselor
community welfare
  worker
religious educator
clergy

sales representative
hairdresser
cosmetologist
restaurant worker
recreation or amusement
  site worker
receptionist
office manager
cashier
bank employee
bookkeeper
accountant
sales
insurance agent
credit counselor
merchandise planner

College majors

health occupations
biology
foreign languages
English

education
psychology
counseling
sociology

religious studies
business
vocational training

ENFP

ENFPs are friendly, creative, energetic, enthusiastic, innovative, adventurous, and fun. They have great people skills and enjoy providing service to others. They are intuitive and perceptive about people. ENFPs are good at anything that interests them and can enter a variety of fields. These types dislike routine and detailed tasks and may have difficulty following through and completing tasks. They enjoy occupations in which they can be creative and interact with people. They like a friendly and relaxed environment in which they are free to follow their inspiration and participate in adventures.

General occupations to consider

creative occupations
marketing
education

counseling
health care

social service
entrepreneurial business

Specific job titles

journalist	public relations	physical therapist
musician	counselor	consultant
actor	clergy	inventor
entertainer	psychologist	sales
fine artist	teacher (health, special	human resources manager
playwright	education, English, art,	conference planner
newscaster	drama, music)	employment development
reporter	social worker	specialist
interior decorator	dental hygienist	restauranteur
cartoonist	nurse	merchandise planner
graphic designer	dietician	environmental attorney
marketing	holistic health practitioner	lawyer
advertising		

College majors

journalism	business (advertising,	religious studies
English	marketing, public	health occupations
drama	relations)	law
art	counseling	vocational training
graphic design	psychology	

ENFJ

ENFJs are friendly, sociable, empathetic, loyal, creative, imaginative, and responsible. They have great people skills and are interested in working with people and providing service to them. They are good at building harmony and cooperation and respect other people's opinions. These types can find creative solutions to problems. They are natural leaders who can make good decisions. They prefer an environment that is organized and structured and enjoy working as part of a team with other creative and caring people.

General occupations to consider

religious occupations	counseling	health care
creative occupations	education	business
communications	human services	

Specific job titles

director of religious
    education
minister
clergy
public relations
marketing
writer
librarian
journalist
fine artist
designer
actor
musician or composer
fund-raiser
recreational director
TV producer

newscaster
politician
editor
crisis counselor
school counselor
vocational or career
    counselor
psychologist
alcohol and drug
    counselor
teacher (health, art,
    drama, English, foreign
    languages)
child-care worker
college humanities
    professor

social worker
home economist
nutritionist
speech pathologist
occupational therapist
physical therapist
optometrist
dental hygienist
family practice physician
psychiatrist
nursing educator
pharmacist
human resources trainer
travel agent
small business executive
sales manager

College majors

religious studies
business (public relations,
    marketing)
art
graphic design
drama

music
journalism
English
foreign languages
humanities
psychology

counseling
sociology
health occupations
business
vocational training

ENTP

ENTPs are creative, ingenious, flexible, diverse, energetic, fun, motivating, logical, and outspoken. They have excellent people skills and are natural leaders, although they dislike controlling other people. They value knowledge and competence. They are lively and energetic and make good debaters and motivational speakers. They are logical and rational thinkers who can grasp complex ideas and theories. They dislike environments that are structured and rigid. These types prefer environments that allow them to engage in creative problem solving and the creation of new ideas.

General occupations to consider

creative occupations
politics

law
business

health care

Specific job titles

photographer	politician	computer professional
marketing professional	political manager	corrections officer
journalist	political analyst	sales manager
actor	social scientist	speech pathologist
writer	psychiatrist	health education
musician or composer	psychologist	practitioner
editor	engineer	respiratory therapist
reporter	construction laborer	dental assistant
advertising director	research worker	medical assistant
radio/TV talk show host	electrician	critical care nurse
producer	lawyer	counselor
art director	judge	human resources planner
new business developer	corporate executive	

College majors

art	music	political science
photography	business (advertising,	psychology
journalism	marketing,	health occupations
drama	management,	computers
English	human resources)	vocational training

ENTJ

ENTJs are independent, original, visionary, logical, organized, ambitious, competitive, hardworking, and direct. They are natural leaders and organizers who identify problems and create solutions for organizations. ENTJs are often in management positions. They are good planners and accomplish goals in a timely manner. These types are logical thinkers who enjoy a structured work environment where they have opportunity for advancement. They enjoy a challenging, competitive, and exciting environment in which accomplishments are recognized.

General occupations to consider

business
finance
law

Specific job titles

executive	manager in city/county/	accountant
manager	state government	auditor
supervisor	management trainer	financial manager
personnel manager	school principal	real estate agent
sales manager	bank officer	lawyer, judge
marketing manager	computer systems analyst	consultant
human resources planner	computer professional	engineer
corporate executive	credit investigator	corrections, probation
college administrator	mortgage broker	officer
health administrator	stockbroker	psychologist
small business owner	investment banker	physician
retail store manager	economist	

College majors

business management	computers	engineering
finance	law	psychology
economics	medicine	vocational training

Other Factors in Choosing a Major

Choosing your college major is one of the most difficult and important decisions you will make during your college years. After assessing their personality types, students often come up with many different options for a major and career. Future chapters will help you to think about your interests, values, and preferred lifestyle. This information will help you to narrow down your choices.

Once you have completed a thorough self-assessment, you may still have several majors to consider. At this point, it is important to do some research on the outlook for a selected career in the future and the pay you would receive. Sometimes students are disappointed after graduation when they find there are few job opportunities in their chosen career field. Sometimes students graduate and cannot find jobs with the salary they had hoped to earn. It is important to think about the opportunities you will have in the future. If you have several options for a career you would enjoy, you may want to consider seriously the career that has the best outlook and pay.

Majors and Earnings[6]

Major	Earnings
Chemical Engineering	$56,269
Electrical Engineering	$53,500
Mechanical Engineering	$51,732
Computer Science	$50,744
Information Sciences and Systems	$47,182
Civil Engineering	$46,084
Accounting	$44,928
Economics/Finance	$44,588
Business Administration Management	$41,155
Political Science and Government	$33,094
History	$33,071
English	$31,385
Sociology	$31,096
Psychology	$30,369

Every career counselor can tell stories about students who ask, "What is the career that makes the most money? That's the career I want!" However, if you choose a career based on money alone, you might find it difficult and uninteresting for a lifetime of work. You might even find yourself retraining later in life for a job that you really enjoy. Remember that the first step is to figure out who you are and what you like. Then look at career outlook and opportunity. If you find your passion in a career that is in demand and pays well, you will probably be very happy with your career choice. If you find your passion in a career that offers few jobs and does not pay well, you will have to use your ingenuity to find a job and make a living. Many students happily make this informed choice and find a way to make it work.

JOURNAL ENTRY #10

Answer one of the following questions:

1. If you have chosen a major, is it one that is suggested by your personality type? If your major is not suggested for your personality type, how can you apply your personality strengths to being successful in your chosen career?

2. If you have not chosen a major, are there some suggested careers that you are interested in considering? How would your personality strengths be an asset in these careers?

Find Your Passion

Mark Twain said, "The secret of success is making your vocation your vacation." Find what you like to do. Better yet, find your passion. If you can find your passion, it is easy to invest the time and effort necessary to be successful. Aviator Charles Lindbergh said, "It is the greatest shot of adrenaline to be doing what you've wanted to do so badly. You almost feel like you could fly without the plane."[7] We may not be as excited about our careers as Charles Lindbergh, but we can find a career that matches our personalities and talents and provides meaning to our lives.

How do you know when you have found your passion? You have found your passion when you are doing an activity and you do not notice that the time is passing. The great painter Picasso often talked about how quickly time passed while he was painting. He said, "When I work, I relax; doing nothing or entertaining visitors makes me tired." Whether you are an artist, an athlete, a scientist, or a business entrepreneur, passion provides the energy needed to be successful. It helps you to grow and create. When you are using your talents to grow and create, you can find meaning and happiness in your life.

Psychologist Martin Seligman has written a book entitled *Authentic Happiness,* in which he writes about three types of work orientation: a job, a career, and a calling.[8] A job is what you do for the paycheck at the end of the week. Many college students have jobs to earn money for college. A career has deeper personal meaning. It involves achievement, prestige, and power. A calling is defined as "a passionate commitment to work for its own sake."[9] When you have found your calling, the job itself is the reward. He notes that people who have found their calling are consistently happier than those who have a job or even a career. One of the ways that you know you have found your calling is when you are in the state of "flow." The state of "flow" is defined as "complete absorption in an activity whose challenges mesh perfectly with your abilities."[10] People who experience "flow" are happier and more productive. They do not spend their days looking forward to Friday. Understanding your personal strengths is the beginning step to finding your calling.

Seligman adds that any job can become a calling by using your personal strengths to do the best

© VR Photos, 2009. Used under license from Shutterstock, Inc.

possible job. He cited a study of hospital cleaners. Although some viewed their job as drudgery, others viewed the job as a calling. They believed that they helped patients get better by working efficiently and anticipating the needs of doctors and nurses. They rearranged furniture and decorated walls to help patients feel better. They found their calling by applying their personal talents to their jobs. As a result, their jobs became a calling.

Sometimes we wait around for passion to find us. That probably won't happen. The first step in finding your passion is to know yourself. Then find an occupation in which you can use your talents. You may be able to find your passion by looking at your present job and finding a creative way to do it based on your special talents. It has been said that there are no dead-end jobs, just people who cannot see the possibilities. Begin your search for passion by looking for possibilities. If the job that you have now is not your passion, see what you can learn from it and then use your skills to find a career where you are more likely to find your passion.

Success is not the key to happiness; happiness is the key to success. If you love what you are doing, you will be successful.

—Anonymous

JOURNAL ENTRIES

Personality

Go to http://www.collegesuccess1.com/ for Word files of the Journal Entries

Success over the Internet

Visit the *College Success Website* at http://www.collegesuccess1.com/

The *College Success Website* is continually updated with new topics and links to the material presented in this chapter. Topics include:

- Personality profiles
- Online personality assessments
- Personality types of famous people in history

- Personality types and relationships
- Personality types and marriage
- Personality and careers
- Personality and communication
- Choosing your major
- Topics just for fun

Contact your instructor if you have any problems in accessing the *College Success Website*.

Notes

1. Judith Provost and Scott Anchors, eds., *Applications of the Myers-Briggs Type Indicator in Higher Education* (Palo Alto, CA: Consulting Psychologists Press, 1991), 51.
2. Ibid., 49.
3. Otto Kroeger and Janet Thuesen, *Type Talk: The 16 Personality Types That Determine How We Live, Love and Work* (New York: Dell, 1989), 204.
4. Ibid.
5. Allen L. Hammer and Gerald P. Macdaid, *MBTI Career Report Manual* (CA: Consulting Psychologist Press, 1998), 57–89.
6. Rob Kelly, "Most Lucrative Degrees for College Grads," CNN Money.com, October 27, 2006.
7. Quoted in Rob Gilbert, ed., *Bits and Pieces,* December 2, 1999.
8. Martin Seligman, *Authentic Happiness* (Free Press, 2002).
9. Martin Seligman, as reported by Geoffrey Cowley, "The Science of Happiness," *Newsweek,* September 16, 2002, 49.
10. Ibid.

Exercise 4.1: Personality Preferences

Name _____   Date _____

Use the textbook and personality assessment to think about your personality type. Place an X on the scale to show your degree of preference for each dimension of personality.

Introvert _____|_____ Extravert

Sensing _____|_____ INtuitive

Thinking _____|_____ Feeling

Judging _____|_____ Perceptive

Write a key word or phrase to describe each preference.

Introvert

Extravert

Sensing

INtuitive

Thinking

Feeling

Judging

Perceptive

What careers are suggested by your personality assessment?

Was the personality assessment accurate and useful to you?

Name _____   Date _____

Look at the charts at the beginning of the chapter that describe the ideal work environment and the section on Personality and Preferred Work Environment. Based on this information and the items you have highlighted, describe your ideal work environment.

Are there other characteristics of your ideal job? For example, do you want a job that provides financial security, helps you stay in the same geographical area, provides opportunity for travel, and lets you have time to be with your family? Write two additional characteristics of your ideal job.

What are the five most important characteristics of your ideal job?

1. _____

2. _____

3. _____

4. _____

5. _____

Look at the careers that match your personality type. List the careers that seem interesting to you. Include any careers that you have been considering, whether they are on the list or not.

Exercise 4.3: Describe Your Personality

Name _____   Date _____

Review the following material to prepare for writing a description of your personality type.

- The material on personality in this chapter

- The results of your "Do What You Are" personality assessment.

- Additional materials provided by your professor or located on the Internet at www.personalitypage.com.

Using the outline below, write a description of your personality type on a separate sheet of paper.

1. In the introduction, give the four-letter abbreviation for your type (such as ISFJ) and explain in your own words what each letter means.

2. Using the material you have reviewed, write a general description of your personality type.

3. Describe the first letter of your code (E or I). Include preferences in the workplace. Give an example of how this preference affects your social life, school, and work.

4. Describe the second letter of your code (S or N). Include preferences in the workplace. Give an example of how this preference affects your social life, school, and work.

5. Describe the third letter of your code (T or F). Include preferences in the workplace. Give an example of how this preference affects your social life, school, and work.

6. Describe the fourth letter of your code (J or P). Include preferences in the workplace. Give an example of how this preference affects your social life, school, and work.

7. Tell how your personality is suited to specific careers and majors.

8. In the last paragraph, tell what you thought of the personality assessment. Was it useful to you? Did it give you ideas for your major or career?

Name _____ Date _____

Directions: Please read the chapter on personality before commenting on these scenarios. Keep in mind the theory that we are all born with certain personality types and there are no good or bad types. Each type has gifts and talents that can be used to be a successful and happy person. Relate your comments to the concepts in this chapter. Your instructor may have you do this exercise as a group activity in class.

Scenario 1 (Sensing vs. Intuitive): Julie is a pre-school teacher. She assigns her class to draw a picture of a bicycle. Students share their pictures with the class. One of the students has drawn a bicycle with wings. Another student laughs at the drawing and says, "Bicycles don't have wings!" How should the teacher handle this situation?

Scenario 2 (Thinking vs. Feeling): John has the almost perfect girlfriend. She is beautiful, intelligent and fun to be with. She only has one flaw. John thinks that she is too emotional and wishes she could be a little more rational. When his girlfriend tries to talk to him about emotional issues, he analyzes her problems and proposes a logical solution. His girlfriend doesn't like the solutions that John proposes. Should John find a new girlfriend?

Scenario 3 (Introvert vs. Extravert): Mary is the mother of 2 children ages 5 (daughter) and 8 (son). The 5-year old is very social and especially enjoys birthday parties. At the last party she invited 24 girls and they all showed up at the party. Everyone had a great time. The 8-year old is very quiet and spends his time reading, doing art work, building models and hanging out with his one best friend. Mary is concerned that her son does not have very many friends. She decides to have a birthday party for her son also. The only problem is that he cannot come up with a list of children to invite to the party. What should Mary do?

Scenario 4 (Judging vs. Perceptive): Jerry and Jennifer have just been married and they love each other very much. Jennifer likes to keep the house neat and orderly and likes to plan out activities so that there are no surprises. Jerry likes creative disorder. He leaves his things all over the house. He often comes up with creative ideas for having fun. How can Jerry and Jennifer keep their good relationship going?

PART TWO

Career Exploration and College Success

CHAPTER QUEST

At the end of this chapter you should be able to:

- Understand the different types of majors

- Learn why students experience difficulty with decision-making

- Realize career options related to specific fields of study

- Discover factors leading to a well-informed career decision

Connecting Majors to Careers

Majors and Degrees...What's the Difference?

Choosing a major is perhaps one of the most important decisions for college students. This decision signals the beginning of specific educational experiences and infers potential career options and paths. The latter causes the greatest concern because most students attach a feeling of finality to their choice of major regarding career options and earning potential. Many students prematurely determine that their choice of major leads to a particular career path they will be "stuck with for life," or they immaturely assume that certain majors automatically lead to high salaries or to a life filled with financial strife. In reality, neither scenario is always true, as career success and earning potential are also impacted by other factors such as interests, skills, abilities, and the realities of the job market and hiring trends. The path to choosing a major is unique to each person, and you should start by exploring majors and how they connect to careers and the world of work.

Before we discuss the different types of majors and relevant career paths, it might be helpful to provide a brief overview of how typical programs at colleges and universities are structured, particularly those at UNF. Simply stated, a college degree, the end result, is the broader category under which various majors are housed, and degrees are labeled by various titles (i.e., a Bachelor of Arts includes majors in psychology, history, and political science, and a Bachelor of Science includes majors like chemistry, communication, and engineering). The four main components of a college degree are:

General Education—a core set of course work required by nearly all universities and colleges. The aim of general education is to enable you to have a broad knowledge base across a variety of disciplines. The added benefit of these courses is your opportunity to explore areas of interest, which proves very useful for selecting the best major.

Prerequisites—required courses to prepare for your chosen major. These courses are taken in conjunction with general education and free electives courses.

Free Electives—courses that round out the total number of credit hours. You can choose electives based on personal interests or courses that will assist you in developing skills or knowledge to enhance your chosen major or career. Most majors will require some free electives to complete your total number of required credit hours for the bachelor's degree.

Major Requirements—whereas general education provides breadth, the major provides depth into a specific field or discipline. It's the primary focal point of the latter portion of your degree.

ACTIVITY 5.1

UNF Majors

This exercise is designed to provide an easy-to-read overview of undergraduate majors and minors available at UNF so you can narrow your focus to a workable list to further explore. Review the list of majors and minors and highlight all that are of interest to you. (Please note the following abbreviations: BA = Bachelor of Arts, BS = Bachelor of Science, BFA = Bachelor of Fine Arts, BM = Bachelor of Music)

COLLEGE OF ARTS AND SCIENCES

Anthropology, BA
Art—Art History Concentration, BA
Art—Ceramics and Sculpture Concentration, BA
Art—Painting and Drawing Concentration, BA
Biology—Biomedical Sciences, BS
Biology—Coastal Biology, BS
Biology—Coastal Environmental Science, BS
Biology—Ecology and Evolution Biology, BS
Biology—Molecular/Cell Bio. & Biotech, BS
Chemistry, BS
Chemistry—Materials Chemistry, BS
Chemistry—Pre-Medical Professions, BS
Communications—Advertising Concentration BS
Communications—Electronic Media Concentration BS
Communications—Journalism Concentration, BS
Communications—Public Relations Concentration, BS
Criminal Justice, BA
Economics, BA
English, BA
English—Drama Concentration, BA
Fine Arts—Ceramics and Sculpture Concentration, BFA
Fine Arts—Graphic Design and Digital Media Concentration, BFA
Fine Arts—Painting and Drawing Concentration, BFA
Fine Arts—Photography Concentration, BFA
French Studies, BA
History, BA
International Studies—Asian Studies, BA
International Studies—European Studies, BA
International Studies—Foreign Language & Culture, BA
International Studies—Intl. Relations & Politics, BA
International Studies—Latin American Studies, BA
International Studies—Middle East-African Studies, BA
Liberal Studies, BA
Mathematics, BA

Mathematics—Discrete Analysis, BS
Mathematics, BS
Music Education, BME
Music—Jazz Studies, BM
Music—Performance—Piano, BM
Music—Performance—Strings (including Harp), BM
Music—Performance—Voice, BM
Music—Performance—Woodwinds, Brass, Percussion, BM
Music Performance—Piano Pedagogy, BM
Philosophy—General, BA
Philosophy—Advanced Studies, BA
Philosophy—Applied Ethics, BA
Philosophy—Historical and Comparative, BA
Philosophy—Legal, Political, and Social Studies, BA
Philosophy—Literary and Cultural, BA
Physics, BS
Physics—Astrophysics, BS
Physics—Civil Engineering Concentration, BS
Physics—Electrical Engineering Concentration, BS
Physics—Mechanical Engineering Concentration BS
Physics—Computing Emphasis Concentration, BS
Physics—Pre-Medical Physics, BS
Political Science—American Politics, BA
Political Science—General, BA
Political Science—International Relations/ Comparative, BA
Politics, BA
Political Science—Public Law, BA
Political Science—Fast Concentration to MPA, BA
Political Science—Public Admin/Public Policy, BA
Psychology, BA
Psychology—Child Psychology, BA
Psychology—Child Psychology, BS
Psychology, BS
Sociology, BA
Sociology—Social Welfare, BA
Spanish, BA
Statistics, BA
Statistics, BS

UNF Majors (continued)

COGGIN COLLEGE OF BUSINESS

Accounting, BBA
Economics, BBA
Finance, BBA
Financial Services, BBA

International Business, BBA
Management, BBA
Marketing, BBA
Transportation and Logistics, BBA

COLLEGE OF COMPUTING, ENGINEERING, AND CONSTRUCTION

Computer and Information Science, BS
Computer Science
Information Science
Information Systems
Information Technology
Civil Engineering, BS

Electrical Engineering, BSEE
Computer Design
System Design
Mechanical Engineering, BS
Building Construction, BS

COLLEGE OF EDUCATION AND HUMAN SERVICES

Art Education (K–12), BAE
Elementary Education—K–6, Pre K-Primary, BAE
English Education—English (6–12), BAE
Middle School—Mathematics and Science, BAE
Mathematics Education (6–12), BAE
Physical Education—K–12, BAE
PreKdg/Primary Education, BAE
Science Education—Physics Education, BAE
Science Education—Biology Education, BAE

Science Education—Chemistry Education, BAE
Secondary Education—Social Studies Education, BAE
Special Education—Deaf Studies, BAE
Special Education—Exceptional Student Education, BAE
Sport Management, BS
Sport Management—Community Sport, BS

BROOKS COLLEGE OF HEALTH

Athletic Training, BSAT
Health Administration, BHA
Health Science—Community Health, BSH
Health Science—Exercise Science, BSH

Nutrition and Dietetics, BSH
Nursing (Traditional Prelicensure, Accelerated Prelicensure, and RN-BSN), BSN

MINORS THE FOLLOWING UNDERGRADUATE MINORS ARE AVAILABLE AT UNF:

COLLEGE OF ARTS AND SCIENCES

Africa/African-American
Diaspora
Anthropology
Applied Statistics
Art History
Asian Studies
Behavioral Medicine
Biology
Chemistry
Classical Civilization
Communications Studies
Creative Writing

Criminal Justice
Culture and Philosophy
Drama
Economics
English
Environmental Studies
Film Studies
French
Gender Studies
History
International Studies
Law and Philosophy

UNF Majors (continued)

Mass Communications	Public Administration
Mathematical Science	Religious Studies
Painting, Drawing, Printmaking	Social Welfare
Philosophy	Sociology
Photography	Spanish
Physics	Statistics
Political Science	Studies in Applied Ethics
Psychology	Urban & Metropolitan Studies

COGGIN COLLEGE OF BUSINESS

Business Administration	Finance
Economics	Geography
Entrepreneurship	International Business

COLLEGE OF COMPUTING, ENGINEERING, AND CONSTRUCTION

Computer Science	Electrical Engineering
Information Science	

COLLEGE OF EDUCATION AND HUMAN SERVICES

Amer Sign Lang/Deaf Studies	Clinical & Applied Movement Sc
Professional Education	Public Health
Sports Management	Health Education
Brooks College of Health	

Types of Majors

While some students enter campus with a major in mind, many students are unsure and experience difficulty with decision-making. A common reason students experience so much difficulty with major and career selection is a lack of information, particularly regarding the connection between majors and careers. Let's make one important distinction: choosing a major and deciding on a career path are not always the same process or the same decision. A college degree provides educational credentials and knowledge that will enhance your competitiveness in the job market, but this does not always mean that a particular major obligates you to a specific job choice. This notion is better understood through an examination of the two basic types of majors:

Occupation-Focused

Do you want your college education to prepare you for a specific job? Career preparation is a popular and valid reason for heading to college. If this sounds like you, then consider a career-focused major like engineering, accounting, graphic design, education, or nursing. Your education will be geared toward a specific vocation, and you'll likely take a job in that field when you graduate.

© Lisa F. Young, 2009. Used under license from Shutterstock, Inc.

Options-Focused

Another reason for attending college is to expand your knowledge and skills in general, without having to initially declare a specific career goal. However, throughout the course of your college career, as you engage in career planning activities, clearer career goals should emerge. Generally, in this case you should consider liberal arts, since these majors emphasize critical thinking, creativity, and integration of information, among other skills. Majors such as psychology, history, literature, and philosophy are not necessarily focused on specific careers, but you'll graduate with a variety of marketable and legitimate skills for entry into a variety of positions and industries.

You might try focusing on both your short- and long-term goals as a way to determine which type of major is best for you. For example, if you want to gain specific skills and knowledge for immediate entry into a career, the Occupations-Focused majors might be best. However, if you want to gain a broader base of skills and knowledge that would lead to many options, focus your exploration on Options-Focused majors. Students express concerns regarding both types of majors. Early commitment to a major that one may later regret is a common source of anxiety for Occupations-Focused majors. With Options-Focused majors, students express concerns about lacking a clear direction due to the variety of options available. To alleviate these concerns, you should take the necessary time to engage in self-assessment and career exploration resources and activities offered by Career Services. It's important to remember that career satisfaction and success are possible with either Occupations-Focused or Options-Focused majors. What's most important is taking the necessary time to engage in the career planning process to explore and discover the best choice for you.

ACTIVITY 5.2
The Type of Major for You

Were the majors you highlighted in the previous activity Options-Focused, Occupations-Focused, or a combination of both? What are your initial thoughts about the type of major that is best for you?

_____

_____

_____

_____

_____

UNF Resources

UNF is a haven of information and resources to chart your course to a suitable field of study. One effective way to explore majors is by enrolling in introductory-type courses. This will allow you to assess your interests in different areas. General education requirements cover many career areas, but here are a few others to consider:

AMH2020—US History Since 1877[*]
ANT2000—Introduction to Anthropology[*]
ART1300C—Drawing I
BCN1251—Construction Drawing
CCJ2002—Crime in America[*]
CGS1570—Microcomputer Software Applications
EDF1005—Introduction to Education
EGN1001—Introduction to Engineering I (Prereq. – Precalculus)
GEB1011—Found. of Business
GEB2112—Planning a New Business
HSC2000—Health Care Careers
HSC2100—Personal Health Issues and Problems
HUN2201—Basic Principles of Nutrition
INR2002—Introduction to International Relations
MMC1004—Media Literacy
PHI2010—Introduction to Philosophy[*]
POS2041—Introduction to American Government[*]
PSY2012—Introduction to Psychology[*]
SYG2000—Introduction to Sociology[*]

[*]General Education Courses (consult your advisor for more options)

Which Comes First . . . the Major or the Career?

You may also discover that while you feel sure about the best major, you may not be ready to set firm career goals. That's perfectly okay, as it may be hard to know the best career choice before you experience the environment. So, as you complete degree requirements, allow the classroom and work experiences you will encounter to help in your career selection process.

As you have discovered, choosing a major is a *process*, and may take several semesters of work on your part. For some students, just taking an introductory course in the subject will tell them what they need to know, while others won't know for sure until they've had experience in the field. Wherever you are in the process, career counselors and academic advisors are available to help along the way.

Information is power, and the more you have, the easier the process will be. You know you are close to making a choice when you feel pretty knowledgeable about yourself and viable career options. This increased competence should lead to your feeling confident enough to make a smart choice. Don't worry so much if you don't feel 100% sure, as that may be an unrealistic goal. Remember, you are still developing and discovering information about yourself.

Other Valuable Resources

Course Catalog—reviewing required coursework for different majors helps you determine your level of interest. Is your interest strong enough to commit to a full load of courses in a particular discipline, or would you prefer one or two courses as electives?

Professors—many of them have worked in your field of interest and can provide a more in-depth perspective on career options and opportunities. You'll be surprised at how willing most will be to speak with you.

Classmates—seek out students who are a little further along in their college career, particularly juniors and seniors who are enrolled in majors of interest to you. They prove especially helpful in providing information they have gathered from a student's perspective. Just be sure to balance their perspective with that of a college or career professional.

UNF Alumni—previous students from your college are invaluable if they are currently working in fields of interest to you. They can help you fully understand the day-to-day perspective of a particular career.

Academic Advisors—the academic perspective on major selection provides much-needed insight to ensure you are on the right track with course selection and your educational goals.

Career Counselors—career professionals complement the insight provided by Academic Advisors. Career Counselors are able to provide you with more in-depth insight into majors and careers through various self-assessment and career exploration activities and resources. You emerge from this process more confident and competent to make a wise choice. As discussed later in this resource, career professionals also assist you in developing employability skills, gaining work experiences, and transitioning effectively from college into careers.

Family and Friends—even those close to you are able to assist in your decision-making process. Family and friends can be a great source of information. They are also valuable in connecting you with professionals in your fields of interest.

One of the most common reasons students experience difficulty with major and career decision-making is a lack of information. Be proactive and take advantage of the full array of information and resources available to you.

Career Paths Overview

An important step to selecting a major is understanding the connection to careers and the world of work. You should always remain optimistic about the many options available to you. Your college degree uniquely qualifies you for many career paths, serving as a springboard to many opportunities. This section does not represent all possibilities, but provides a great foundation for realizing the potential and value of UNF degrees and majors as they relate to various career paths. Activity 5.1 provided a comprehensive list of the undergraduate majors and minors offered at UNF. The five colleges housing these majors are detailed below with connections to relevant careers and workplace environments.

© DUSAN ZIDAR, 2009. Used under license from Shutterstock, Inc.

The College of Arts and Sciences

The College of Arts and Sciences is the bedrock of UNF, provides a dynamic liberal arts curriculum that lays the foundation for all further advanced academic study, and is the largest college at UNF in both size and number of programs offered. Each of the College's programs provides opportunities for intellectual discovery and career preparation in a variety of areas. You'll have access to some of the brightest and best professors in the country, as evidenced by recognition in their areas of expertise by the Fulbright Award, the International Jazz Educators Hall of Fame, and the National Academy of Public Administration. Graduates of the College are knowledgeable, articulate, and discerning, having an education that will serve them for a lifetime. The College's mission focuses on the long-term, total educational experience of each student.

Source: UNF Office of Admissions

Typical Job Titles for Liberal Arts Graduates

Anthropologist
Field Archaeologist
Museum Education Director
Art Historian
Catalog Illustrator
Costume Designer
Fashion Designer
Graphic Designer
Photographer
Biochemist
Public Health Worker
Wildlife Biologist
Water Purification Chemist
Radio Announcer
Sports Reporter
Border Patrol Agent
Drug Enforcement Agent
State Trooper
Financial Planner
Book Editor
Cartoonist
Film Animation Artist
Counselor
Legislative Aide
Disc Jockey

Social Worker
Historic Site Interpreter
Child Psychologist
Public Relations Representative
Advertising Copywriter
Internal Revenue Agent
Editor
Film Music Editor
Game Designer
Journalist
Sales Representative
City Manager
College Professor
Art Director
Public Information Officer
CIA Agent
Insurance Underwriter
Purchasing Agent
Actuary
Music Promoter
Nursing Home Director
Technical Writer
Toxicologist
Teacher
Foreign Service Officer

Typical Work Settings for Liberal Arts Graduates

Government Agencies
Museums
National Park Services
Art Galleries
Film/Motion Picture Industry
Chemical Companies
Drug Companies
Medical Centers
Biotechnology Firms
Advertising Agencies
Newspapers
Public Relations Firms

Television/Radio Stations
State Police Departments
County Sheriff Offices
Federal Bureau of Investigation
Libraries
Retirement Communities
Insurance Firms
Banks/Financial Institutions
Magazines
Orchestras
Corporations
Nonprofit Organizations

Coggin College of Business

The Coggin College of Business is emerging as one of the premier business programs in the United States; it is endorsed by the distinctive accreditation of AACSB International, the Association to Advance Collegiate Schools of Business, and maintains high standards for academic quality. Undergraduate students obtain a great classroom education in a variety of business areas, while also having the opportunity for internships with some of North Florida's most successful business and nonprofit organizations. The College is also committed to providing its students with opportunities to experience various aspects of business and has established several student and faculty exchange programs with schools in China, India, France, Brazil, Germany, Argentina,

© Yuri Arcurs, 2009. Used under license from Shutterstock, Inc.

Poland, and many more. The faculty at the College consists of experienced professionals who have cultivated theoretical learning with practical real-world expectations.
Source: UNF Office of Admissions

Typical Job Titles for Business Graduates

Actuary
Internal Auditor
Financial Analyst
Bank Examiner
Controller
Public Accountant
Chief Financial Officer
Budget Officer
Estate Planner
Foreign Trade Analyst
Insurance Underwriter
Claims Adjuster
Personnel Manager

Human Resources Manager
Bank Manager
Stock Broker
Mortgage Loan Officer
Distribution Manager
Logistics Specialist
Director of Transportation
Advertising Executive
Sales Manager
Financial Planner
International Account Representative
International Purchasing Agent

Typical Work Settings for Business Graduates

Accounting Firms
Government Agencies
Advertising Agencies
Federal Reserve Board
Insurance Companies
Law Firms
Investment Firms
Small Businesses

Trade Associations
Nonprofit Agencies
Transportation Companies
Distribution Centers
Trade Associations
Marketing Research Firms
Corporations
International Businesses

© Jaimie Duplass, 2009. Used under license from Shutterstock, Inc.

Medical Agencies   Political Action Groups
Banks   Fundraising Firms
Department of the Treasury   Colleges and Universities
Labor Unions   Environmental Associations

Brooks College of Health

The Brooks College of Health is dedicated to providing high-quality health care education and preparing students who are dedicated to serving the community and its patients. Outstanding programs are offered in a wide range of health care fields. These courses of study are each directed and enhanced by the use of the most current technologies, innovative faculty and student research, and opportunities for hands-on learning experiences in clinical settings and laboratories. The College continues to develop its growing national reputation for excellence in academic, clinical, and scientific studies.

Source: UNF Office of Admissions

Typical Job Titles for Health Graduates

Massage Therapist   Health and Wellness Educator
Personal Trainer   Nurse
Athletic Trainer   Geriatric Administrator
Exercise Physiologist   Nutrition Counselor
Fitness Consultant   Family Services Manager
Physical Therapist   Social Services Manager
Occupational Therapist   Clinical Researcher
Health Officer   Vocational Rehabilitation Counselor
Health Administrator   Mental Health Counselor
Hospital Personnel Director   Substance Abuse Counselor
Health Educator   Case Manager
Clinical Researcher   Hospital Risk Manager

Typical Work Settings for Health Graduates

High Schools
Colleges/Universities
Professional Sports Teams
Health and Fitness Centers
Hospitals
Nursing Homes
Rehabilitation Hospitals
Disease Centers
Insurance Companies
Health Clinics
Social Service Agencies
Government Agencies

Adult Day Care Centers
Health Management Organizations
Hotels and Restaurants
Pharmaceutical Companies
Food Manufacturers
Correctional Facilities
Public Health Organizations
Personal Care Facilities
Consulting Firms
Private Practices
Commercial Wellness Centers
Physician Management Organizations

© Monkey Business Images, 2009. Used under license from Shutterstock, Inc.

The College of Education and Human Services

The vision of the College of Education and Human Services is to be active leaders and responsive partners in the study and enhancement of teaching and learning within diverse communities. The research, critical debate, and hands-on experience required by the College of Education and Human Services in its undergraduate, master's, and doctoral programs have created a community of compassionate and responsible educators, well respected for their classroom creativity and excellence. Students complete extensive educational programs, including comprehensive clinical experiences in local schools, led by an active and engaged faculty. The College is active in developing international alliances permitting our students to travel and experience education and human services in other countries. Over 75% of our graduates either become or are already employed in local schools and school districts. Alumni of the College have received Milken National Educator Awards and have consistently been named Teachers of the Year in Northeast Florida.

Source: UNF Office of Admissions

Typical Job Titles for Education Graduates

Preschool Teacher
Kindergarten Teacher
Elementary School Teacher
Middle School Teacher
High School Teacher
College Instructor/Professor
Community College Instructor
Adult Education Instructor
Adult Literacy Specialist
Coach
School Psychologist
Fitness Trainer

College Administrator
School Administrator
Instruction Coordinator
School Counselor
Speech Pathologist
Sports Camp Director
Sports Promoter
Sportscaster
Historic Site Administrator
Curriculum Specialist
Child Life Specialist
Physical Education Teacher

Typical Work Settings for Education Graduates

Colleges
Universities
Private Schools
Public Schools
Day Care Centers
Board of Education
Montessori Schools
Libraries
Department of Defense Schools
Private Learning Centers

Correctional Facilities
Sheltered Workshops
Mental Health Facilities
Fitness Centers
Professional Sports Teams
Stadiums/Arenas
YMCA/YWCA
Sporting Goods Stores
City Recreation and Parks Departments
Community Care Facilities

© Lisa F. Young, 2009. Used under license from Shutterstock, Inc.

College of Computing, Engineering, and Construction

The College of Computing, Engineering, and Construction offers nationally recognized and accredited academic areas of study. Students are given opportunities for a wide range of educational experiences through co-ops, internships, study abroad, research activities, student clubs, and community-based service learning. These programs enjoy exceptional support from local industry organizations, companies, and business leaders, and offer students real-world educational experiences. Over 75% of the College's graduates enter the growing computing, engineering, information systems, and building construction management job markets in Jacksonville. The learning environment resembles the most current engineering and construction industry practices, and classes are taught by a dedicated faculty that excels in teaching, research, and service.

Source: UNF Office of Admissions

Typical Job Titles for Computing, Engineering, and Construction Graduates

Field Engineer	Teacher/Professor
Estimator	Safety Engineer
Cost Control Engineer	Electrical Engineer
Project Engineer	Mechanical Engineer
Civil Engineer	Mainframe Technician
CAD Drafter	Research Analyst
Project Manager	Artificial Intelligence Programmer
Director of Transportation	Database Administrator
Systems Analyst	Control Systems Engineer
Computer Programmer	Plasma Engineer
Software Support Specialist	Digital Signal Processor
Robotics Programmer	Electromechanical Test Engineer

Typical Work Settings for Computing, Engineering, and Construction Graduates

Residential Construction	Nonprofit Agencies
Commercial Construction	Small Businesses
Engineering Firms	Law Firms
Architectural Firms	Information Technology Industry
Utility Companies	Aeronautical/Aerospace Industry
Oil Companies	Automotive Industry
Telecommunications Businesses	Nuclear Plants
Manufacturing Companies	Pulp and Paper Industry
Consulting Firms	Glass, Ceramics, and Metal Industry
Railroads	Chemical and Petrochemical Plants
Government Agencies	Water and Wastewater Treatment
Medical Companies	Plants
Colleges/Universities	

Career Exploration

You now have a good idea of potential career options often pursued by students from various UNF colleges and majors. However, you should now allocate time for more in-depth exploration of the career options presented. This can be an overwhelming process if your list is still broad and diverse. Focus on exploring a narrower list of careers based on insight you gained during the self-assessment phase of the career planning process and the major exploration process. Engaging in different exploration

activities will help you discover the wide variety of career options available while learning the specifics about job responsibilities and qualifications.

If you are like most students, you have a "need to know" what you are getting into before you make the final decision. While it is the responsibility of UNF Career Services to ensure you have access to the appropriate resources, it is your responsibility to actively gain an understanding of career information and current trends. What do you need to know? See if you can relate to the statements below:

"I need to know more about what different careers are out there."
(career titles by major, career descriptions)

"I need to know more about the job."
(job duties and responsibilities, work environment)

"I need to know more about what it takes to get the job."
(degree level, skills, years of experience)

"I need to know the rewards offered by different jobs."
(entry level salary, salary increases, benefits)

"I need to know if I will be able to get a job when I graduate."
(employer profiles, job market, geographical restrictions)

Gaining this type of knowledge allows you to eliminate options that conflict with your needs and preferences while focusing on options that are a good fit.

Salary Data

Gaining access to knowledge about the rewards offered by different jobs is a key consideration for many career decision-makers. The self-assessment phase of career planning often reveals a high personal and professional value placed on the salary of various career options. To ensure that needs, desires, and expectations are congruent with the realities of the job market, it's important to understand the different types of salary data discovered during the career exploration process.

Entry Level or Starting Salaries reflect specific amounts or monetary ranges targeted to job candidates with minimal or no experience in the field.

Local or Regional Salaries reflect specific amounts or ranges offered in a specific city, state, or region.

Top Salaries reflect the earnings of professionals typically holding many years of experience in the field.

National Average Salaries and Salary Ranges reflect a summarized combination of multiple salaries and are inclusive of entry-level through top salaries. The salary actually offered to a candidate could be on the high or low end of the range based on experience level or region.

Career explorers should carefully weigh all information to ensure a clear understanding of which type of salary data is being reviewed. Salary data will not only assist in your decision-making process, but will also prove helpful during the career implementation phase. The job search and interview process require a strong knowledge of salary data and a realistic understanding of your worth (i.e., skills, experience) in relation to the specific positions you may seek. This knowledge will enhance your stance and success during salary negotiations. The following websites may be consulted for current salary data:

State of Florida Agency for Workforce Innovation: http://labormarketinfo.com/library/oes.htm

Florida Research and Economic Database: http://fred.labormarketinfo.com

Florida's Labor Market Statistics: http://www.whatpeopleareasking.com/index.shtm

NACE (National Association of Colleges Employers): http://www.jobweb.com

JobStar Central: http://jobstar.org/tools/salary

SalaryList: http://www.salarylist.com

Remember, your career "fit" must also fit into the realities of the world of work. The information and trends you discover in the self-assessment and career exploration phase will work to your advantage in determining where you are most compatible and competitive with employment demands. This allows you to discover and target key skill areas to develop in order to acquire the qualifications future employers desire in job applicants.

Use the process of elimination and narrow your options further by taking the time to research careers. Research all potential options, as decisions based solely on initial perceptions could result in prematurely eliminating good opportunities or selecting unrealistic options. UNF Career Services offers the following two valuable resources:

Career Library

We house many books, directories, and other resources on almost any career to help you get the information you need (see Table 5.1).

Career Services Website: www.unf.edu/dept/cdc

This useful online tool answers the question "*What can I do with a major in . . . ?*" For each college, there is a list of majors, and for each major, there is a list of possible careers. Our website also provides answers to specific details about career options through links to career exploration sites that provide information such as the nature of the work, employment trends, training, qualifications, earnings, and job outlook for specific careers.

Table 5.1 UNF Career Services—Career Library Resources

This Career Library houses hundreds of books organized by the following categories:

Advertising/Public Relations	International
Animal Care	Languages
Building Construction/Architecture	Law
Business (including Accounting, Finance, Marketing, Real Estate)	Liberal Arts
Communications	Life and Physical Sciences
Computers and Math	NonProfit/Human Services/Psychology
Education	Protective Services
Engineering	Social Sciences
Entertainment	Space and Technology
Entrepreneur	Sports/Outdoors/Cars
Government	Travel/Hospitality Services
Health Care	Visual/Fine Arts
	Writing/Journalism

Information Interviews

To take career exploration to the next level, you should conduct information interviews. This experience allows you to connect with professionals in a particular field

© icyimage, 2009. Used under license from Shutterstock, Inc.

and get practical information to help you evaluate your career. Books and websites are useful and provide valuable information, but they are no substitute for getting information directly from a person working in the field. It is best to talk to more than one person in a particular occupation to get a diverse outlook on that field. Sometimes an information interview might lead to a job shadowing experience allowing you to spend extended time in work settings to experience a "typical day" in a career. Your Career Counselor can assist in this process by providing an information interview guide and sample questions. They may also be able to connect you with local employers or former UNF students. In the final analysis, you will be the one doing the work, so get information directly from professionals working in fields of interest to you before making a final decision.

Exploring Majors and Careers Suitable for You

This chapter has focused on various factors related to choosing a major and exploring career options. Hopefully you have discovered that there is not "one right choice," but that you can make a wise choice based on the information you gather and the way you process that information with resources such as Academic Advisors and Career Counselors. Here are some final points to consider.

When Exploring Majors, Consider This . . .

- Can you complete the required prerequisites and core courses with good grades?
- Are you considering certain majors because they are strongly recommended by your parents or significant others?
- Which topics do you normally like to read about?
- Are you really interested or passionate about the subject matter?
- Do you look forward to tasks and projects related to the major?
- Which specific or unique skills will you gain from the major?
- What types of jobs/careers will you be qualified for?
- Do you know which careers are a good fit for you?

© Pling, 2009. Used under license from Shutterstock, Inc.

Choosing a Minor

"What should I choose as a minor?" This is a very popular question posed to Academic Advisors and Career Counselors. Depending on the major you select, you may also have the opportunity to choose a minor. One option is to choose a minor that increases your skills, thus enhancing job marketability toward your career goals. If you desire a career in the international arena, you might consider a foreign language minor. Another option is to focus on a recreational interest or something fun. This latter option may allow you to "balance" a difficult courseload. Perhaps you want to hone your photography skills or enhance your art and design skills. Please consult your Academic Advisor to ensure your choice is in line with university guidelines.

Warning Signs That a Major May Not Be for You

- A consistent pattern of poor grades
- Low interest level
- Repeated withdrawal from a course
- A nagging doubt or gut feeling

If you can relate to one or more of the above, you may want to rethink your initial major and career selections and explore options suitable to your interests and abilities. You are unique and have to consider which options are best for you. Exercise your freedom to choose a major you will enjoy, one that leads to careers where you can use your abilities and be satisfied.

University of North Florida

Career Discoveries

Career Services
Founders Hall, Bldg 2, Room 1100
www.unf.edu/dept/cdc
904-620-2955

Explore Careers, Discover

Career Decision-Making Steps

1. **Know yourself:** what you like, what you can do, what you want, and what's important to you in a career.

2. **Identify acceptable alternatives.** If you don't have at least two, it's time for research or action.

3. **Evaluate** the information you already have and seek new information, but don't let this become a way of avoiding a decision. There will always be some unknowns.

4. **Choose** by weighing alternatives, narrowing down, and confirming by experience or contact.

5. **Commit** yourself to one alternative first, so you can develop a strategy to reach your goal. Set the other(s) aside, at least until you come to another decision point.

6. **Develop** a timeline and follow through, don't just think or talk about it.

7. **Re-evaluate** after a while to see if it's still what you want.

CHECKLIST

🍎 I am aware of my personal characteristics and have used what I know about myself to narrow my career options. (i.e., interest, personality, abilities/skills and values).

🍎 I have explored my career options in depth through a variety of resources (i.e., online, career library, networking, and internship).

🍎 I have chosen an alternative(s) major or career path.

🍎 I am able to give many reasons why I choose my major over any alternative choices.

REMEMBER...
Decisions are not permanent!

New options may open up and new choices can be made. Most of us go through this process periodically; the result may be a change or a renewed commitment to the career choice.

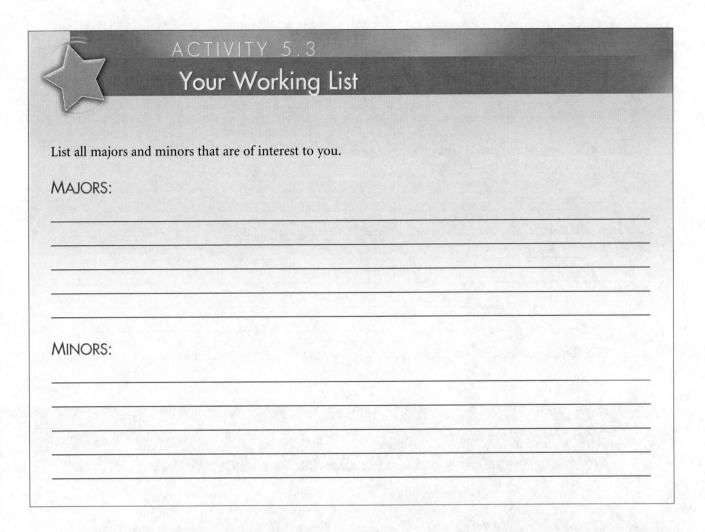

ACTIVITY 5.3
Your Working List

List all majors and minors that are of interest to you.

MAJORS:

_____

_____

_____

_____

MINORS:

_____

_____

_____

_____

ACTIVITY 5.4
Major Research

Allocate time to research majors in your working list to learn about prerequisite coursework, core academic requirements, and any application procedures. Make a list of the resources you would like to use.

_____

_____

_____

_____

_____

ACTIVITY 5.5
Your Top Five Majors

Major exploration resources used in the previous activity most likely decreased options from your working list. List your top five majors in rank order.

_____

_____

_____

_____

_____

_____

ACTIVITY 5.6
Analyze Your Information

Task 1: Using self-assessment data gained from activities in previous chapters, list your top three values, interests, and skills/abilities and personality characteristics that are most influential with your decision-making.

Values: _____   _____   _____

Interests: _____   _____   _____

Skills: _____   _____   _____

Personality: _____   _____   _____

Task 2: Compare your self-assessment data to your top five majors in Activity 5.5. Do you notice any patterns or conflicts? Do some options seem better suited than others? Discuss your findings below. If you need assistance, review this activity with a Career Counselor.

_____

_____

_____

_____

_____

ACTIVITY 5.7

What's Next?

Take time to evaluate and reflect on what you have discovered so far. Plan your next actions and list additional steps you should take to continue on your path to career planning success.

_____

_____

_____

_____

_____

_____

Career Discoveries

University of North Florida   **Career Services**

Founders Hall, Bldg 2, Room 1100

www.unf.edu/dept/cdc

904-620-2955

Explore Careers, Discover

CareerWings

- Go to **http://www.unf.edu/dept/cdc/**
- Click "Career Wings" logo; Again, click on "Career Wings" logo
- Log in with the email you used when you registered. If you don't remember your password, call Career Services to have your password reset.

ONET Online

- Go to **http://online.onetcenter.org**
- Enter an occupation title in the search box

Occupational Outlook Handbook

- Go to **www.bls.gov/oco/**
- Click on either "Search Box" or "A-Z Index" to begin browsing occupations
- Enter an occupation title in the word search

Facts: Florida Choices Planner

- Go to **www.facts.org**
- Click a link the "College Students" link
- Choose options from the "Explore Careers" section

Vault

- Go to **http://www.vault.com**
- Browse and follow instructions on page to navigate between various options

My Plan

- Go to **www.myplan.com**
- For taking assessments, you will need to enter license code: speak with your Career Counselor first.

My Skills

- Go to **www.myskillsmyfuture.com**
- To explore new career options based on the skills you've used in a past job

My Next Move

- Go to **http://www.mynextmove.org/**

Name _____   Date _____

ACROSS

1. Type of major that prepares you for a specific job

4. Where you can find many books, directories, and other resources on almost any career to help you get the information you need

5. The selection of a _____ allows you to focus on a subject that increases your skills or focus on a recreational interest or something fun

6. The most popular major at UNF with over 3000 students

7. Houses approximately 75% of all majors at UNF

8. Choosing a major is a _____

9. Introductory courses that cover many career areas

10. Highly selective programs that limit applicants by selecting only the top candidates

DOWN

1. Type of major that builds marketable skills and prepares you for a variety of careers

2. This experience allows you to connect with professionals in a particular field

3. Programs that limit the number of applicants that are allowed to enroll in major each year

Key Discoveries

- A college degree is the broader category of formal education under which various majors are organized.
- The four main components of a college degree are general education, prerequisites, free electives, and major requirements.
- General education provides breadth to your education, whereas your major provides depth into a specific field or discipline.
- The two basic types of majors are Occupations-Focused and Options-Focused.
- One effective way to explore majors is by enrolling in introductory-type courses.
- Some majors require specific admissions criteria. A part of your major exploration process should include learning about admission requirements and the application process.
- Salary data discovered during the career exploration varies based on experience and geographical region.
- Valuable resources for major and career exploration include books, Internet sites, university faculty, staff, current and previous students, and personal contacts.
- The selection of a minor allows you to focus on a subject that increases your skills or focus on a recreational interest or something fun.
- Your college degree uniquely qualifies you for many career paths, serving as a springboard to many opportunities.
- Career success and satisfaction are not only connected to major selection, but are also impacted by other factors such as interests, skills, abilities, and the realities of the job market.
- Increasing your competence through major and career exploration increases your confidence in making a wise decision.

Career Connections: Internet Links

- http://www.unf.edu/dept/cdc/info/majors.html (*UNF Career Services: What can you do with a major in _____?*)
- http://mymajors.com/index.html (*My Major Quiz: College Planning*)
- http://online.onetcenter.org (*O*NET*)
- http://www.facts.org (*Florida Choices Planner*)
- http://www.bls.gov/oco/ (*Occupational Outlook Handbook*)
- http://www.jobprofiles.org (*Job Profiles*)
- http://www.princetonreview.com/careers-after-college.aspx (*The Princeton Review*)
- http://www.vault.com/cb/careerlib/careerlib_main.jsp?parrefer=1023 (*Vault Online Career Library*)
- http://www.myplan.com (*My Plan*)

CHAPTER 6

CHAPTER QUEST

At the end of this chapter you should be able to:

- Understand the changes taking place in the workplace

- Recognize the differences in generational employees

- Realize the impact that education has on earning potential

- Define diversity and equal opportunity

- Discover the many faces of discrimination

- Realize the issues and concerns of women in the workplace

- Know the impact that technology will make on the world of work

- Explore the "hot" careers and "not so hot" careers of the future

- Understand local, state, and national occupational trends

- Recognize the skills needed to be successful in the workplace of the future

The Changing World of Work

Changes in the Workplace

As you begin to explore potential careers, it is important to understand the changes that are taking place in today's workplace. Many jobs that existed just five to 10 years ago have been phased out and new jobs are being created. More women and minorities are assuming upper-level positions, and technology will continue to shape the future. There will be some interesting dynamics affecting the workplace in the future as a result of population patterns such as multigenerational workforces, shifting populations, diversity, technology, and occupational trends. Being a "lifelong learner," developing new skills, and being able to adapt to these changes will be critical for future success.

Generations

Baby Boomers*

© Losevsky Pavel, 2009. Used under license from Shutterstock, Inc.

According to the U.S. Census Bureau, after World War II, from 1946 to 1964, approximately 76 million people were born. This generation is referred to as the "baby boomers." Their parents planned to create opportunities for their children to have more than they did. Education became an important priority. Most boomers were raised by stay-at-home mothers and fathers who were the main breadwinners. The baby boomer generation experienced major social and political upheaval during the 1960s, including the civil rights movement, the women's movement, and the war in Vietnam. Also referred to as the "me generation," baby boom employees tend to be self-absorbed, prefer face-to-face interaction, dislike conflict, and prefer building consensus. They tend to focus on group decision making and the process. Boomers are high achievers, they dedicate themselves to the project at hand, and they expect the same from others. This generation gave us the term "workaholic." Baby boomers have been faced with raising their children and caring for their elderly parents, and have thus been called the "sandwich generation."

Generation X*

From 1965 to 1980, there was a marked decrease in the number of births. According to The Learning Cafe and American Demographics Enterprising Museum 2003, there were approximately 51 million people born during this time frame. This generation is referred to as the "baby bust." It is also known as "Generation X." Generation Xers grew up in a time when technology (i.e., high-speed copiers, calculators, and desktop computers) started impacting the workplace. Referred to as "latchkey kids," Gen Xers were often at home alone or taking care of siblings while their parents worked. This generation favors autonomy and self-reliance. They hit the workforce during an economic downturn and faced a very competitive job market. Many had to move back in with their parents and were referred to as the "boomerang generation." Single-parent and blended families helped this generation better understand and deal with diversity issues in the workplace. Gen Xers tend to favor a balance between work and life, and prefer more flexible hours and work schedules. They are technologically savvy and are very productive. Having seen their baby boom parents downsized from jobs, this generation holds no loyalty to their employers and changes jobs frequently to better their situation. They are very independent, tend to be outspoken, and are willing to take risks. They might clash with baby boomer managers who tend to micromanage and avoid conflict.

Generation Y (The Millennials)*

From 1980 to 2000, about 75 million people were born. This generation is referred to as the "baby boom echo," "Generation Y" or the "Millennials." They have always known cable television, cell phones, pagers, answering machines, laptop computers, video games, and the Internet. Impacted by events such as the Columbine High School shooting, this generation resonated to marketing slogans such as "live for today" and "just do it." Generation Y workers tend to expect recognition and reward for minimal effort. These young workers maintain very close relationships with their parents, who have been referred to as "helicopter parents" because they tend to "hover" over their children. This generation is also very opportunistic, and they tend to change jobs for their own gain. This generation prefers to work in teams, and because they are very ethnically diverse, they are very accepting of diversity. They are creative, innovative, inclusive of others, and have a global perspective. They will be the prime-aged workforce by 2014.

Sources: http://www.valueoptions.com
Five Sweeping Trends That Will Shape Your Company's Future: The New Workforce, *by Harriett Henkin, American Management Association, Amacom Books, 2005*

Population*

U.S. Population Projections: 2005–2050

If current trends continue, the population of the United States will rise to 438 million in 2050 from 296 million in 2005; 82% of the increase will be due to immigrants arriving from 2005 to 2050 and their U.S.-born descendants, according to new projections developed by the Pew Research Center.

Of the 117 million people added to the population during this period due to the effect of new immigration, 67 million will be the immigrants themselves and 50 million will be their U.S.-born children or grandchildren.

Among the other key population projections:

- Nearly one in five Americans (19%) will be an immigrant in 2050, compared with one in eight (12%) in 2005. By 2025, the immigrant or foreign-born share of the population will surpass the peak during the last great wave of immigration a century ago.
- The major role of immigration in national growth builds on the pattern of recent decades, during which immigrants and their U.S.-born children and grandchildren accounted for most population increase. Immigration's importance increased as the average number of births to U.S.-born women dropped sharply before leveling off.
- The Latino population, already the nation's largest minority group, will triple in size and will account for most of the nation's population growth from 2005 through 2050. Hispanics will make up 29% of the U.S. population in 2050, compared with 14% in 2005.
- Births in the United States will play a growing role in Hispanic and Asian population growth; as a result, a smaller proportion of both groups will be foreign-born in 2050 than is the case now.
- The non-Hispanic white population will increase more slowly than other racial and ethnic groups; whites will become a minority (47%) by 2050.
- The nation's elderly population will more than double in size from 2005 through 2050, as the baby boom generation enters the traditional retirement years. The number of working-age Americans and children will grow more slowly than the elderly population, and will shrink as a share of the total population.

Source: Pew Research Center

Diversity, Discrimination, and Equal Opportunity

The workplace will mirror changes in all aspects of our lives with a much more diverse population. Workers in the future can expect to have much more interaction with minorities and women, and diversity, discrimination, and equal opportunity will continue to be important issues. Here are some brief definitions to help put some of these issues into perspective:

Diversity: The concept of diversity encompasses acceptance and respect. It means understanding that each individual is unique and recognizing our individual differences. These can be along the dimensions of race, ethnicity, gender, sexual orientation, socioeconomic status, age, physical abilities, religious beliefs, political beliefs, or other ideologies. It is the exploration of these differences in a safe, positive, and nurturing environment. It is about understanding each other and moving beyond simple tolerance to embracing and celebrating the rich dimensions of diversity contained within each individual. *Source: University of Oregon, May 1999*

Discrimination is the failure to treat people in the same way because of bias toward some of them because of some characteristic—such as race, religion, sex, national origin, sexual orientation, disability—which is irrelevant. *Source: www.unmc.edu/ethics/words.html*

Racial discrimination differentiates between individuals on the basis of real and perceived racial differences. *Source: http://www.wikipedia.com*

Age discrimination is discrimination against a person or group on the grounds of age. *Source: http://www.wikipedia.com*

Gender discrimination is the discrimination against a person or group on the grounds of sex or gender identity. *Source: http://www.wikipedia.com*

Disability discrimination: People with disabilities face discrimination in all levels of society. The attitude that disabled individuals are inferior to non-disabled individuals is called "ableism." *Source: http://www.wikipedia.com*

Equal opportunity is a descriptive term for an approach intended to provide a certain social environment in which people are not excluded from the activities of society, such as education, employment, or health care, on the basis of immutable traits. Equal opportunity practices include measures taken by organizations to ensure fairness in the employment process. *Source: http://www.wikipedia.com*

The Americans with Disabilities Act of 1990 (United States Public Law 101-336 Statute 327) was signed into law by President George H.W. Bush. This law prohibits discrimination based on disability.

A nontraditional career is defined as one where more than 75% of the workforce is of the opposite gender (or fewer than 25% of the workforce is your gender). Some examples of nontraditional jobs:

Nontraditional Careers

Women

Airline Pilots
Announcer
Carpenters/Construction Workers
Chefs
Clergy
Dentists
Engineers

Film Directors
Firefighters
Mathematicians
Security Guards
Truck Drivers
Welders

Men

Bank Tellers
Cashiers
Child Care workers
Clerical Support Workers
Cosmetologists
Dental Assistants and Hygienists
Elementary and Middle School Teachers

Flight Attendants
Hair Stylists
Librarians
Nurses
Receptionists
Social Workers

Reference: U.S. Department of Labor: Women's Bureau, Bureau of Labor Statistics, Unpublished data, Annual Averages 2003, Current Population Survey

Labor Force*

The civilian labor force is projected to grow by 12.6 million between 2008 and 2018, to 166.9 million persons.

As the members of the large baby boom generation grow older and continue their trend of increased labor force participation, the number of persons age 55 years and older in the labor force is expected to increase by 12.0 million, or 43.0%, during the 2008–18 period. Persons in the 55 years and older age group are projected to make up nearly one-quarter of the labor force in 2018. Young people (age 16–24) are expected to account for 12.7% of the labor force in 2018, and persons in the prime-age working group (age 25 to 54) are expected to account for 63.5% of the 2018 labor force.

The labor force in 2018 will be more diverse. As a result of higher population growth among minorities—due to higher birth rates and increased immigration, along with higher labor force participation rates by Hispanics and Asians—the share of the labor force held by minorities is projected to increase significantly. Whites will remain the largest race group in the labor force in 2018 (79.4%) despite growing by just 5.5% between 2008 and 2018. The number of Asians in the labor force is projected to increase by 29.8% and the number of blacks by 14.1%. In 2018, Asians are projected to comprise 5.6% of the labor force and blacks to make up 12.1%.

Hispanics (who can be of any race) will join the labor force in greater numbers than non-Hispanics. The number of Hispanics in the labor force is projected to grow by 7.3 million or 33.1%. Their share of the labor force will expand from 14.3% in 2008 to

© Yuri Arcurs, 2009. Used under license from Shutterstock, Inc.

17.6% in 2018. In contrast, the number of persons in the labor force not of Hispanic origin is expected to grow by 4.0%, and their share of the labor force to decline to 82.4%.

*Sources: U.S. Department of Labor, Bureau of Labor Statistics

Women in the Workforce

From 2008 to 2018, the women's civilian labor force is projected to increase by 9.0%, or 6,462,000. The number of women aged 65 to 74 in the civilian labor force is projected to increase more than the number of women in any other age group—increasing by 89.8%, or 2,030,000. Although projected to be the smallest in number among all age groups, the number of women in the civilian labor force aged 75 years and older is projected to have the second highest increase—61.4%, or 336,000. The numbers of women aged 16 to 19 and 35 to 54 in the labor force are projected to decrease over that same period.

Ratio of Women's to Men's Earnings by Occupation

The ratio of women's to men's earnings, for all occupations, was 81.2% in 2010. The ratio varies by occupation. In occupations such as personal financial advisors, retail salespersons, insurance sales agents, and lawyers, for example, the earnings ratios are lower than the overall ratio of women's to men's earnings. In occupations such as stock clerks and order fillers, bill and account collectors, and combined food preparation and serving workers, women earn more than men.

© Kurhan, 2009. Used under license from Shutterstock, Inc.

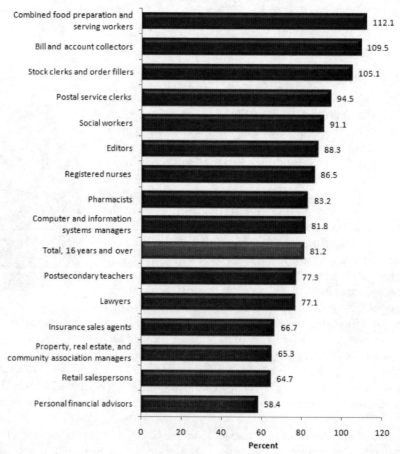

Ratio of women's to men's earnings, selected occupations, 2010

Occupation	Percent
Combined food preparation and serving workers	112.1
Bill and account collectors	109.5
Stock clerks and order fillers	105.1
Postal service clerks	94.5
Social workers	91.1
Editors	88.3
Registered nurses	86.5
Pharmacists	83.2
Computer and information systems managers	81.8
Total, 16 years and over	81.2
Postsecondary teachers	77.3
Lawyers	77.1
Insurance sales agents	66.7
Property, real estate, and community association managers	65.3
Retail salespersons	64.7
Personal financial advisors	58.4

Sources: U.S. Department of Labor, Bureau of Labor Statistics   *www.bls.gov*

How Does Education Affect Earnings?

Ever wonder how important your education is in terms of earnings? Education pays in higher earnings and lower unemployment rates. The chart below shows the impact education has on monthly earnings.

Education pays

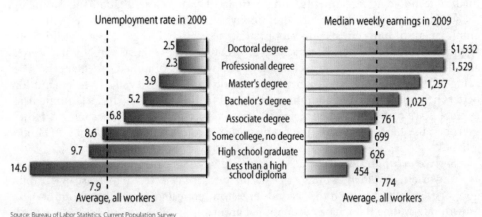

© karen roach, 2009. Used under license from Shutterstock, Inc.

Source: Bureau of Labor Statistics, Current Population Survey

Future Occupational Trends

Employment Projections: 2008–2018

According to the U.S. Bureau of Labor Statistics, total employment is projected to increase by 15.3 million, or 10.1%, from 2008 to 2018. More than half of the new jobs will be in professional and related occupations and service occupations.

Where to Look for Jobs of the Future

Employment Change by Occupation

Management, business, and financial occupations. Workers in management, business, and financial occupations plan and direct the activities of business, government, and other organizations. Their employment is expected to increase by 11% by 2018.

Professional and related occupations. This occupational group, which includes a wide variety of skilled professions, is expected to be the fastest-growing major occupational group, at 17%, and is projected to add the most new jobs—about 5.2 million. Employment among health care practitioners and technical occupations, a subgroup of the professional and related category, is expected to increase by 21%.

Employment in *community and social services occupations* is projected to increase by 16%, growing by roughly 448,400 jobs.

Employment in *arts, design, entertainment, sports, and media occupations* is expected to grow by 12% from 2008 to 2018, resulting in almost 332,600 new jobs.

Employment in *life, physical, and social science occupations* is projected to increase by nearly 277,200 jobs over the 2008–18 projection period. About 116,700 of these jobs are expected to be created among social science and related occupations, led by strong growth among market and survey researchers.

Architecture and engineering occupations are projected to add roughly 270,600 jobs, representing a growth rate of 10%. Much of this growth will occur among engineering occupations, especially civil engineers, as greater emphasis is placed on improving the nation's infrastructure.

Legal occupations will add the fewest new jobs among all professional and related subgroups, increasing by about 188,400. However, with a growth rate of 15%, this group will grow faster than the average for all occupations in the economy. Of the new jobs created, lawyers will account for 98,500 while paralegals and legal assistants will account for 74,100.

Developments from biotechnology research will continue to be used to create new medical technologies, treatments, and pharmaceuticals. As a result, demand for medical scientists and for biochemists and biophysicists will increase. However, although employment of biochemists and biophysicists is projected to grow rapidly, this corresponds to only 8,700 new jobs over the projection period. Increased medical research and demand for new medical technologies also will affect biomedical engineers. The aging of the population and a growing focus on health issues will drive demand for better medical devices and equipment designed by these workers. In fact, biomedical engineers are projected to be the fastest-growing occupation in the economy. However, because of its small size, the occupation is projected to add only about 11,600 jobs.

Service occupations. The duties of service workers range from fighting fires to cooking meals. Employment in service occupations is projected to increase by 4.1 million, or 14%, which is both the second-largest numerical gain and the second-largest growth rate among the major occupational groups.

Employment in **personal care and service occupations** is anticipated to grow by 20% over the projection period, adding more than 1 million jobs. Personal and home care aides will experience increased demand as a growing number of elderly individuals require assistance with daily tasks. Child care workers, in addition, will add jobs as formal preschool programs, which employ child care workers alongside preschool teachers, become more prevalent.

Employment in **food preparation and serving** and related occupations is projected to increase by roughly 1 million jobs from 2008 to 2018, representing a growth rate of 9%.

Employment **in building and grounds cleaning and maintenance** occupations is expected to grow by almost 483,900 jobs over the projection period, representing a growth rate of 8%.

Protective service occupations are expected to gain the fewest new jobs among all service subgroups: about 400,100, or 12% growth. These workers protect businesses and other organizations from crime and vandalism. In addition, there will be increased demand for law enforcement officers to support the growing U.S. population.

Sales and related occupations. Sales and related workers solicit goods and services for businesses and consumers. Sales and related occupations are expected to add 980,400 new jobs by 2018, growing by 6%.

Employment in **management, scientific, and technical consulting services** is anticipated to expand at a staggering 83%, making up about 31% of job growth in this sector. Demand for these services will be spurred by businesses' continued need for advice on planning and logistics, the implementation of new technologies, and compliance with workplace safety, environmental, and employment regulations.

Office and administrative support occupations. Office and administrative support workers perform the day-to-day activities of the office, such as preparing and filing documents, dealing with the public, and distributing information. Employment in these occupations is expected to grow by 8%, adding 1.8 million new jobs by 2018. Customer service representatives are anticipated to add the most new jobs, 399,500, as businesses put an increased emphasis on building customer relationships.

Farming, fishing, and forestry occupations. Farming, fishing, and forestry workers cultivate plants, breed and raise livestock, and catch animals. These occupations are projected to decline by about 1%, losing 9,100 jobs, by 2018.

Construction and extraction occupations. Construction and extraction workers build new residential and commercial buildings and also work in mines, quarries, and oil and gas fields. Employment of these workers is expected to grow 13%, adding about 1 million new jobs.

Installation, maintenance, and repair occupations. Workers in installation, maintenance, and repair occupations install new equipment and maintain and repair older equipment. These occupations are projected to add 440,200 jobs by 2018, growing by 8%.

Production occupations. Production workers are employed mainly in manufacturing, where they assemble goods and operate plants. Production occupations are expected to decline by 3%, losing 349,200 jobs by 2018.

Transportation and material moving occupations. Transportation and material moving workers transport people and materials by land, sea, or air. Employment of these workers is anticipated to increase by 4%, accounting for 391,100 new jobs.

Source: U.S. Department of Labor, Bureau of Labor Statistics, Occupational Outlook Handbook, http://www.bls.gov

Information and Technology

Employment in **computer systems design and related services** is expected to increase by 45%, accounting for nearly one-fourth of all new jobs in this industry sector. Employment growth will be driven by growing demand for the design and integration of sophisticated networks and Internet and intranet sites.

Computer and mathematical science occupations are projected to add almost 785,700 new jobs from 2008 to 2018. As a group, these occupations are expected to grow more than twice as fast as the average for all occupations in the economy. Demand for workers in computer and mathematical occupations will be driven by the continuing need for businesses, government agencies, and other organizations to adopt and utilize the latest technologies.

Employment in the **information sector** is expected to increase by 4%, adding 118,100 jobs by 2018. The sector contains fast-growing computer-related industries. The data processing, hosting, and related services industry, which is expected to grow by 53%, includes establishments that provide Web and application hosting and streaming services. Internet publishing and broadcasting is expected to grow rapidly as it gains market share from newspapers and other more traditional media. Software publishing is projected to grow by 30% as organizations of all types continue to adopt the newest software products.

© Franck Boston, 2009. Used under license from Shutterstock, Inc.

The information sector also includes **the telecommunications industry**, whose employment is projected to decline 9%. Despite an increase in demand for telecommunications services, more reliable networks along with consolidation among organizations will lead to productivity gains, reducing the need for workers. In addition, employment in the publishing industry is expected to decline by 5%, which is the result of increased efficiency in production, declining newspaper revenues, and a trend towards using more freelance workers.

Two of the fastest-growing detailed occupations are in the computer specialist occupational group. **Network systems and data communications analysts** are projected to be the second-fastest-growing occupation in the economy. Demand for these workers will increase as organizations continue to upgrade their information technology capacity and incorporate the newest technologies. The growing reliance on wireless networks will result in a need for more network systems and data communications analysts as well. Computer applications software engineers also are expected to grow rapidly from 2008 to 2018. Expanding Internet technologies have spurred demand for these workers, who can develop Internet, intranet, and Web applications.

The Impact of Technology

- Information technology will continue to have a global impact on all aspects of our lives. The average U.S. worker spends at least one third of his/her workday at a computer and one fourth of the day on the Internet.
- An integration of the telephone, television, and computer into one home information appliance is already taking place. By the year 2012, 250 million Americans and 1.5 billion people worldwide will be online as a result of new Internet-capable cell phones. Telecommunications experts agree that, 80% to 90% of all Internet access will be from wireless mobile devices such as laptop computers, webphones, Palm Pilots, cell phones, pagers, and video cameras.
- Most Americans will retain a home computer to store their financial, medical, and personal records to protect them from loss, theft, or unauthorized access.
- Broadcast, copper wire, fiber-optic cable, Wi-Fi/Wi-Max, infrared, microwave, cellular, ultra-wideband, satellite, etc. will grow both in the United States and globally.
- Within 10 years, Radio Frequency Identification Technology (RFID) will become a new trillion-dollar technology-based industry. This technology involves electronic labeling of all types of items. These labels will be used to track inventory, match medications to prescriptions, and program appliances.
- By 2012, state and local governments will offer tax incentives to encourage "telecommuting" or working from home in order to alleviate traffic, conserve energy, and reduce air pollution. Full-time telecommuters will make up 10% of the white collar workforce. Home-based employment will also help to reduce office space costs. By 2015, 40 million salaried employees will be working at home at least once a week.
- In the near future, all job search application, screening, and recruitment will be done online. Newspaper want ads will most likely disappear by the end of the decade. Personal websites might take the place of the traditional paper resume.

Sources: United States Department of Labor, Bureau of Labor Statistics, August 2005. "Living in the USA-2000–2010: 110 Million Households in Revolutionary Times; Changing Realities Confronting America's Consumers and Constituents," by David Pearce Snyder, Lifestyles Editor, The Futurist

What Are the "Hot Jobs" of the Future?

Table 6.1. Occupations with the largest numerical growth

Occupations	Number of new jobs (in thousands)	Percent change	Wages (May 2008 median)	Education/training category
Registered nurses	581.5	22	$ 62,450	Associate degree
Home health aides	460.9	50	20,460	Short-term on-the-job training
Customer service representatives	399.5	18	29,860	Moderate-term on-the-job training
Combined food preparation and serving workers, including fast food	394.3	15	16,430	Short-term on-the-job training
Personal and home care aides	375.8	46	19,180	Short-term on-the-job training
Retail salespersons	374.7	8	20,510	Short-term on-the-job training
Office clerks, general	358.7	12	25,320	Short-term on-the-job training
Accountants and auditors	279.4	22	59,430	Bachelor's degree
Nursing aides, orderlies, and attendants	276.0	19	23,850	Postsecondary vocational award
Postsecondary teachers	256.9	15	58,830	Doctoral degree
Construction laborers	255.9	20	28,520	Moderate-term on-the-job training
Elementary school teachers, except special education	244.2	16	49,330	Bachelor's degree
Truck drivers, heavy and tractor-trailer	232.9	13	37,270	Short-term on-the-job training
Landscaping and groundskeeping workers	217.1	18	23,150	Short-term on-the-job training
Bookkeeping, accounting, and auditing clerks	212.4	10	32,510	Moderate-term on-the-job training
Executive secretaries and administrative assistants	204.4	13	40,030	Work experience in a related occupation
Management analysts	178.3	24	73,570	Bachelor's or higher degree, plus work experience
Computer software engineers, applications	175.1	34	85,430	Bachelor's degree
Receptionists and information clerks	172.9	15	24,550	Short-term on-the-job training
Carpenters	165.4	13	38,940	Long-term on-the-job training

Source: BLS Occupational Employment Statistics and Division of Occupational Outlook

Source: U.S. Department of Labor, Bureau of Labor Statistics, Occupational Outlook Handbook, http://www.bls.gov

Globalization

According to the Bureau of Labor Statistics, the United States is shifting from a manufacturing-based economy to a service-based economy. The Internet and telecommunications advances have made it easier to conduct business all across the world. Companies continue to expand and develop into other countries, creating a demand for employees who understand the languages and cultures of other countries and have knowledge of international business. Companies are turning to outsourcing and offshoring to cut their costs and raise their profit margins.

© Yuri Arcurs, 2009. Used under license from Shutterstock, Inc.

Outsourcing Versus Offshoring

According to Wikipedia, the free encyclopedia, *"Outsourcing is the practice of hiring an external organization to perform some business functions in a country other than the one where the products or services are actually developed or manufactured. Offshoring refers to when functions are performed in a foreign country by a foreign subsidiary."* Companies typically outsource and offshore functions such as data entry, computer programming, customer service, information technology, business processing, software research and development, etc. Companies that outsource usually take advantage of lower wages in the outsource country. Jobs from the United States have been outsourced to countries such as China, India, Brazil, Argentina, Indonesia, Russia, Pakistan, Bulgaria, Malaysia, Ukraine, and many others.

The Global Time Clock: 24/7

The standard 8:00 a.m. to 5:00 p.m. work schedule no longer fits with the global workplace. In order to communicate with counterparts around the world in different time zones, companies will have workers available 24 hours a day, seven days a week. Computers and the Internet have made these connections much easier.

Ecommerce

With the click of a mouse, a person can order products on the other side of the world and have it shipped to their home within a week. Companies continue to expand their businesses through ecommerce. The Internet allows their customers to customize the items they want to order. Dell Computer was one of the leaders in this trend customizing and shipping personal computers.

Local and Statewide Trends:

Florida Facts and Figures

- By 2030, Florida should pass New York as the third most populous state.
- No place in Florida is more than 90 miles from one or more of 14 deep-water ports.
- Florida land transportation includes four interstate highways, 40,000 lane-miles of state highway, and nearly 3,000 miles of rail.
- With $73.2 billion in 2003 trade and its multicultural population, Florida is the national leader in international commerce.
- Florida hosts some 2,000 firms from other countries, including 300 regional headquarters.
- Machinery exports from Florida totaled more than $7.4 billion in 2003.
- Florida is the number three state in dollar value of its high-tech exports and fourth in high-tech workers.
- Defense-related spending (direct and indirect) accounts for $44 billion (9.8%) of Florida's GSP.
- With deposits of $90 billion-plus, about 550 financial institutions, banks, S&Ls, and credit unions operate in Florida.

Source: www.bringyouhome.com
Other Sources:
Sales and Marketing Management *magazine, September 2003*
Global Insight Inc.
Enterprise Florida
Florida Trend Magazine

© Katherine Welles, 2009. Used under license from Shutterstock, Inc.

Jacksonville, Florida

Jacksonville is the largest city in the state of Florida and the county seat of Duval County. Since 1906, Jacksonville has been the largest city in land area in the contiguous United States; this resulted from the consolidation of the city and county government, along with corresponding expansion of the city limits to include almost the entire county. As of the 2006 census estimate, the city proper had an estimated population of 794,555 with a metropolitan population of 1.3 million. Jacksonville is the third most populated city on the East Coast, after New York City and Philadelphia.

Jacksonville Economy

Jacksonville's location on the St. Johns River and the Atlantic Ocean led to providential growth for the city and its industry. The largest city in the state, Jacksonville is a transportation hub, with a 38-foot deepwater port that ranks with New York as one of the top two vehicle-handling ports in the nation. It is served by four airports, three seaports, a highway system that links the city to three major interstates, and three railroads: CSX, Norfolk Southern, and Florida East Coast. The hub of seven major highways—I-10, I-95, I-295, and U.S. Highways 1, 17, 90, and 301—Jacksonville has straight shipping lines to the Midwest, West, and Northeast. It is served by more than 100 trucking lines, three major railroads, and Jacksonville International Airport.

The automotive parts and accessories industry is attracted by this logistics network, as well as by the fact that less than 2% of the city's manufacturing industry is unionized. However, the strength of the city's economy lies in its broad diversification. The area's economy is balanced among distribution, financial services, biomedical technology, consumer goods, information services, manufacturing, and other industries.

Lumber, phosphate, paper, cigars, and wood pulp are the principal exports; automobiles and coffee are among the imports.

Three important naval air stations within the city limits and Kings Bay Submarine Base nearby give Jacksonville one of the largest military presences in the country, topped only by Norfolk, Virginia and San Diego, California. The total economic impact of the bases in the community is about $6.1 billion annually.

World Trade Center, Jacksonville, one of six trade centers in the state, assists Florida companies to enter or expand into overseas markets.

The Jacksonville Film and Television Office was formed to attract film and video production to the area and help streamline the production process. As a result, numerous motion pictures, television movies, commercials, and videos have been produced in Jacksonville in recent years. Each movie or television series can add millions of dollars to the local economy.

Jacksonville Careers

Among the most common occupations in Jacksonville are management, professional, and related occupations (31%); sales and office occupations (28%), and service occupations (14%). Approximately 77% of workers in Jacksonville work for companies, 12% work for the government, and 5% are self-employed.

Jacksonville Industries

The leading industries in Jacksonville are educational services, health care, and social assistance, 16%; finance, insurance, real estate, rental, and leasing, 13%; and retail trade, 11%.

Jacksonville Salaries

According to government data, the average salary for jobs in Jacksonville, Florida is $35,948, and the median income of households is $44,173.

Sources:
http://www.simply hired.com
http://www.city-data.com/US-Cities/The South

May 2009 Metropolitan and Nonmetropolitan Area Occupational Employment and Wage Estimates—Jacksonville, FL

Occupation Code	Occupation Title	Employ-ment (1)	Median Hourly	Mean Hourly	Mean Annual (2)
00-0000	All Occupations	581,450	$15.04	$18.97	$39,460
11-0000	Management Occupations	17,720	$42.22	$49.43	$102,810
13-0000	Business and Financial Operations Occupations	33,310	$25.25	$27.80	$57,820
15-0000	Computer and Mathematical Science Occupations	14,690	$28.67	$30.76	$63,970
17-0000	Architecture and Engineering Occupations	9,230	$30.11	$31.51	$65,550
19-0000	Life, Physical, and Social Science Occupations	3,460	$24.66	$27.56	$57,330
21-0000	Community and Social Services Occupations	6,080	$17.52	$19.37	$40,290
23-0000	Legal Occupations	4,310	$26.06	$33.39	$69,450
25-0000	Education, Training, and Library Occupations	28,090	$19.47	$22.13	$46,020
27-0000	Arts, Design, Entertainment, Sports, and Media Occupations	5,850	$19.33	$22.78	$47,390
29-0000	Healthcare Practitioner and Technical Occupations	32,020	$25.98	$31.00	$64,480
31-0000	Healthcare Support Occupations	14,640	$12.25	$13.02	$27,090
33-0000	Protective Service Occupations	14,350	$15.60	$17.83	$37,090
35-0000	Food Preparation and Serving Related Occupations	51,580	$8.63	$9.66	$20,090
37-0000	Building and Grounds Cleaning and Maintenance Occupations	19,270	$10.05	$11.27	$23,450
39-0000	Personal Care and Service Occupations	15,900	$9.40	$11.08	$23,050
41-0000	Sales and Related Occupations	71,640	$12.28	$17.57	$36,540
43-0000	Office and Administrative Support Occupations	122,610	$14.10	$15.03	$31,270
45-0000	Farming, Fishing, and Forestry Occupations	460	$13.32	$14.33	$29,800
47-0000	Construction and Extraction Occupations	27,860	$16.20	$17.73	$36,870
49-0000	Installation, Maintenance, and Repair Occupations	23,620	$18.26	$19.01	$39,540
51-0000	Production Occupations	24,820	$14.53	$15.77	$32,800
53-0000	Transportation and Material Moving Occupations	39,940	$13.27	$15.17	$31,560

Source: U.S. Department of Labor, Bureau of Labor Statistics

Largest Employers (Duval County)	Number of Employees
Naval Air Station	19,537
Naval Station Mayport	15,293
Duval County Public Schools	15,000
City of Jacksonville	8,019
Winn-Dixie Stores, Inc.	7,238
Blue Cross Blue Shield of Florida	7,000
Publix Distribution Center	6,615
Baptist Health System	5,600
CSX Corporation	4,400
Citibank	4,000
Bank of America	4,000

Source: http://www.city-data.com/US-Cities/The South

The Rise of Temporary Staffing/ Employment Agencies

As another way to cut costs, many companies are shifting their human resource functions to temporary staffing agencies. The staffing agency takes on the responsibility of screening, interviewing, and hiring workers that will work in short-term or long-term assignments with a given company. Often, the temporary employee does not receive any benefits. If the company chooses to hire the temporary employee, they must pay the staffing agency a "finder's fee," but this is usually after a set time, such as six months. This gives the original company an opportunity to "try out" the temporary employee before making a hiring decision. They can terminate the assignment at any time. Often, working through a temporary agency is an effective way to gain entry into large companies.

Employment in this sector is expected to grow by 18% by 2018. The employment services industry ranks fifth among industries with the most new employment opportunities in the nation over the 2008–18 period and is expected to grow faster than the average for all industries. Projected growth stems from the strong need for seasonal and temporary workers and for specialized human resources services.

Small Businesses

A small business is defined by the U.S. Small Business Administration (SBA) as one that is organized for profit; has a place of business in the United States; makes a significant contribution to the U.S. economy by paying taxes or using American products, materials, or labor; and does not exceed the numerical size standard for its industry. The business may be a sole proprietorship, partnership, corporation, or any other legal form. The SBA has established size standards for most industries in the U.S. economy. The most common size standards are as follow:

- 500 employees for most manufacturing and mining industries
- 100 employees for all wholesale trade industries
- $6.5 million for most retail and service industries
- $31 million for most general & heavy construction industries
- $13 million for all special trade contractors
- $0.75 million for most agricultural industries

There are over 20 million small businesses in the United States compared to over 15,000 large corporations. It is estimated that over 60–70% of new hires will be by small businesses.

Lifelong Learning and Skill Development

The world of work will continue to be impacted by changes in technology and the ways that people around the world communicate with one another. Jobs will constantly change, and the skill sets of workers will continue to change. Many experts predict that today's generation will change jobs more than 10 times and change careers three to five times during their working years. Engaging in a continual, lifelong learning process to develop new skills and knowledge will help you position yourself for these changes in the workplace.

Employee of the Future: What Skills Will Employers Look For?

The National Association of Colleges and Employers conducted a survey asking employers to rate the importance of candidate qualities/skills on a scale of 1–5. Below are the top 15 results:

Communication skills (verbal)	4.65
Strong work ethic	4.61
Teamwork skills (works well with others)	4.59
Analytical skills	4.56
Initiative	4.50
Problem-solving skills	4.48
Communication skills (written)	4.48
Interpersonal skills (relates well to others)	4.40
Computer skills	4.38
Flexibility/adaptability	4.37
Detail-oriented	4.18
Technical skills	4.16
Organizational skills	4.05
Leadership	4.04
Self-confidence	3.96

Scale: 1 = Not Important, 2 = Not Very Important, 3 = Somewhat Important,
4 = Very Important, 5 = Extremely Important

Source: NACE Research; Job Outlook 2011

What Separates One Candidate from Another

In the same survey, employers were asked to rate the influence of attributes when deciding on two equally qualified candidates:

Attribute	2011 Average Influence Rating
Major	4.1
Has held leadership position	4.1
High GPA (3.0 or above)	3.8
Has been involved in extracurricular activities (clubs, sports, student government, etc.)	3.8
School attended	3.2
Has done volunteer work	3.2

72.4% of employers also indicated that they preferred to hire candidates with relevant work experience.

An additional 17.6% said they preferred to hire candidates with any type of work experience (doesn't matter if it's relevant or not, just some type of experience).

Source: NACE Research; Job Outlook 2011

Key Discoveries

- Workers in the future will experience a very diverse, multigenerational workplace.
- Discrimination of all types will continue to influence both hiring and the workplace.
- There is a direct correlation between the level of education and earnings.
- Employers will seek candidates with effective communication, a strong work ethic, teamwork and leadership, problem-solving, computer and technical skills, and flexibility and adaptability skills.
- Technology will continue to impact and shape the global workplace of the future.
- The United States will continue to shift from a manufacturing-based economy to a service-based economy.
- Jacksonville's leading industries will be transportation and logistics, financial services, biomedical technology, consumer goods, information services, and manufacturing.
- Health care occupations will account for seven of the 20 fastest-growing occupations of the future.
- More and more companies will use temporary staffing agencies to manage their human resource function.
- Small business will account for close to 70% of all new hires.

Career Connections: Internet Links

http://www.valueoptions.com
http://www.dol.gov *(U.S. Department of Labor)*
http://www.bls.gov *(Bureau of Labor Statistics)*
http://www.dol.gov/wb *(U.S. Department of Labor Women's Bureau)*
http://www.bls.gov/oco *(Occupational Outlook Handbook)*
http://www.census.gov *(U.S. Census Bureau)*
http://www.wikipedia.com
http://en.wikipedia.org/wiki/Jacksonville,_Florida
http://www.simplyhired.com
http://www.sba.gov *(U.S. Small Business Administration)*
http://www.bringyouhome.com
http://www.stateofflorida.com

Name _____   Date _____

For each of the generations listed below, identify three famous people or celebrities:

A. Baby Boomers (born 1946–1964)

1. _____

2. _____

3. _____

B. Generation X (The Baby Bust) (born 1965–1980)

1. _____

2. _____

3. _____

C. Generation Y (Baby Boom Echo or The Millenials) (born 1980–2000)

1. _____

2. _____

3. _____

Name _____   Date _____

Looking at nontraditional careers, list below three famous people who are working in nontraditional careers or jobs:

Nontraditional Careers for Women

1. Job/Career: _____

   Famous Person: _____

2. Job/Career: _____

   Famous Person: _____

3. Job/Career: _____

   Famous Person: _____

Nontraditional Careers for Men

1. Job/Career: _____

   Famous Person: _____

2. Job/Career: _____

   Famous Person: _____

3. Job/Career: _____

   Famous Person: _____

CHAPTER 7

CHAPTER

CHAPTER QUEST

At the end of this chapter you should be able to:

- Make sound career decisions

- Manage stress effectively

- Develop effective time management skills

- Manage your finances effectively

© Kaminskiy, 2009. Used under license from Shutterstock, Inc.

Career Decisions: Managing Your Life and Career

You will be in your "career" for the better part of your life. Your career becomes a part of who you are and it incorporates a variety of life management skills such as making decisions, managing your time, handling stress, and managing your finances. As you develop and improve these life management skills, you will quickly advance both professionally and personally.

Making Career Decisions

We are faced with all kinds of decisions every day. Some of these decisions are minor (i.e., what to wear, what to eat, what to do that day) and some (career-related decisions) will have a major impact on our future (i.e., choosing to go to a college or university, accepting job offers, etc.). People make decisions in all kinds of ways with all kinds of results.

What Type of Decision Maker Are You?

Plan Your Work, Work Your Plan

You use a step-by-step process, getting a lot of information, looking at options, and putting together a plan of action.

Wing It

You don't really give it much thought and don't really look at options. Usually, you end up choosing the first option or alternative that presents itself.

Intuition

You go with your "gut feeling." If it feels right, you go for it. Intuitive/Perceptive types tend to make decisions this way.

Let Someone Else Decide

The easiest way out is to let someone else make decisions for you. As we are growing up, our parents, teachers, and others make important decisions for us. Many individuals, even as adults, continue to want others to make important decisions for them.

Procrastination

Some people prefer to put off the decision until the last possible moment, working up to the deadline. By putting off the decision, they are hoping something might happen that will help make the decision easier.

Destiny or Fate

Many people believe that our lives are preordained or things were just "meant to be." They tend to go with the first option that comes along thinking that it was "fate."

Lost at Sea Approach

The decision is too overwhelming and there is too much to consider resulting in a feeling of being "lost" and unable to make a decision.

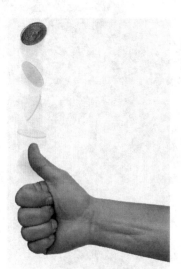

© James Steidl, 2009. Used under license from Shutterstock, Inc.

Rational/Logical Decision-Making Process

For the majority of people, a step-by-step decision making process can be very effective in terms of making important career decisions. Completing each step in a logical progression makes each of the tasks easier to manage and ensures that all of the needed information is gathered and analyzed. Information is power and is the key to being able to make a sound decision. Here is an example of a step-by-by step decision-making model:

Step One: Identify the decision to be made
Step Two: Know yourself (factor who you are into the decision)
Step Three: Begin identifying options
Step Four: Gather information and data about the options
Step Five: Evaluate all options
Step Six: Select one of the options (make a decision)
Step Seven: Design a course of action to implement the decision

Intuitive/Perception Decision-Making

The step-by-step works very well for most people, but for those creative, intuitive, and artistic types whose personality leans more toward spontaneity and possibilities, another approach is needed. They tend to look at the bigger "picture" in terms of the options and prefer to gather information by talking with people and experiencing the environments. They make the decision based on their "gut feeling," or a hunch. It just feels right to them based on what they have learned or experienced. Here are some ideas for intuitive decision making:

© maigi, 2009. Used under license from Shutterstock, Inc.

Brainstorming: Bounce our ideas off of other people. Use people in your network (friends, family members, mentors, faculty) to get the creative juices going. The give-and-take enables you to talk through the pros and cons of different options and to project outcomes.

Talk it out with other people: Gather information by talking to people with that experience. For example, if you are trying to choose a major, talk to faculty members of those majors; if you are thinking about a specific job or career, conduct an informational interview or "shadow" a professional in that field. Job Fairs are great places to talk to people about job and career options.

Mind Mapping: A mind map is a diagram used to put your thoughts and ideas on paper allowing you to visualize and organize your ideas. It allows you the freedom to connect various thoughts and ideas in a way that makes sense to you and does not follow any logical order.

What Is Keeping You from Making Your Decision?

Looking at the decision making model, think of the decision you are trying to make. What information do you need to make an informed decision? Do you need to know more about you: your skills, interests, values, or personality? Or do you need more information about the options you are considering? Being able to zero in on what information you need will help move you to the decision making point.

© Andresr, 2009. Used under license from Shutterstock, Inc.

Managing Your Time

With the development of computers, cell phones, the internet, and other technologies, life is moving at a much faster pace, placing more and more demands on your time. Learning how to manage your time can help you ultimately manage your life and career more effectively.

24 Hours in a Day

There are 24 hours in a day and only one of you to handle everything. One of the first keys to time management is mapping out how much time you will devote to the demands on your time. For example, what percentage of your time do you devote to: school/studies, commuting, work/job, recreation/activities, job hunting, eating, sleeping, going to church, chores/shopping/laundry/etc.?

Procrastination

The number one enemy of time management is procrastination. More time is wasted because people put off to tomorrow what they could have done today. Managing your time by planning out what you need to do will pay huge dividends in the end. Plan the day: Do this the night before and prioritize the things that need to be done. Plan the week: Do this on Friday. Plan the year: Do this with continuous updates. Remember, everyone is different and you need to set a planning schedule that fits your life style and personality.

Energy Levels

Handling a lot of commitments does require certain amounts of energy. Know your high points and low points for energy and plan around it. Tackle those tough tasks or assignments for times you have high energy and save the simple tasks for low energy times.

Work Rate

The pace at which you work or handle tasks can affect the way you feel. If you work at a very slow pace, you will feel more tired and drained. Working at a fast pace tends to energize you and make you feel more upbeat. If you feel yourself slowing down, take a break, go outside, and get some fresh air and come back at a new pace.

Paper Shuffle?

How many times do you pick up the same piece of paper or read an email? To gauge how many times you are shuffling the same papers around, put a check in the upper corner of a page every time you pick it up. This will help you think about your work patterns and become more efficient. Imagine if you can develop a system where you only handle that piece of paper once. The same goes for email. A lot of time can be saved by dealing with email only once.

Plan Your Work, Work Your Plan (Familiar Theme?)

Our work or jobs require a lot of time management skills to be successful. We are often faced with big projects and short deadlines. The key is to take a big task and break it down into steps that can be handled one at a time. Devote so much time to various aspects of the project each day. There are always jobs/tasks you hate to do but they need to get done. Prioritize your tasks and do those jobs or tasks you dislike first during times you have high energy. Save the jobs you enjoy for low-energy times.

How Many Passwords?

Technology was supposed to make our lives easier but it appears to have only complicated things. How many passwords do you have for all the different accounts you have. An easy time saver is to set your password so you can type it with one hand and use the same password for multiple accounts.

Waiting for a Reply

Need a response from someone? Stop procrastinating. Make the request verbally by picking up the phone or going in person. In the time you would take for all those emails, you could have received your information as a result of a few minutes on the telephone.

Study Schedule

As a college student, for every hour of class time, you should spend 4 hours studying or preparing for classwork. With all of your other commitments, this requires prioritizing your time. Remember to schedule regular study times. Handle those tough assignments or projects during high-energy times and the easy classes or projects during low-energy times. Develop a study schedule. Create incentives for yourself with a reward for completion of a task such as a soda, candy bar, movie, or even a vacation in Bermuda. Make it appropriate to the task.

Maintaining That Balance in Your Life

The old saying goes, "All work and no play makes Jack/Jill a dull boy/girl." Maintaining a balance is important. Minimize the amount of work that spills over to the weekend. Plan your weekends and make the most of your time away from work-related tasks.

Standing Up

According to the University of Southern California, your brain processes 5%–20% faster and heart beats increase 10 beats per minute while standing up. Next time you are on the telephone, try standing up, and see if it makes a difference.

Draw a Picture

Facing a large problem? Draw a picture with links that relate—use scribbles, arrows, whatever fits, anything that helps you see the "big picture" and all the related tasks. This will help you see what needs to get done and can help you set priorities.

Planning a Job Search

Job hunting requires a lot of time and energy. An effective job search can take anywhere from 3 to 9 months of intensive looking. Effective time management can bring about a successful conclusion much quicker. Record keeping is also an important part of any job search. Here is an example of a job search schedule: Monday through

Thursday plan to make three employer contacts each day. This would include either sending a letter, conversing by phone, or interviewing with a potential employer. If you held to this schedule, you would have 12 contacts per week and a total of 48 per month. Over a 6-month period, you would have close to 300 employer contacts. And the nice thing is you have Friday, Saturday, and Sunday for other activities and to recharge your batteries. Most job searches drag on because people do not maintain any type of time management schedule.

© iofoto, 2009. Used under license from Shutterstock, Inc.

Interesting Time Management Facts

- 78% of workers in America wish they had more time to "smell the roses"
- 25% of sick days are taken for illness and the remaining 75% of sick days are taken for other reasons
- The average worker gets 6 hours and 57 minutes of sleep per night
- The average worker spends 35 minutes per day commuting
- 70% of business and professional people use a "to do" list on a regular basis
- 1 hour of planning will save 10 hours of doing
- It almost always takes twice as long to complete a task as what we originally thought it would take

Taken from: www.balancetime.com, Dr. Donald E. Wetmore, Professional Speaker, Productivity Institute Time Management Seminars, 60 Huntington St. P.O. Box 2126, Shelton, CT 06484

Handling and Managing Stress

Managing your time effectively should help reduce your stress. But there are plenty of things in our daily lives that stress us out. The term "stress" was first defined by Hans Selye in 1936 as "the non-specific response of the body to any demand or change." Our body naturally reacts to both external and internal factors and demands being placed on us. It is natural and in many cases can be a good thing since it helps to energize us to face challenges and to accomplish our goals. Without stress we could become complacent and bored. And stress is different for all of us. What is stressful for one might be energizing or relaxing to someone else. Managing your stress is important since too much stress begins to interfere with our day-to-day coping abilities. The key to managing stress is to recognize, manage it, and control it so that it energizes us and doesn't harm us.

© Edyta Pawlowska, 2009. Used under license from Shutterstock, Inc.

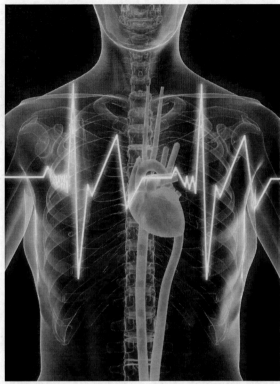

© Sebastian Kaulitzki, 2009. Used under license from
Shutterstock, Inc.

Causes of Stress

Other People

A lot of stress is caused by our relationships with other people: our family, roommates, friends, coworkers, faculty members, and others around us. Things people say and do can greatly affect us and cause stress.

Things

Many times things will start to get to us. The weather, the place we live, our car, appliances, cell phone, computer. The list is endless. Our interaction with all of the things in our lives can stress us out.

Self-Inflicted

Many times we cause our own stress by things we think, say, feel, and do. Sometimes we have unrealistic expectations, and we are often disappointed when we can not meet them.

What Are Some of the Signs of Stress?

Our bodies react to stress in different ways including heart palpitations, headaches, muscle tension, skin outbreaks, shortness of breath, fatigue, restlessness, lack of sleep, and digestive disorders. Other signs include depression, anxiety, irritability, mood swings, crying, feeling pressured, emotional outbursts, anger, sensitivity, being emotional, being impatient, having no humor, lack of self-esteem, poor concentration, lack of interest, procrastination, forgetfulness, indecision, withdrawal from others, loneliness, buying things you don't need, alcohol, tobacco, and drug use, loss of direction or purpose, emptiness, and apathy.

© Dallas Events Inc, 2009. Used under license from Shutterstock, Inc.

Strategies for Managing Your Stress
Take Care of Your Body

Pay attention to your diet, and try to eat healthy foods. Be sure to eat regular meals throughout the day. Start the day with a good breakfast. They say that, "breakfast is the most important meal of the day." Proper nutrition will help you to maintain your energy levels. Getting the proper amount of sleep each night is also important to maintaining a healthy body. Eight hours of sleep for adults is the recommended average per night. Exercise and other physical activity help in so many ways, giving you energy, improving your sleep, and relaxing muscles. Taking deep, relaxed breaths in through your nose out through your mouth also help to slow things down and reduce stress.

The Power of Positive Thinking

Avoid the self-fulfilling prophecy, "I am going to fail the exam today" and use positive self-talk, "I am going to ace this exam!" Set realistic goals and keep expectations you have for yourself reasonable. The world is constantly changing and is part of the natural order of things, so always be prepared to deal with those changes. Everyone makes mistakes so avoid beating yourself up for making mistakes. By maintaining a positive outlook you can see these challenges as opportunities for personal and professional growth. Developing effective time management strategies can also help you meet the numerous demands that are coming your way. Maintaining a sense of humor is a great way to manage your stress. Developing a strong self-esteem is another important aspect of handling stress.

Don't Go It Alone

Having a support network of family and friends can keep you grounded, make you feel good about yourself, and help you face any challenges. Be sure to make time to spend with others. Don't be afraid to ask others for help or advice. Don't keep things bottled up inside; talking things out with someone you trust helps to keep stress levels low. If you are a spiritual person, prayer and meditation are also very powerful. As they say, "faith can move mountains."

Taking Time for You

Be sure to make time for recreational activities that you enjoy (i.e., sports, running, fishing, sewing, reading, going to the movies, dancing, etc.). Maintain pleasant surroundings (your room, your apartment, your house, your work space, etc.) to maintain a positive outlook. Sometimes, being by yourself and getting away from everything can help you look at things from a different perspective. Taking walks and being alone with your thoughts can be very relaxing. Listening to soft music or taking a hot bath can soothe away a lot of stress.

References:

Stress, Definition of Stress, Stressor, What is Stress? The American Institute of Stress; http://www.stress.org/topic-definition-stress.htm

Common Symptoms of Stress, Systematic Stress Management; The American Institute of Preventive Medicine; http://aipm.wellnesscheckpoint.com/library/banner_main.asp?P=987ECASMC2

How To Go From Stressed to Unstressed; College of Saint Benedict/Saint John's University, Counseling And Health Promotions, http://www.csbsju.edu/chp/stress.htm

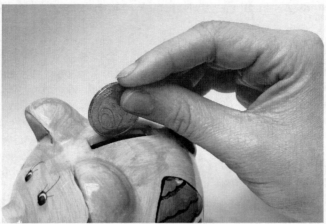

© Rafa Irusta, 2009. Used under license from Shutterstock, Inc.

Managing Your Money

As you make the transition from college to the world of work, you will also change the way you handle all of your finances. Completing your degree tends to be the top priority, and oftentimes it takes a combination of student loans, part-time work, and seasonal employment to get through. When you start your career you will manage an annual salary and benefits and juggle a wide range of expenses such as housing, transportation, clothing, etc. If you don't like living "pay check to pay check," learning how to manage your money will help you to maintain the lifestyle you want, reduce stress caused by finances, and prepare for your future and retirement.

Money In, Money Out

In a perfect situation, you will earn more money than you spend. In today's economy and with the rising cost of living, it is a very challenging proposition. The first step is to figure out your income. How much money do you have coming in? This can include your student loans or grants, money from your parents, and any type of employment. After graduation and after you find a full-time, career position, you will be calculating your annual salary and monthly take-home pay. Calculating all of your expenses or creating a monthly budget is the next step. See Exercise 7.6: Developing A Monthly Budget.

Money Management Tips

Staying in "the black," or maintaining a positive balance, should always be your goal. Now that you have your monthly budget, you should know which bills are top priority (mortgage payment, apartment rent, car payment, insurance, etc.). Money should be set aside for these expenses first. Once the critical bills are taken care of you can determine how much money you have for other things: food, entertainment, gas for the car, etc. It can be very challenging to stretch a dollar to pay for all the things you want. Here are some tips:

- When grocery shopping, use coupons from the newspaper and circulars on items you normally buy. Consider the store's generic brands. In most cases, the generic brands are cheaper and taste just as good as

© Andresr, 2009. Used under license from Shutterstock, Inc.

name brands. Avoid shopping when you are hungry; it will cut down on "impulse buys."
- Consider packing your lunch; eating at a restaurant every day will "eat up" a lot of your income.
- Create and maintain a savings account. Even if it is only a small amount each month. You would be surprised at how much it will add up.
- How much driving do you do? Gas is pretty expensive these days. Can you use public transportation? Can you plan your trip to accomplish several errands and avoid multiple trips?
- Prioritize your expenses into "need" and "want." Spending mostly on what you need versus things you want can save you considerably. Rewarding yourself once in a while with things you want is OK, but always spending on unneeded items can throw you off budget.

Credit Cards

According to The American Bankers Association, the average credit card debt among American households has more than doubled over the past decade. Today, the average family owes roughly $8000 on their credit cards. This debt has helped generate record profits for the credit card industry—last year, more than $30 billion before taxes. If you have fallen into the credit card trap, here are some tips:

- If you have more than one credit card, pay off the one with the highest interest rate. Try to consolidate your credit cards into as few as possible.
- If you must have and use a credit card, shop around and look for cards that offer the lowest interest rates. Be weary of introductory rates that offer a low interest rate to start and then charge a very high rate after so many months. You might save a little on the front end and then spend a lot on the back end.
- Having a line of credit should not be seen as a source of revenue for your budget. When you use a credit card you are basically loaning yourself money that needs to be paid back later.
- Pay your credit card payments on time even if it is only the minimum payment. Making payments on time will help you build a strong credit rating. Any late payments, even if they are "once in a while" can bring your credit score down.

© Olga Kolos, 2009. Used under license from Shutterstock, Inc.

Having Good Credit

Decisions you make about your finances now will come back into play later on when you look to buy a house, new car, or another major expense requiring credit terms. The lower your credit score, the higher the interest rate you will receive on the money you borrow. Paying all bills on time and in full will help you build a great credit rating.

Reference:
Managing Your Finances; College Summit; http://www.collegesummit.org/students-alumni/alumni-staying-in-college/managing-your-finances

 Key Discoveries

- Information about yourself and the options being considered are the keys to making decisions.
- A step-by-step decision-making approach can help you process the information needed for a decision.
- Effective time management enables you to accomplish more and reduce your stress.
- One hour of planning will save 10 hours of doing a task or assignment.
- Stress is our body's natural reaction to changes in our lives. Stress can energize us if we know how to recognize, manage, and control it.
- Developing a monthly budget and using it to manage your finances will enable you to maintain the lifestyle you want, build a solid credit rating, and prepare for your future.

 Career Connections: Internet Links

- http://career.berkeley.edu/Plan/MakeDecisions.stm
- http://www.csbsju.edu/chp/stress.htm *College of Saint Benedict/Saint Johns University, Counseling and Health Promotions*
- http://www.collegesummit.org/students-alumni/alumni/staying-in-college/managing-your-finances
- http://www.stress.org/topic-definition-stress.htm (*The American Institute of Stress*)
- American Institute of Preventive Medicine

Exercise 7.1: Decision-Making

Name _____ Date _____

Use the 7-step career decision making model to work through the career decision you are trying to make:

STEP ONE: IDENTIFY THE DECISION TO BE MADE
_____

STEP TWO: KNOW YOURSELF (Self-Assessment)

My values: _____

My skills: _____

My interests: _____

My goals: _____

STEP THREE: BEGIN IDENTIFYING OPTIONS

1. _____

2. _____

3. _____

STEP FOUR: GATHER INFORMATION AND DATA
_____
_____
_____
_____

STEP FIVE: EVALUATE OPTIONS THAT WILL SOLVE THE PROBLEM

Option 1: Pros: _____

Option 1: Cons: _____

Option 1: Risks: _____

Option 1: Future consequence: _____

Option 2: Pros: _____

Option 2: Cons: _____

Option 2: Risks: _____

Option 2: Future consequence: _____

Option 3: Pros: _____

Option 3: Cons: _____

Option 3: Risks: _____

Option 3: Future consequence: _____

STEP SIX: SELECT ONE OF THE OPTIONS

_____

STEP SEVEN: DESIGN A COURSE OF ACTION TO IMPLEMENT THE DECISION

Identify steps to implement the decision

1. _____

2. _____

3. _____

4. _____

5. _____

Name _____ Date _____

Start in the center of the page. Write down the most important idea, concept, or decision being made and draw a circle around. Next write down words or concepts that are related. Use diagrams or pictures to help the flow of ideas. Connect related ideas of concepts with lines or arrows. Continue until you have run out of ideas and/or your map is complete.

Exercise 7.3: Time Management Inventory

Name _____   Date _____

Test your time management skills: Answer Questions 1–10 on scale of 1–5

1 = Almost never   2 = Seldom   3 = Sometimes   4 = Usually   5 = Almost always

1. I map out how much time I will devote to the demands on my time (school/studies, commuting, work/job, recreation/activities, job hunting, eating, sleeping, going to church, chores/shopping/laundry/etc.).

        1   2   3   4   5

2. I manage my time by planning out what I need to do. (Plan the day the night before and prioritize the things that need to be done. Plan the week on Friday. Plan the year with continuous updates.)

        1   2   3   4   5

3. I tackle those tough tasks or assignments for times when I have high energy and save the simple tasks for low-energy times.

        1   2   3   4   5

4. I work at a fast pace that tends to energize me and makes me feel more upbeat.

        1   2   3   4   5

5. I save a lot of time dealing with paper or email only once.

        1   2   3   4   5

6. I take a big task and break it down into steps that can be handled one at a time.

        1   2   3   4   5

7. I have set my password so I can type it with one hand and use the same password for multiple accounts.

        1   2   3   4   5

8. When I need a response from someone, I make the request verbally by picking up the phone or going in person.

        1   2   3   4   5

9. I schedule regular study times.

        1   2   3   4   5

10. I create incentives for myself with a reward for completion of a task such as a soda, candy bar, movie, or even a vacation in Bermuda.

        1   2   3   4   5

11. I maintain a balance in my life and minimize the amount of work that spills over to weekend. I plan my weekends and make the most of my time away from work-related tasks.

$$1 \qquad 2 \qquad 3 \qquad 4 \qquad 5$$

12. When facing a large problem, I draw a picture with links that relate; I use scribbles, arrows, whatever fits, anything that helps me to see the "big picture" and all the related tasks.

$$1 \qquad 2 \qquad 3 \qquad 4 \qquad 5$$

Determine your score by adding the number circled together. How did you score?

1–20: Uh oh! 21–30: Time to spend more time managing your time

31–40: Average 41–50: Pretty good

51–60: EXCELLENT!

Name _____   Date _____

Weekly Study Schedule

Time	Monday	Tuesday	Wednesday	Thursday	Friday
6:00 a.m.					
7:00 a.m.					
8:00 a.m.					
9:00 a.m.					
10:00 a.m.					
11:00 a.m.					
12:00 noon					
1:00 p.m.					
2:00 p.m.					
3:00 p.m.					
4:00 p.m.					
5:00 p.m.					
6:00 pm					
7:00 p.m.					
8:00 p.m.					
9:00 p.m.					
10:00 p.m.					
11:00 p.m.					
12:00 a.m.					

Exercise 7.5: Stress Test

Name _____   Date _____

Read each sentence and, in the space to the right, place your score based on this scale:
4 = Always   3 = Frequently 2 = Sometimes 1 = Never

Do you try to do as much as possible in the least amount of time?   _____

Do you become impatient with delays or interruptions?   _____

Do you always have to win at games to enjoy yourself?   _____

Do you find yourself speeding up the car to beat the red light?   _____

Are you unlikely to ask for or indicate you need help with a problem?   _____

Do you constantly seek the respect and admiration of others?   _____

Are you overly critical of the way others do their work?   _____

Do you have the habit of looking at your watch or clock often?   _____

Do you constantly strive to better your position and achievements?   _____

Do you spread yourself "too thin" in terms of your time?   _____

Do you have the habit of doing more than one thing at a time?   _____

Do you frequently get angry or irritable?   _____

Do you have little time for hobbies or time by yourself?   _____

Do you have a tendency to talk quickly or hasten conversations?   _____

Do you consider yourself hard-driving?   _____

Do your friends or relatives consider you hard-driving?   _____

Do you have a tendency to get involved in multiple projects?   _____

Do you have a lot of deadlines in your work?   _____

Do you feel vaguely guilty if you relax and do nothing during leisure?   _____

Do you take on too many responsibilities?   _____

                                        Add Up Your Score: _____

Answer Key:
-If your score is between 20 and 30, chances are you are nonproductive or your life lacks stimulation.
-A score between 31 and 50 designates a good balance in your ability to handle and control stress.
-For a score between 51 and 60, your stress level is marginal and you are bordering on being excessively tense.
-If your total number of points exceeds 60, you may be a candidate for heart disease.
Source of Quiz: Unknown

Name _____   Date _____

To effectively evaluate a job offer, you will also need to examine your financial situation. Will the salary and benefits meet your financial needs? Use the list below to help construct an overall budget. BE REALISTIC!

Your Anticipated Monthly Take Home Pay: _____

Expense Items	**Estimated Expense**
Mortgage Payment or Apartment Rent	_____
Home or Apartment Insurance	_____
Gas (utilities)	_____
Electric (utilities)	_____
Water (utilities)	_____
Telephone	_____
Student Loan Payment	_____
Car Payment	_____
Car Insurance	_____
Gasoline	_____
Car Maintenance	_____
Food	_____
Clothing	_____
Drugs/Medical Expenses	_____
Child Care	_____
Tuition Expenses	_____
Subscriptions, Magazines	_____
Household Needs	_____
Personal Needs	_____
Life Insurance Premiums*	_____
Medical Insurance Premiums*	_____
Laundry and Dry Cleaning	_____
Taxes	_____
Club and Association Memberships	_____
Entertainment	_____
Other:	_____
Other:	_____
Total Monthly Expenses	_____

When evaluating a job offer, fringe benefits are an important part of the compensation package and should be carefully reviewed. Listed below are some examples of what might be included in a job offer.

HEALTH INSURANCE COVERAGE

Most employers offer two or three options for health coverage, and this is the most expensive benefit. The employer pays part of the premium and the employee the remainder. The stronger plans also include dental and vision coverage. Three of the most common options are:

Health Maintenance Organization (HMO)
Under this plan, the employee selects a physician from a list specified by the insurer. The physician serves as a gatekeeper and refers patients to certain specialists. In an HMO, there is no deductible, and you pay small copayments for each visit. An HMO is the least expensive to you, but is a controlled system.

Preferred Provider Organization (PPO)
Under this plan, a group of doctors, hospitals, and pharmacies are contracted at a higher discount than traditional health insurance. Under this plan, oftentimes you are allowed to select your own physician. There is usually an annual deductible, you might pay a percentage of certain expenses, and there might be other copayments involved.

Traditional Health Insurance
Under this plan, you have total freedom of choice of doctors and hospitals. The insurance covers 70%–80% of the expenses and there is a deductible. This is the most expensive coverage.

PENSION PLAN

Under a pension plan, an employer contributes a portion of your salary, and you contribute a portion of your salary in pretax dollars. These dollars are invested in real estate, bonds, stocks, and money market accounts to provide an annuity for your retirement. It is important to understand how a company handles the money invested in a pension plan if you leave the organization.

GROUP LIFE INSURANCE

A life insurance plan provides a payment to your beneficiary if you die or are seriously disabled while in the employment of the organization. This is usually based on a formula of your salary. Group life insurance is to replace the loss of your wages for several years to your beneficiary. Group life rates are age-rated and are lower for younger people.

SHORT-TERM AND LONG-TERM DISABILITY

If you become permanently disabled and are not able to work, long-term disability provides you a percentage of your salary to age 65. In most cases, long-term disability starts 6 months after you become disabled. Short-term disability replaces the loss of salary for serious illnesses that last up to 6 months.

EDUCATIONAL BENEFITS

Some employers will reimburse employees for the costs of taking courses at local colleges. After you have been employed at a company, you may want to continue your education and take graduate courses. With the escalating cost of tuition, this can be a very valuable benefit.

CHILD CARE

This is the new benefit of the 1990s. With both members of a family working outside the home, there is a need to find quality care for children during the day. Child care may include a company-operated center, a discount with a local provider, or a reimbursement for direct costs.

OTHER BENEFITS

Vacation Time	Sick Time	Employee Discounts
Profit Share Plans	Flex Time	Maternity/Parental Leave
Recreational Programs	Relocation Programs	Cafeteria Benefits Plan

Name _____   Date _____

You will be evaluating each team presentation on Blackboard. This worksheet is for you to take notes to help you complete the online evaluation. THIS WORKSHEET WILL NOT BE ACCEPTED FOR CREDIT FOR THE ONLINE EVALUATIONS.

PRESENTATION #1: DECISION MAKING

Question 1. Content: Did the group adequately cover the required content? Was the information easy to understand and apply?

Ratings: 5–Excellent   4–Very Good   3–Average/Good   2–Fair/Below Average   1–Needs Improvement

Question 2. Handouts: Were they visually appealing? Did they include key presentation points/tips/strategies, etc.?

Ratings: 5–Excellent   4–Very Good   3–Average/Good   2–Fair/Below Average   1–Needs Improvement

Question 3. Teamwork: Were group members in sync with each other? Was team collaboration evident? Did the presentation flow from beginning to end?

Ratings: 5–Excellent   4–Very Good   3–Average/Good   2–Fair/Below Average   1–Needs Improvement

Question 4. Creativity/Visual Aids: Was the presentation original? Was it presented in a unique and interesting way?

Ratings: 5–Excellent   4–Very Good   3–Average/Good   2–Fair/Below Average   1–Needs Improvement

Question 5. Communication Skills/Presentation Style: Did the presenters engage the audience and maintain eye contact? Did they use their own words to illustrate points and avoid merely reading the presentation?

Ratings: 5–Excellent   4–Very Good   3–Average/Good   2–Fair/Below Average   1–Needs Improvement

Comments

PRESENTATION #2: TIME MANAGEMENT

Question 1. Content: Did the group adequately cover the required content? Was the information easy to understand and apply?

Ratings: 5–Excellent   4–Very Good   3–Average/Good   2–Fair/Below Average   1–Needs Improvement

Question 2. Handouts: Were they visually appealing? Did they include key presentation points/tips/strategies, etc.?

Ratings: 5–Excellent   4–Very Good   3–Average/Good   2–Fair/Below Average   1–Needs Improvement

Question 3. Teamwork: Were group members in sync with each other? Was team collaboration evident? Did the presentation flow from beginning to end?

Ratings: 5–Excellent   4–Very Good   3–Average/Good   2–Fair/Below Average   1–Needs Improvement

Question 4. Creativity/Visual Aids: Was the presentation original? Was it presented in a unique and interesting way?

Ratings: 5–Excellent   4–Very Good   3–Average/Good   2–Fair/Below Average   1–Needs Improvement

Question 5. Communication Skills/Presentation Style: Did the presenters engage the audience and maintain eye contact; used ? Did they use their own words to illustrate points and avoid merely reading the presentation?

Ratings: 5–Excellent   4–Very Good   3–Average/Good   2–Fair/Below Average   1–Needs Improvement

Comments

PRESENTATION #3: STRESS MANAGEMENT

Question 1. Content: Did the group adequately cover the required content? Was the information easy to understand and apply?

Ratings: 5–Excellent   4–Very Good   3–Average/Good   2–Fair/Below Average   1–Needs Improvement

Question 2. Handouts: Were they visually appealing? Did they include key presentation points/tips/strategies, etc.?

Ratings: 5–Excellent   4–Very Good   3–Average/Good   2–Fair/Below Average   1–Needs Improvement

Question 3. Teamwork: Were group members in sync with each other? Was team collaboration evident? Did the presentation flow from beginning to end?

Ratings: 5–Excellent   4–Very Good   3–Average/Good   2–Fair/Below Average   1–Needs Improvement

Question 4. Creativity/Visual Aids: Was the presentation original? Was it presented in a unique and interesting way?

Ratings: 5–Excellent   4–Very Good   3–Average/Good   2–Fair/Below Average   1–Needs Improvement

Question 5. Communication Skills/Presentation Style: Did the presenters engage the audience and maintain eye contact? Did they use their own words to illustrate points and avoid merely reading the presentation?

Ratings: 5–Excellent   4–Very Good   3–Average/Good   2–Fair/Below Average   1–Needs Improvement

Comments

PRESENTATION #4: MANAGING YOUR FINANCES

Question 1. Content: Did the group adequately cover the required content? Was the information easy to understand and apply?

Ratings: 5–Excellent   4–Very Good   3–Average/Good   2–Fair/Below Average   1–Needs Improvement

Question 2. Handouts: Were they visually appealing? Did they include key presentation points/tips/strategies, etc.?

Ratings: 5–Excellent   4–Very Good   3–Average/Good   2–Fair/Below Average   1–Needs Improvement

Question 3. Teamwork: Were group members in sync with each other? Was team collaboration evident? Did the presentation flow from beginning to end?

Ratings: 5–Excellent   4–Very Good   3–Average/Good   2–Fair/Below Average   1–Needs Improvement

Question 4. Creativity/Visual Aids: Was the presentation original? Was it presented in a unique and interesting way?

Ratings: 5–Excellent   4–Very Good   3–Average/Good   2–Fair/Below Average   1–Needs Improvement

Question 5. Communication Skills/Presentation Style: Did the presenters engage the audience and maintain eye contact? Did they use their own words to illustrate points and avoid merely reading the presentation?

Ratings: 5–Excellent   4–Very Good   3–Average/Good   2–Fair/Below Average   1–Needs Improvement

Comments

PRESENTATION #5: DEVELOPING A BUDGET

Question 1. Content: Did the group adequately cover the required content? Was the information easy to understand and apply?

Ratings: 5–Excellent   4–Very Good   3–Average/Good   2–Fair/Below Average   1–Needs Improvement

Question 2. Handouts: Were they visually appealing? Did they include key presentation points/tips/strategies, etc.?

Ratings: 5–Excellent   4–Very Good   3–Average/Good   2–Fair/Below Average   1–Needs Improvement

Question 3. Teamwork: Were group members in sync with each other? Was team collaboration evident? Did the presentation flow from beginning to end?

Ratings: 5–Excellent   4–Very Good   3–Average/Good   2–Fair/Below Average   1–Needs Improvement

Question 4. Creativity/Visual Aids: Was the presentation original? Was it presented in a unique and interesting way?

Ratings: 5–Excellent   4–Very Good   3–Average/Good   2–Fair/Below Average   1–Needs Improvement

Question 5. Communication Skills/Presentation Style: Did the presenters engage the audience and maintain eye contact? Did they use their own words to illustrate points and avoid merely reading the presentation?

Ratings: 5–Excellent   4–Very Good   3–Average/Good   2–Fair/Below Average   1–Needs Improvement

Comments

PRESENTATION #6: FRINGE BENEFITS

Question 1. Content: Did the group adequately cover the required content? Was the information easy to understand and apply?

Ratings: 5–Excellent   4–Very Good   3–Average/Good   2–Fair/Below Average   1–Needs Improvement

Question 2. Handouts: Were they visually appealing? Did they include key presentation points/tips/strategies, etc.?

Ratings: 5–Excellent   4–Very Good   3–Average/Good   2–Fair/Below Average   1–Needs Improvement

Question 3. Teamwork: Were group members in sync with each other? Was team collaboration evident? Did the presentation flow from beginning to end?

Ratings: 5–Excellent   4–Very Good   3–Average/Good   2–Fair/Below Average   1–Needs Improvement

Question 4. Creativity/Visual Aids: Was the presentation original? Was it presented in a unique and interesting way?

Ratings: 5–Excellent   4–Very Good   3–Average/Good   2–Fair/Below Average   1–Needs Improvement

Question 5. Communication Skills/Presentation Style: Did the presenters engage the audience and maintain eye contact? Did they use their own words to illustrate points and avoid merely reading the presentation?

Ratings: 5–Excellent   4–Very Good   3–Average/Good   2–Fair/Below Average   1–Needs Improvement

Comments

CHAPTER QUEST

At the end of this chapter you should be able to:

- Develop a plan for exploring careers outside of the classroom environment

- Understand the different types of work experience opportunities

- Identify the value of extracurricular activities to skill development

- Understand how skill development impacts career planning outcomes

© Stephen Coburn, 2009. Used under license from Shutterstock, Inc.

Making the Most of Your College Career

© emin kuliyev, 2009. Used under license from Shutterstock, Inc.

Career Exploration outside of the Classroom

Students often consider major selection as the most important factor for career planning success. While the selection of a major has a direct relationship to the type of career opportunities available to you at graduation, it is only one factor of many that will determine your success. Your major will expose you to a climate of learning within the classroom setting relative to a particular discipline. You will gain in-depth knowledge and skills that uniquely qualify you for a wide variety of career options. However, relying solely on academic knowledge often limits your ability to build workplace skills. Majors that incorporate internship requirements compensate for such limitations, allowing you to gain practical experience and skills. Employers will expect you to demonstrate a wide variety of knowledge and skills during the job interview process. If your major does not incorporate an internship, there are other options outside of the classroom environment that will help you develop workplace skills. These opportunities also serve as valuable career exploration tools to validate or eliminate current career possibilities.

© AVAVA, 2009. Used under license from Shutterstock, Inc.

GETTING REAL . . . Experience

Mark, a graduating senior, met with a Career Counselor for a resume critique and practice interview. Through a professional association he was a member of, he found the perfect job and desired an opportunity to interview. A week prior, Mark managed to contact the human resources manager at a major national news organization to discuss the available position. The position was extremely competitive, and Mark knew the prestigious nature of this company would result in a large and select pool of applicants, including those from Ivy League schools.

Mark learned about Career Services as a sophomore. A representative visited one of his classes to discuss the value of internships and co-op opportunities. He chose Communications-Public Relations (PR) as a major and knew to expect keen competition in his field. Only the cream of the crop would get top high-paying jobs at the best companies. Mediocrity wasn't Mark's trademark. He was competitive by nature, a star quarterback in high school, and president of his fraternity. He wasn't threatened by his competitive major, because he was passionate about Public Relations and knew he had the potential for success. But all the potential in the world wouldn't get Mark the PR Assistant job at a major national news organization unless he played his cards right. His ace was maximizing his experience in his field *before* graduating in order to become a top candidate *after* graduation. Mark joined the PR club on campus and quickly became the president. He also joined two professional associations in PR and picked up a couple of volunteer projects related to his major. One such project was writing articles for Habitat for Humanity in the community pages of the local newspaper. He was published, and this was something he could put on his resume! As a sophomore, he had yet to gain any direct practical experience in a PR department. Since he had a love for sports, Mark connected with the local professional football team's human resources department and landed a summer internship in the marketing and PR department soon after his sophomore year. This experience confirmed that he had chosen the right major. The next summer, Mark pursued another internship with a professional football team. With two solid internships under his belt, Mark felt more confident about his career prospects. He knew the environment, work tasks, lingo, PR-related computer programs, and salary potential in the field.

Within a week of submitting his resume to the major national news organization, Mark was invited to interview. Using the skills and knowledge he gained through work experience programs, as well as practice interview assistance, he was able to present himself professionally and clearly communicate that he was the best fit for the position. Two weeks later, a day before graduation, Mark received the call he had been waiting for. He had been selected for the position of PR Assistant at a major national news organization. He was well on his way to becoming a top PR executive, and he was barely 22. His supervisor later mentioned how impressed they were with Mark during the interview and noted that the level of involvement in his field and the amount of relevant experience set him apart from other applicants. He was the top choice for the position.

Discussion Points

1. What are some actions you can initiate to create future career opportunities?
2. Are you familiar with clubs and professional associations in your major?
3. How would you go about searching for an internship or co-op relating to your field of study?
4. If your major requires an academic internship, what would be the value of adding a career internship?
5. In what ways do you think Mark's internship experience prepared him for his future career as a PR Assistant?

Work Experience Programs and Opportunities

During your college career, you should engage in active skill building through various work experience programs. These experiences allow you to "test the waters" and explore careers from a hands-on perspective. You are then better able to confirm career interests and clarify your work values while building valuable skills.

Academic Internships

Experiences required for certain majors. Consult your Academic Advisor for specific requirements.

Co-Operative Education

Experience related to your major. Although it is not required for any major, you may opt to register for 0–3 academic credit hours. Program requirements and eligibility vary by college.

© Gina Sanders, 2009. Used under license from Shutterstock, Inc.

Career Internships

Paid or nonpaid experiences you voluntarily pursue that are related to your major or career interests.

Part-Time Employment

Jobs designed to assist with college and living expenses. These experiences are not necessarily related to your major or career interests, but help you establish and develop your work ethic and work style.

Volunteerism

Nonpaid, informal experiences exposing you to various work settings to gain workplace skills and knowledge. The UNF Volunteer Center, an agency of Student Government, is a valuable on-campus resource for learning about volunteer opportunities. Contact them at 620-2755, volctr1@unf.edu, or www.unf.edu/groups/volctr.

Ideally, developing your skills by participating in all of these opportunities is strongly encouraged throughout your college years. Table 8.1 provides a detailed comparison chart of each option.

Remember:

In today's market economy, you need more than just a degree to get a good job. Practical experience can give you the edge you need to be successful. It will allow you to stand out in the crowd and get noticed in a large group of applicants. Additionally, relevant experience can help confirm whether you have made the correct career choice by providing real experiences in your chosen field.

Table 8.1 UNF Work Experience Progams and Opportunities

	Academic Internships	Co-Operative Education	Career Internship	Part-Time Job	Volunteerism
Definition	Practical work experience relevant to your major	Practical work experience relevant to your major	Practical work experience relevant to your major or career goals	Work experience not necessarily related to your major or career goals	Work experience not necessarily related to your major or career goals
When to Apply	Within the last year of your program of study*	**Undergraduate:** after the completion of 60 semester hours (transfer students must have one term at UNF) ***Graduate:** after one term at UNF	Anytime	Anytime	Anytime
GPA Eligibility Requirements	Determined by each department	**Undergraduate:** minimum 2.5 **Graduate:** minimum 3.0	Determined by employer	Determined by employer; usually not a factor	Determined by organization; usually not a factor
Supervision	Faculty and site supervisor	Co-op coordinator and site supervisor	Employer only	Employer only	Organization only
Grade	Letter grade*	Pass/Fail	N/A	N/A	N/A
Transcript Notation	Shows on transcript	Shows on transcript	N/A	N/A	N/A
Time Commitment	One or more semesters	One or more semesters	Varies	Varies	Varies
Total Hours Required	Varies by department	Varies by credit hours	Varies	Varies	Varies
Work Schedule	Flexible around classes	Flexible around classes	Flexible around classes	Flexible around classes	Flexible around classes
Compensation	May or may not be paid	Paid*	May or may not be paid	Paid	Nonpaid
Initial Contact	Academic Department	Career Services	Career Services	Career Services or UNF Human Resources	Volunteer Center

*Some exceptions may apply.

Career Wings

Career Wings is an online system offered by UNF Career Services to connect students with employers for full-time, part-time, co-op, and internship opportunities. Registering with this system is the best first step to learning about the many opportunities available to help you explore careers, build your skills, and gain valuable work experience. To get started, visit http://www.unf.edu/dept/cdc.

Benefits of Work Experience Programs

There are numerous benefits to participating in work experience programs and other skill and knowledge building activities. The most beneficial options are those related to your major or career interests. These experiences can enhance your academic knowledge and professional preparation, resulting in increased job marketability upon graduation. These valuable opportunities allow you to:

© Orange Line Media, 2009. Used under license from Shutterstock, Inc.

- Enhance course knowledge in a practical way
- Develop new skills
- Gain exposure to new environments
- Test out theories learned in the classroom
- Explore career options
- Discover specific job requirements and qualifications
- Learn practical information about the job market in your field
- Establish a professional network

You are encouraged to take advantage of as many of these opportunities as possible during your college career. Gaining various types of educational and work experiences is essential to ensuring a smooth transition from college to the world of work, as your marketability will be greatly enhanced. Many students receive offers of full-time employment upon graduation as a result of these experiences. Remember, you may begin some of these options as early as your freshman year, so be proactive and discover your path to success.

DID YOU KNOW?

UNF offers Transformational Learning Opportunities (TLOs). The importance of seizing these opportunities is underscored by the notion that learning occurs best when facilitated within the context of a practical situation or problem. It is direct experience that impacts how students understand their contributions to work or educational environments. A key distinguishing aspect of TLOs from other experiences is often the level of university faculty and staff involvement. When students actively pursue and engage in learning experiences, personal and professional development occurs. In addition to some of the opportunities described in Table 8.1, here are some additional activities and programs to inquire about:

Study Abroad
Community-Based Learning
Service Learning
Leadership Development
Independent Study
Research
Field Experience

© Monkey Business Images, 2009. Used under license from Shutterstock, Inc.

ACTIVITY 8.1
Current Work Experience

Task 1: Discuss your current work experiences. Are they related to your major or career interests?

_____

_____

_____

_____

_____

_____

Task 2: Which categories from Table 8.1 does your work experience relate to?

_____

_____

_____

_____

_____

_____

© Monkey Business Images, 2009. Used under license from Shutterstock, Inc.

Skill Development through Extracurricular Activities

Student clubs and organizations are an effective option for building or enhancing workplace skills. These student groups include options that are relevant to your academic, recreational, social, or civic interests. Connecting with activities relevant to your major is typically preferred, but don't underestimate the value of other activities as well. Student organizations provide opportunities to develop teamwork and leadership skills. Organizations centered around civic interests can enhance organizational skills as a result of coordinating community-based projects. UNF currently has over 175 recognized student clubs and organizations. For a complete listing visit http://www.unf.edu/groups/.

DID YOU KNOW?

If you do not discover a student club or organization of interest to you, you may be able to start one here at UNF. Club Alliance, an Agency of Student Government at UNF, provides oversight to student clubs on campus. They also assist in providing information for starting and registering new student clubs and organizations. For more information, visit http://www.unf.edu/groups/cluballiance.

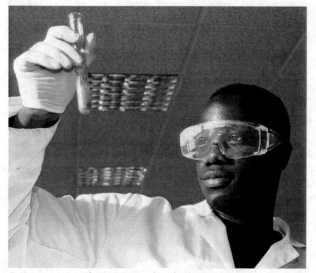

© Laurence Gough, 2009. Used under license from Shutterstock, Inc.

A Proactive College Career

Successful students are proactive students. Proactive students are those who make the most of their college career by taking advantage of the many opportunities to develop personally and professionally. During job interviews, employers typically incorporate behavioral-based questions that target specific behaviors relevant to the job you are applying for. The basic premise of these questions is the belief that past performance equals future behavior. For example, you may be asked to describe how you responded to a team situation where a major conflict arose. Your answer should reflect the positive actions you took to ensure a successful outcome. Engagement in the activities presented in this chapter provides ample opportunity for you to build teamwork skills. If you believe teamwork is currently one of your assets, engaging in multiple experiences ensures you have several examples to offer in support of this skill. On resumes and during job interviews, employers will expect you to state solid evidence to support your skills and experiences. This type of evidence takes time to develop. Start now by discovering activities well suited to you and your career plans. Table 8.2 recommends activities to pursue on a year-by-year basis. You are not obligated to follow this plan in a strict manner. It is possible that you are a freshman who has already completed activities recommended for later years, or you may be a junior or senior just learning about or starting this process. It is never too late to start using this plan as a general guide to ensure a proactive college career. A proactive college career leads to career planning success. As you review Table 8.2, place a check mark next to activities you have already completed.

Table 8.2 Working the 4-Year Plan at UNF

First Year—FRESHMAN

Explore Self, Majors, and Careers

Your first year at UNF will be filled with excitement, anticipation, and a vast amount of new information and experiences. While acclimating to college life, focus on the following:

✓	Recommended Activities
	Meet with an Academic Advisor to discuss general education course requirements.
	Meet with a Career Counselor and start the career planning process.
	Take introductory or elective courses to explore potential majors.
	Visit the Career Library and the Career Services website to begin researching careers.
	Start developing relationships with professors; meeting with them during office hours.
	Attend Career Services Events (e.g., Explore-A-Major, Career Expo, Pre-Med Day, Pre-Law Day).
	Register in Career Wings (update each semester).
	Pursue work experience or volunteer opportunities.
	Review your first year. What sparked an interest? What did you learn about yourself regarding majors and careers?

Second Year—SOPHOMORE

Confirm Major and Complete Prerequisites

As you start your second year, you typically have a better understanding of your academic abilities, but you may have discovered that your interests have changed or that you need more information. While you **continue with activities from the first year,** here are some additional things to focus on:

✓	Recommended Activities
	Talk with professionals in your career field(s) of interest.
	Join student clubs/organizations related to your major to network and grow in your field.
	Try out your career interests through part-time jobs or volunteering.
	Start researching possible internships and co-operative education positions.
	In the last semester of your sophomore year, meet with an upper-level Academic Advisor in your intended college for a degree evaluation (may be accessed via your myWings account).
	Explore study abroad options as an experience for building life and workplace skills.

Third Year—JUNIOR

Develop Employability Skills and Gain Relevant Work Experience

By this point, you should be in the "Career Implementation" phase of the career planning process, which includes making sure you are on track academically while gaining work experience related to your major and career interests.

✓	Recommended Activities
	See an upper-level Academic Advisor in your college to receive class recommendations.
	Meet with your Career Services "College Liaison" to develop your career action plan.
	Secure an internship or co-operative education position to gain relevant work experience.
	Take required tests (i.e., GRE, LSAT, MCAT) for graduate or professional schools.
	Participate in the S.T.A.R. Program for workshops on job search, resume writing, and interviewing.
	Develop a targeted resume and reference list.
	Network with professionals in your fields of interest and establish contacts for future job openings.
	Join student organizations to further develop transferable skills and enhance your personal traits.

Fourth Year—SENIOR

Commence the Job Search Process

Now, you can apply all of the career development activities you engaged in the first three years to your job search plan and get the job you want.

✓	Recommended Activities
	Meet with your Academic Advisor to make sure you are on track for graduation.
	Meet with your Career Services "College Liaison" to develop your job search plan.
	Participate in the S.T.A.R. Program for workshops on job search, resume writing, and interviewing.
	Review and update your resume to ensure it targets your career interests.
	Seek job openings related to your career interests.
	Research companies with job opportunities related to your career interests.
	Update your profile in Career Wings to fully maximize recruiting programs and services.
	Attend job fairs and additional Career Services events, workshops, and employer-sponsored sessions.
	Complete appropriate steps for graduate or professional school. Remember, the application process for some schools could take up to a year.

ACTIVITY 8.2
Your Action Plan

Task 1: Review your selections in Table 8.2. Do you seem to be on track based on your year in college? Did you notice any major gaps? Discuss your findings.

_____

_____

_____

_____

_____

_____

Task 2: What activities have you discovered that you should pursue to ensure career planning success? Why?

_____

_____

_____

_____

_____

_____

Key Discoveries

- Non-coursework experiences are important career exploration activities that help confirm career goals.
- Participation in work experience programs provides practical knowledge and builds skills helpful for career planning success.
- Practical experience in your field of study during your college career greatly enhances your competitiveness in the job market after graduation.
- Joining student clubs and organizations is an effective strategy for building workplace skills.
- Gaining practical work experience can begin as early as your freshman year in college.

Career Connections: Internet Links

- http://www.unf.edu/dept/cdc (*UNF Career Services—Career Wings*)
- http://www.unf.edu/groups (*UNF Clubs and Organizations*)
- http://careers.state.gov/students/programs.html#SIP/ (*U.S. Department of State Student Internship Program*)
- http://www.careerbuildercollege.com (*Career Builder*)
- http://www.monster.com (*Monster*)
- http://www.simplyhired.com (*Simply Hired*)

PART THREE

Job Search Skills, Tools, and Techniques

CHAPTER 9

© Gilles DeCruyenaere, 2009. Used under license from Shutterstock, Inc.

30 Seconds to "Hit the Target": Resumes and Cover Letters

CHAPTER QUEST

At the end of this chapter you should be able to:

- Understand the purpose of a resume and the different types

- Create a resume that passes the 30 second test

- Know how to format and layout your resume

- Create the most effective type of resume: the targeted resume

- Learn what categories to include on your resume

- Use action verbs to highlight your skills and qualifications

- Understand the purpose of cover letters and the different types

- Write an effective cover letter to apply for a job

- Be able to critique your own resume and cover letter

Your College Career on One Page: Your Resume

Your resume is like an advertisement of yourself to a prospective employer. You want your resume to look and sound appealing to enhance your chances of being selected for an interview. Your resume should be one page in length, free of spelling errors, produced on high-quality bond paper, and organized so that it is easy to read. Since your resume presents a combination of your skills, abilities, and qualifications, you want it to show your best assets.

30 Seconds to Get Your Resume on the "Yes" Pile

Employers receive hundreds of resumes for job openings and the screening process is usually quick and decisive: within 30 seconds your resume goes into one of three piles: "yes," "no," or "maybe." The "yes" candidates have succeeded in communicating to the employer that they have the skills and qualifications needed for the job and have an excellent chance of receiving an interview. Your resume is the first formal introduction between you and hiring organizations. It is imperative that your resume clearly and concisely spells out your career objective, skills, education, and achievements. The "targeted resume" is the most effective resume format for getting and keeping the attention of the employer.

"Targeting" Your Resume

Targeting your resume essentially involves choosing particular career goals or objectives and designing a resume to achieve them. If you have done a complete inventory of your qualifications, you should be able to identify strengths that can translate into potential career directions. By creating multiple experience categories (i.e., "Administrative Experience," "Teaching Experience," "Other Experience," etc.) you can help employers focus on those experiences most relevant to the position you are applying for. If your job search includes multiple job objectives, you can have two or three different resumes which place emphasis on different targeted objectives.

Types of Resumes

Chronological

In the "olden days," the chronological resume was the format most commonly used. This format lists all of your educational and work experience in reverse chronological order. By listing your experience all in one "Experience" category, oftentimes unrelated experience ends up distracting from more important experience. For example, your most recent experience might be that restaurant job you have to help pay for college expenses, and the employer will see that before other relevant experience such as an internship or co-operative education experience.

Functional Resume

This resume features an approach that emphasizes capabilities, skill levels, and accomplishments, rather than job titles or time spent at various jobs. This format is effective if you are changing fields, re-entering after an absence from the job market, or seeking a different emphasis in your career. Note: Most employers view functional resumes with suspicion, since the actual employment history may be unclear. If you feel this format is the most effective one for you, be sure to make your skills clear and your language concise and include an employment history either before or after your skills breakdown.

Combination Resume

This format combines the best features of the other two formats. One option is when experience is listed in chronological order but is organized under skills or topical headings. In some cases, a functional heading is more effective than your job title (e.g., "Administration" heading used in place of "Staff Assistant"). Another option allows you to list your skills and qualifications first, followed by your employment history. This type of resume highlights relevant skills, but also provides the chronological work history that most employers prefer.

The Scannable Resume

In today's fast-paced job market, companies are increasingly turning to computers to do the initial screening through a scannable computer database system that searches for key words. For example, a sample job description may state:

- Five years experience as a salesperson
- College Bachelor degree
- Traveling
- Self-starter
- Team Leader

The computer checks a database of resumes searching for these key words. Tip: Fill your resume with as many of these key words as possible. You can develop your list of key words by checking newspaper and internet job postings and look for the qualifications listed. In this case, it is wiser to focus on nouns that indicate your accomplishments rather than verbs that focus on your job duties.

Some key points to think about when writing a scannable resume:

- Use 8½" x 11" white paper, printed on one side only
- Use black ink
- Avoid italics, scripts, and underlined words or phrases
- Do not fold or staple; it is best to send resume in a flat large envelope
- Choose standard typefaces like Helvetica, Times, or Arial
- Use a font size between 10 and 14 points
- Choose your key words carefully
- Avoid vertical and horizontal lines, graphics, gray shading, and boxes
- Use boldface and/or all capital letters only for section headings
- Avoid 2-column format
- 20 lb or slightly heavier paper is recommended for scanning
- Place your name at the top of the page and address and phone number below, each on its own line

Which Format Is Right?

There is no "right" or "wrong" way of doing a resume. However, people are used to reading resumes a certain way and if your format is far off the "beaten path," they might not bother taking the time to figure it out. By going with a recognizable and readable format, you will maximize your chances of getting an interview. **Note:** You should decide on choice of format after you have conducted an inventory of your qualifications. Your experience, skills, and qualifications can be categorized in a number of different ways. You need to select the layout and format that presents your qualifications as effectively as possible. Try different versions and see which makes the best presentation. Design it with the reader in mind. Your resume needs to answer this fundamental question: "WHY SHOULD THEY HIRE *YOU*?"

Building Your Resume

Your resume is like an advertisement of yourself to a prospective employer. You want your resume to look and sound appealing to enhance your chances of being selected for an interview. Ultimately, your resume presents your skills, abilities, and qualifications as they relate to the position you are applying for. Before developing your resume, it is important to know what skills employers are seeking.

Skills Commonly Sought by Employers

- Verbal communication skills
- Ability to organize and coordinate
- Creativity
- Ability to motivate others
- Listening skills
- Counseling skills
- Group dynamics knowledge
- Leadership ability
- Flexibility/adaptability
- Written skills
- Interpersonal skills
- Mathematical ability
- Computer skills
- Language skills
- Persuasive skills
- Teamwork skills
- Analytical skills
- Motivation/initiative

Using Action Verbs to Highlight Skills and Accomplishments

Yes, believe it or not, there is something known as "resume language." Action verbs are used to emphasize your skills and accomplishments, avoids personal pronouns, and uses action words to describe duties.

Effective Action Verbs—A Few Examples

- **Conduct** individual, small, and large group counseling sessions.
- **Advise** students regarding college majors and admission requirements.
- **Designed, selected,** and **implemented** instructional materials for course unit, "Columbus Sailed the Ocean Blue."
- **Constructed, administered,** and **evaluated** formal and informal tests.
- **Developed** software for emerging growth welding robotics firm.
- **Used** SEI software development model to outline system specification, create code, and ensure quality.
- **Designed** new lab apparatus for engineering coursework.
- **Conducted** analysis of processes and procedures on existing equipment.
- **Redesigned** a cereal packaging line.
- **Provided** line sketches and equipment recommendations.
- **Designed** equipment interface, **configured** automated scales, and **recommended** line flow alterations that decreased cycle time by 10%.
- **Reconciled** bank statements for operating and payroll accounts.
- **Conducted** research on market potential and demographics.
- **Met** and **exceeded** $200,000 sales quota set by sales supervisors and management.
- **Directed** and **supervised** three plant superintendents and 25 production supervisors in a 300,000 square foot facility consisting of 525 employees.

  See the "Resume Verb List" in the Chapter 9 Appendix for More Ideas

Elements of a Resume

The following elements are often included in resumes. Your unique educational and work experiences should be considered when deciding which categories will be most effective. Arrange whichever categories you use to reflect your strengths in the most advantageous way.

Contact Information

Your name, address(es), and phone number(s) with area code(s). It is acceptable to include your e-mail address.

Objective

One sentence stating the kind of position you want, the task(s) you want to perform, or the environment in which you wish to work.

Education

Include name of institution, city, state, degree, major, and month and year of graduation. Other information you may wish to include would be schools attended overseas, course work directly applicable to the desired job, minor, and GPA (overall or departmental). The highest degree earned should be listed first, then continue backward.

Certification

Include your area/level of certification and date received.

Experience

Include name of organization, job title, city, state, dates of employment or service, and active verb descriptions (*) of responsibilities and duties usually in bullet form. For Targeted Resumes, you can highlight specific experience: **"Administrative Experience," "Management Experience," "Engineering Experience," "Volunteer Experience," "Internships," "Related Experience," "Other Experience,"** etc.

Skills

Provide a list of skills or qualifications that you would like the employer to know about you that may not come through in other headings. List computer languages, programs, systems, etc. For example: excellent team player; works well independently while also in team situations; excellent oral and written communication skills; punctual, reliable, and dependable.

Honors/Awards

Academic scholarships, grants, academic honors, awards (e.g., Geology Student of the Year) and Dean's List may be included in this category to draw more attention to them.

Languages

List foreign languages and define the level of your ability: "Fluent," "Literate," "Conversant."

Professional Memberships

Include professional and community affiliations, clubs/organizations, and student groups. Include the names of organization, dates of membership, and offices held, if any.

Interests/Activities

Space permitting, add special interests, activities, or travel experiences. **Note:** personal information has the potential to be used in a discriminatory way. Be cautious about listing religious or other group activities that might not be universally accepted.

References

Not necessary but if you want to, the statement "references available upon request" is preferred. Do not list the names of your references. Choose three individuals who can speak to your academic and work skills and qualifications (i.e., former supervisor, college instructor, coworker). Be sure to notify your references and leave them a copy of your resume and an idea of the work you would like to enter as a professional. List references on a separate page (name, address, and phone) which matches your resume paper. Do not send with initial resume and cover letter; make them available upon request!

Other Headings

"Special Skills," "Publications," "Professional Development" (training, seminars, conferences, workshops), "Class Projects," "Study Abroad," etc. If you have something else to add that would be relevant, make a heading that's appropriate and include it!

Points to Consider

An effective resume should attract attention, stimulate interest, create desire, and generate action. Therefore, follow these basic guidelines:

Be brief: Your resume should be as complete as possible without being redundant or irrelevant. Usually, the resume will be one page long. As a rule of thumb, for each additional degree and/or 7 years of experience, you can add another page. If you do have a two-page resume, be sure that the essential or primary information can be scanned quickly and appears on the front page.

Be consistent in style and content: Stylistic gimmicks (e.g., underlining, asterisks, indenting, boldface type) can be used effectively but should not be overused.

Be logical: You have some latitude in the way you set up your resume but make sure the information flows smoothly and sensibly. Be aware that information presented on the first page, at the beginning of a section, on the left hand margin, or in a column, gets extra emphasis. For example, dates in the left hand margin are emphasized. If your job chronology is not something you want to highlight, place the dates in a less conspicuous place. If you consider your experience more important than your education, place it first on your resume. Remember: YOU determine how a person reads your resume. We read left to right, top to bottom. Prioritize and arrange your information accordingly.

Be conscious of image: Remember that your resume and cover letter are often your first contacts with a prospective employer. Resumes should be visually appealing and should not contain typographical or grammatical errors.

Layout, Format, and Printing: Quick Check

Format

Are general headings (education, experience, etc.) consistently presented and set apart in some way from the other material (by capitalizing, underlining, spacing, boldfacing, etc.)?

Does the order of material presented emphasize what you intend it to? Is the order logical? Are the items in reverse chronological order (i.e., most recent experience first)?

Is the length of the resume appropriate to the amount of material presented and to the job objective?

Does the resume have an overall neat, readable appearance? Is it easy to scan? Is there sufficient but not excessive white space?

Content

- Are the topic headings specific enough to invite reader interest?
- Is the information specific and concise? Is it quantitative where appropriate?
- Are accomplishments and problem-solving skills emphasized?
- Are your name, address, telephone number, and e-mail address at the top of the first page? If there is a second page, is your last name and "Page 2" at the top?
- Is all important information included?

- Is extraneous material eliminated? Extraneous information includes hobbies, marital status, age, irrelevant memberships, repetitious information, and information that is assumed or information that is out-of-date.

Style

- Do sentences begin with action verbs or prominently contain action verbs?
- Is grammatical style consistent throughout?
- Is choice of vocabulary appropriate to your job target?
- Are punctuation and spelling correct?
- Are sentences and paragraphs of a readable length? (Paragraphs ideally should be no longer than a few lines.)
- Have extraneous phrases, such as "duties included" been eliminated?
- Do any of your phrases or sentences contain personal pronouns?

Printing

Your resume should be word-processed. Have it printed on "resume paper" (stationery stores or office supply stores have a selection of paper for resume writing). Use pale colors such as white, ivory, gray, cream, beige, or off-white. Avoid loud and garish colors and bright white. Test your resume by photocopying it. Oftentimes, employers copy your resume and pass it on to others in the organization.

Layout

- Fonts: Avoid using Courier: it is a wide font and takes up too much room. Common resume fonts include Times Roman, Helvetica, Palatino, and Arial. There are many new fonts that look great too. Experiment with your font menu!
- **Font Size: 11 pt** is a good size for a one page resume. 12 pt is probably too big and 10 pt too small.
- **Margins: 0.5 inch margins top, bottom, right, and left** are recommended for most resumes to give you the maximum amount of space for text. In Microsoft Word, go to "File" then "Page Setup" and change each margin. The default margins are too much, and it is almost impossible to have a one page resume with the default margins.
- **Bullets** are used to highlight verb statements on a resume. It is recommended to go to "Insert" and then select "Symbol" and insert a bullet where you want it. The bullet wizard in Word adds too much spacing that takes away valuable space on your resume.

FINALLY . . . Proofread, Proofread, Proofread!! Always have someone else proof your resume. You have worked so much with your resume you will just not see those typos or mistakes that someone else can spot in seconds!

Sample Resumes
Example: Combination Resume

THOMAS JEFFERSON
123 Central Avenue
Jacksonville, FL 32224
904-555-1234, tjefferson@gmail.com

QUALIFICATIONS   Organization and Implementation of recruitment functions, marketing seminars, and admissions programs. Extensive administrative experience. Strong interpersonal public, speaking, interviewing, and evaluating skills.

EDUCATION   **UNIVERSITY OF NORTH FLORIDA,** Jacksonville, FL
Bachelor of Arts in Psychology May, 2012

EXPERIENCE   **DIGITAL EQUIPMENT CORPORATION,** Jacksonville, FL (7/11–present)
Evaluation: Research and evaluate the effectiveness of a technical training course for computer engineers. Created and distributed questionnaires to control and experimental groups. Compiled, analyzed, evaluated, and presented research findings to middle management in Education and Training and Electronic Storage Departments.

UNIVERSITY OF NORTH FLORIDA CAREER SERVICES, Jacksonville, FL (9/09–6/11)
Administration: Organized and oversaw an annual Career Fair for 250 employers and students and two Career Networking Receptions for over 200 students and alumni. Prepared invitation lists, maintained phone and written contact with employers and alumni, made arrangements for receptions, and evaluated effectiveness of programs.

WEST NOTTINGHAM ACADEMY, Colora, MD (3/06–6/09)
Training and Development: Designed and implemented the Nottingham Admissions Network. Instructed four regional alumni and parent groups of 10–25 people byinstructing them on strategies for contacting prospective students, advertising in local newspapers, and interacting with local public school counselors.
Recruiting and Marketing: Developed marketing strategies that increased enrollment by10%, phone and written contacts with students and consultants by 12%, and number of interviews by 8%. Traveled extensively in the Mid-Atlantic region to public and private schools. Met with educational consultants to recruit students. Interviewed, counseled, and evaluated prospective students.
Administration: Managed admissions/financial aid office procedures and guidelines. Supervised student tour guides. Researched and presented data to Board of Trustees on current enrollment and demographic trends.

ALBRIGHT COLLEGE, Reading, PA (6/04–3/06)
Training and Development: Coordinated the Albright Alumni Liaison program. Instructed five regional alumni groups of 20–30 people on admissions recruiting and procedures. Evaluated effectiveness of program. Coordinated and operated seminar for state-wide conference of the Pennsylvania Association of College Admissions Counselors.
Recruitment and Marketing: Interviewed, counseled, and evaluated applicants. Represented Albright at numerous high schools while speaking to counselors and students. Traveled extensively in New England and Mid-Atlantic regions.
Administration: Coordinated and oversaw open house for 750 prospective students and families. Oversaw various admissions receptions, staff college night schedule, and recruitment travel schedule.

COMPUTER   Solid computer experience in statistical analysis (SAS, WORMSTAT, BASIC).
SKILLS

INTERESTS   Running, cycling, and swimming; photography, camping, backpacking and canoeing; cooking, music, and creative writing.

Example: Combination Resume

Franklin D. Roosevelt
123 All American Way
Jacksonville, FL 32224
904-123-2345
Frooseve@aol.com

OBJECTIVE

A position in public relations that will utilize strong analytical, planning, and communication skills.

AREAS OF EFFECTIVENESS

ANALYTICAL SKILLS
- Have passed three parts of the Florida CPA license and will be taking the fourth part in January 2010.
- Prepared tax returns and extensions and preliminary audit review.
- Able to maintain accounts payable, receivables, and general ledger.
- Adept in MS Word, Excel, Lotus, WordPerfect, and Power Point.

ORGANIZATIONAL/PLANNING SKILLS
- Collaborated with local children's charity to assist with math tutoring.
- Coordinated, implemented, and supervised a raffle to raise $1000.00 for local children's charity.
- Reorganized file system to improve office administration.
- Arranged guest speakers for student organization.
- Planned and organized a social event for employers and students.
- Able to maintain above average GPA while working 25–30 hours per week and participating in various activities.

COMMUNICATION SKILLS
- Invited guest speaker for student organization.
- Able to communicate effectively with customers and employees.
- Prepared and delivered speech to help raise funds for charity.
- Served as spokesperson for student organization.

EDUCATION

UNIVERSITY OF NORTH FLORIDA, Jacksonville, Florida
Master of Accountancy, August 2012, GPA: 3.8
Dean's List

Bachelor of Business Administration, May 2010
FICPA Scholarship, Dean's List, Phi Kappa Phi Honor Society

EMPLOYMENT HISTORY

WILLIAM & ASSOCIATES, Jacksonville, Florida, *Customer Service Representative,* June 2011–Present
COOPERS & LYBRAND, Jacksonville, Florida, *Accounting Intern,* Fall 2010
JACKSONVILLE INSURANCE COMPANY, Jacksonville, Florida, *Office Assistant,* January 2006–August 2010

ACTIVITIES

FICPA—student member
Alpha Sigma Pi—treasurer/public relations officer

Example: Targeted: Social Work/Human Services

Sarah Sunshine
123 Brandnewday Road
Jacksonville, Florida 32256
(904) 620-1234
ssunshin@hotmail.com

EDUCATION
>
> **University of North Florida,** Jacksonville, Florida
> *Bachelor of Art, Major in Sociology; Minor in Psychology,* May 2012
> GPA: 3.7/4.0, Dean's List and Psi Chi National Honor Society
> Graduated Cum Laude

RELATED EXPERIENCE
>
> **Duval County Family Resource Center** (DCFRC), Jacksonville, Florida
> *Intern,* Spring 2012
> • Prepared resource manual to be used by the Center.
> • Provided child care information.
> • Researched and translated social insurance programs of clients.
> • Obtained medical supplies for clients not covered by medical cards.
> • Provided counseling to a caseload of 20–25 clients per week.
> • Initiated a program to inform the school children about the DCFRC.
> • Worked in conjunction with other social service agencies to obtain needed services for clients.
>
> **Brighten Center,** Jacksonville, Florida
> *Intern,* Fall 2011
> • Maintained small caseload with teen parents.
> • Conducted home visits and counseled teen parents.
> • Co-led teen parenting classes.
> • Prepared a variety of materials taught at the parenting classes.
>
> **Camp Sunny Day,** Boone, North Carolina
> *Camp Counselor,* Summer 2010 and 2011
> • Worked with physically handicapped children ages 5–7 years old.
> • Organized activities for children.
> • Learned basic sign language while working with deaf impaired child.

RESEARCH EXPERIENCE
>
> **University of North Florida, Professor B. F. Skinner,** Jacksonville, Florida
> *Research Assistant,* January 2011–August 2011
> • Helped develop coding system for behavioral assessment of 8-year-olds
> • Tested 40 research participants for ability to complete various motor tasks
> • Assisted with data analysis using SPSS-X

VOLUNTEER EXPERIENCE
>
> **Mental Health Services,** Jacksonville, Florida
> *Volunteer* (June 2011–present)
> • Work with mentally handicapped people in daily activities including personal hygiene, eating, and recreation
> • Learned to take care of and communicate with the mentally challenged
>
> **Boys and Girls Club of Duval County,** Jacksonville, Florida
> *Volunteer* (May 2010–January 2011)
> • Assisted children with homework and facilitated their learning
> • Organized recreational activities

MEMBERSHIPS
>
> American Psychological Association, Student Member, 2011–present
> UNF Psychology Club, President, 2010–present

SKILLS
>
> Above average understanding of American Sign Language
> Proficient with SPSS-X, ACCESS Data Base

Example: Targeted: Human Services/Counseling

OZZIE OSPREY

4567 All American Drive   Phone: (904) 620-1000
Jacksonville, Florida 32224   Email: ozzie123@unf.edu

OBJECTIVE
Seeking a Program Coordinator position in youth services.

EDUCATION
University Of North Florida   Jacksonville, Florida
Bachelor of Arts, Psychology   Expected: 12/2013
GPA 3.5/4.0, Dean's List, FICPA Scholarship

RELEVANT COURSES
Advanced Adolescent Psychology   Learning Theory   Behavior Modification
Personality Theories   Social Psychology   Mentor of Urban Youth

RELEVANT EXPERIENCE
Boys and Girls Club   Jacksonville, Florida
Office Assistant   6/2010–Present
Provide the public with information about various services. Coordinate recreational events. Assist counselors
with Mentor Youth Training seminars. Manage various office and administrative tasks.

University of North Florida   Jacksonville, Florida
Experimental Social Psychology Class Project   Spring 2010
Worked in a group setting to plan a research project. Conducted research on religious and sexual attitudes.
Collected data via surveys of 18- to 40-year-old college students

University of North Florida   Jacksonville, Florida
Behavior Modification Class Project   Fall 2009
Worked to develop a behavior modification plan to stop inappropriate behavior. Research possible plans of
action and chose two plans to limit behavior. Implemented plans with positive reinforcement.

University of North Florida Psychology Club   Jacksonville, Florida
Special Events Coordinator   Fall 2009
Oversaw the financial operations of outreach marketing projects; maintained budget. Coordinated Adopt-a-
Kid Day, a recreational event for inner city children. Successfully raised funds for children's charity.
Arranged guest speakers for meetings.

OTHER WORK EXPERIENCE
Hallmark Cards   Jacksonville, Florida
Merchandiser   6/2007–5/2009
Merchandised 8–10 retail stores daily to ensure visual appeal of product displays. Assisted sales representa-
tives with servicing accounts. Processed customer-billing statements. Handled customer inquiries and
resolved any existing problems.

Jacksonville Insurance Company   Jacksonville, Florida
Office Assistant   8/2005–5/2007
Provided information to clients regarding insurance policies. Improved office administration process by
reorganizing file system.

Targeted: Engineering

Albert Einstein
(904) 555-1212 aeinstein@aol.com
2657 Uphill Ave, Jacksonville, Florida 32244

OBJECTIVE

An entry-level automotive engineering position requiring strong analytical and organizational skills.

EDUCATION

UNIVERSITY OF NORTH FLORIDA   Jacksonville, Florida
Bachelor of Science in Mechanical Engineering   May 2012
Honors: Daniel M. Joseph Prize in Mechanical Engineering, 2008
Top Five Finisher in the ASME Region XI Student Section Website Competition

RELATED COURSEWORK

Thermodynamics, Deformable Solids, Statics, Materials Science, Basic Circuits, Fluids Mechanics, Controls, Heat Transfer, Vibrations, Statistics, Design, Turbo Machinery, Automotive Structural Design

RELATED EXPERIENCE

AUTOCRAFTERS, INC.   Jacksonville, Florida
Co-op Engineer   August 2012
• Worked on advanced test project that involved mechanical design, CAD/CAM technology, automobile structures, and coordination among project groups

UNIVERSITY OF NORTH FLORIDA   Jacksonville, Florida
Senior Design Project   Spring 2012
• Designed a data acquisition system to monitor solar panels installed on roof of the UNF Engineering building
Mini-Baja Team participant   Fall 2010
• Worked on 6-member team to design and build a miniature stock car for National Society of Automotive Engineers competition
Pressure Vessel Project   Spring 2009
• Measured the discharge pressure when one pressure vessel discharged to the next at the instant it reached choke flow or subtonic velocity

GENERAL MOTORS CORPORATION   Detroit, Michigan
Intern   Summer 2006
• Assisted in experimental and literature research
• Prepared data for technical papers
• Computed engineering calculations

SKILLS

• Windows Operating System	• HTML	• AutoCAD
• Java	• ProE	• Matlab
• Ideas	• Labview	• C++

ACTIVITIES

• Society of Automotive Engineers, President, 2009–Present
• American Society of Mechanical Engineers (ASME), 2008–Present

SKILLS

Computer: MS Word, Excel, Power Point, Word Perfect, Photo Shop, Internet
Language: Fluent in Spanish, Conversational French and American Sign Language

Example: Targeted: Business

WILBUR WRIGHT
123 Appledumpling Avenue
Jacksonville, Florida
(904) 555-5555
EDUCATION

UNIVERSITY OF NORTH FLORIDA   Jacksonville, Florida
Bachelor of Business Administration, Business Administration   August 2012
G.P.A. 3.5 Dean's List

RELATED EXPERIENCE

ABC ORGANIZATION   Jacksonville, Florida
Intern   August 2011–August 2012
• Assisted with the design and research of several marketing projects
• Created a survey for the general public to be used for a marketing research study
• Attended a 2 week advertising seminar
• Effectively worked as a team player while also maintaining top performance on individual projects

SMALL BUSINESS DEVELOPMENT CENTER   Jacksonville, Florida
Business Analyst   Summer 2011
• Assisted in business planning to small start-up and existing businesses
• Conducted research on market potential and demographics
• Performed business valuations used for buying and selling small businesses
• Prepared financial statements for tax and lending purposes

UNIVERSITY OF NORTH FLORIDA   Jacksonville, Florida
Strategic Management and Business Policy Class Project   Spring 2011
• Worked in a group setting on the marketing and promotion of the Maytag Corporation
• Collected data via a survey on the marketing methods currently used by the Maytag Company
• Researched the history of their marketing strategies and conferred with other professionals in the field
• Received a grade of A, individually and as part of the team, on the project

OTHER WORK EXPERIENCE

UNIVERSITY OF NORTH FLORIDA   Jacksonville, Florida
Student Assistant/Career Services   May 2010–Present
• Greet students, answer phones, and file
• Maintain the career library and assist students in the computer lab
• Assist staff with running errands, typing, and scheduling student appointments

SKILLS

Proficient in Lotus and WordPerfect
Excellent oral and written communication skills
Receive and carry out instructions and tasks in a timely manner
Organized, with attention to detail
Ability to adapt to a changing work environment and deal with pressure comfortably

ACTIVITIES

Alpha Sigma Pi, Accounting Fraternity, *Member*	2010–present
Student Government Association, *Member*	2010–present
American Marketing Association, *Member*	2010–present
United Way Student Fund Raising Committee, *Member*	2010–present

Example: Targeted: Communications/Journalism

HARRIET OSPREY

1111 University Dr., #000, Jacksonville, FL 32246
Phone: (904) 123-1234, Email: hosprey@aol.com

OBJECTIVE
To obtain a journalism internship with Billboard magazine.

EDUCATION
UNIVERSITY OF NORTH FLORIDA   Jacksonville, FL
Bachelor of Science in Communication, Journalism   May 2012
Current GPA 3.96/4.0

WRITING EXPERIENCE
FLORIDA TIMES UNION   Jacksonville, FL
Freelance Writer   8/2011–present
- Research, write, and edit stories for all sections of the Jacksonville daily newspaper which has a circulation of over 165,000 readers
- Develop working relationship with members of Jacksonville media community
- Write articles highlighting the Hope Fund which has helped more than 760 local families in need

THE SPINNAKER, UNIVERSITY OF NORTH FLORIDA STUDENT
NEWSPAPER   Jacksonville, FL
Assistant News Editor and Writer   1/2012–present
- Assign stories for news section of weekly student newspaper
- Assisted with various editorial decisions and story budgets
- Generate new story ideas
- Edit stories of other writers
Staff Writer   1/2011–12/2011
- Wrote hard news
- Write news articles on political, academic, and social topics

COX COMMUNICATIONS   Atlanta, GA
Writer (Internship)   5/2010–12/2010
- Wrote articles for employee publication
- Wrote and posted articles to updated intranet
- Wrote press releases and personnel announcements
- Conducted research for speeches and presentations
- Involved with strategic planning related to communication issues and challenges

JACKSONVILLE BUSINESS JOURNAL   Jacksonville, FL
General Assignment Reporter (Internship)   Summer 2009
- Wrote articles for a number of different beats
- Wrote profiles and feature articles on local area business professionals

OTHER WORK EXPERIENCE
OLIVE GARDEN, **Server/Trainer/Shift Leader,** Jacksonville, FL   8/2010–Present
PULTE HOMES, **Office Assistant,** Jacksonville, FL   6/2009–8/2009
BENNIGAN'S RESTAURANT, **Server/Bartender,** Jacksonville, FL   4/2006–8/2008
SAWGRASS COUNTRY CLUB, **Server/Houseman,** Jacksonville, FL   5/2004–8/2005

ORGANIZATIONS/CLUBS
Golden Key International Honor Society   1/2011–present
UNF Ad Club, Vice President and Charter Member   8/2010–present

SKILLS
MS Word, Excel, PowerPoint, Outlook, Explorer Internet, News Edit Pro

INTERESTS
Artist and repertoire, artist management, promotions, tracking of "Top 10 Artists"

Example: Targeted: Computer Programming

William Gates

4567 St. Johns Bluff Road, South   Jacksonville, Florida 32256   (904) 620-1234   aein@unf.edu

OBJECTIVE

To obtain an entry-level position in computer programming.

EDUCATION

UNIVERSITY OF NORTH FLORIDA, Jacksonville, FL
Bachelor of Science in Computer and Information Science, May 2012
Major: Computer Science GPA: 3.5

COMPUTER SKILLS

- COBOL, Assembly, Qbasic, C, Pascal, Basic, C++
- UNIX, MS-DOS, MS Windows, TSX/RSX
- DEC Alpha, PC, PDP-11, IMB Mainframe
- MS Word, Excel, WordPerfect, Lotus, dBase, PageMaker

RELATED EXPERIENCE

BLUE CROSS BLUE SHIELD OF FLORIDA, Jacksonville, FL
Server Management Team Intern, 7/2011–present
- Automate in-office Service Center reports using Excel macros and VBA
- Help with maintenance and hardware support for production Proliant servers, including hot-swap parts replacement and other forms of troubleshooting
- Participated in complete hardware assembly of HP/Compaq Proliant DL series servers, including racking and cable management

UNIVERSITY OF NORTH FLORIDA, Jacksonville, FL
OFFICE OF COMPUTING SERVICES
Help Desk Programmer Analyst, August 2010–present
- Install and maintain various computer software
- Assist in solving technical problems with University computers
- Train new employees and assist with hiring
- *Programmer Assistant*   January 2005–August 2007
- Promoted to Programmer Analyst
- Installed hardware
- Assisted with various software support

CLASS PROJECTS
- Developed software for pseudo inventory management system using the RUP
- Designed client/server using sockets/RPC
- Constructed a C-compiler and a cross assemble using C
- Designed programs featuring forking, semaphores, and pipes using C
- Designed a variant of the game "connect five" using artificial intelligence paradigms
- Created various multimedia projects using PHP, HTML, Director, Premiere, Authorward
- Designed FTP client/server using C

ACTIVITIES

Association of Information Technology Professionals, *Member, 2011–present*
University of North Florida Computing Society, *Treasurer, 2010–present*
BACCHUS—the campus alcohol awareness group, *Volunteer, 2009–present*

OTHER WORK EXPERIENCE

BELK DEPARTMENT STORE, *Accounting Clerk,* Jacksonville, FL, 5/2009–4/2010
UNITED PARCEL SERVICE, *Loader,* Jacksonville, FL, 5/2008–4/2009
BOUNDLESS LIGHT PRODUCTIONS, *Web Designer,* 1/2007–5/2008

HONORS

Dean's List, 2010, 2011, 2012
Upsilon Pi Epsilon Award for Academic Excellence, 2011
Golden Key National Honor Society, 2010–2012
Math Student of the Year Award, 2010

Example: Targeted: Chemistry Internship

Carl Sagan
124 Galaxy Way
Jupiter, Florida 32256
(123) 123-4546

OBJECTIVE

An internship in laboratory research.

EDUCATION

University of North Florida, Jacksonville, Florida
Bachelor of Science in Chemistry, Expected May 2012
Major GPA: 3.8, Overall GPA: 3.68
Relevant Courses:

- Organic Chemistry I & II
- Calculus I & II
- Chemistry I & II
- Biology I & II
- Physics I & II
- Inorganic Chemistry
- Quantitative Analytical Chemistry

HONORS

Dean's List; Golden Key National Honor Society; UNF Academic Scholarship

RELEVANT WORK EXPERIENCE

University of North Florida, Jacksonville, Florida
Chemistry Research Assistant, Summer 2010
Constructed multistage vacuum system and computer-interfaced, pulsed, supersonic gas injector for molecular collision experiments.

Eckerd Drug Store, Jacksonville, Florida
Pharmacy Technician, January 2010–May 2010
Assisted pharmacist with filling prescriptions. Dispensed medication and determined volumes for solutions and suspensions. Maintained inventory. Completed appropriate insurance paperwork. Provided customer service and operated the cash register.

SKILLS

Computer: Microsoft Word, Excel, and Power Point
Strong skills in interpreting complex and/or technical information and problem solving
Work well independently while also a positive team player
Strong organizational skills with attention to detail
Punctual and reliable

MEMBERSHIPS

American Chemical Society
Student Member, 2010–Present

Pre-Med Society
Student Member, 2010–Present

OTHER WORK EXPERIENCE

Winston Barney Corporation, Data Processor, Jacksonville, Florida, 9/2009–12/2010
The Gap, Night Manager, Jacksonville, Florida, 1/2009–12/2009
McDonald's, Cashier, St. Augustine, Florida, 1/2008–12/2008

Example: Targeted: Teaching

George Washington
1 American Way
Jacksonville, Florida 32224
(904) 123-4567

EDUCATION

University of North Florida, Jacksonville, Florida
Bachelor of Education (NCATE and State Approved Program), May 2012
Major: Special Education   Track: Varying Exceptionalities, (K–12)

TEACHER CERTIFICATION

Florida Teaching Certificate in Secondary Social Science (6–12)

TEACHING EXPERIENCE

Duval County School System, Jacksonville, Florida (January 2012–Present)
Substitute Teacher, 2 days per week
• Teach middle and high school classes in history, English, and exceptional education.

Mandarin High School, Jacksonville, Florida, (August 2011–December 2011)
Social Sciences Intern, Grades 10–11, 400 hours/5 classes
• Developed lesson plans and taught Geography and American Government
• Coadvisor to Student Government Association
• Participated in parent teacher conferences
• Developed a unit plan on the importance of voting
• Tutored students in social sciences

Ed White Middle School, Jacksonville, Florida (January 2011–May 2011)
Preintern II in Social Sciences, Grade 7, 50 onsite hours
• Developed and taught 5 lesson plans on Civics
• Assisted with field trip to the Duval County Court House
• Cochaperoned 50 students on social sciences field trip to Washington, DC

Landon Middle School, Jacksonville, Florida (August 2010–December 2010)
Preintern I in Psychology, Grade 9 (50 onsite hours)
• Taught 5 lessons and team taught with supervising teacher other lessons
• Assisted teacher in administrative duties: attendance and testing

RELATED WORK EXPERIENCE

Museum of Science and History (MOSH), Orlando, Florida (Summer 2009)
Museum Guide
• Assist with daily presentations and tours
• Give presentation to summer camp students
• Provide customer service and operate cash register

OTHER WORK EXPERIENCE

Olive Garden Restaurant, *Server/Host,* Mandarin, FL (2008–2010)
Yotagi Toyota Dealers, *Sales Representative,* Orange Park, FL (Summer 2008)
Pizza Hut Restaurants, *Training Specialist,* Kansas City, MO (2007–2008)

COMPUTER SKILLS

• Word Perfect
• Page Maker
• Excel
• Page Microsoft

PROFESSIONAL ORGANIZATIONS

• Student Council for Exceptional Children
• Student Government Association
• History Club
• Best Buddies Volunteer

HONORS

• Dean's List
• Golden Key National Honor Society
• Junior Achievement Scholarship
• Phi Alpha Theta

Example: Targeted: Sport Management

Derek Jeter

2345 Bulldog Terrace
Jacksonville, FL 32223
Email: djeter@aol.com

Home Phone: (345) 234-5555
Work Phone: (345) 234-1234

EDUCATION

UNIVERSITY OF NORTH FLORIDA
Bachelor of Arts Degree: Sports Management

Jacksonville, FL
May 2012

FLORIDA COMMUNITY COLLEGE AT JACKSONVILLE
Applied Associates of Science, General Studies/Education

Jacksonville, FL
May 2010

COACHING EXPERIENCE

YOUNG MEN'S CHRISTIAN ASSOCIATION
Youth Soccer Head Coach

Jacksonville, FL
9/2011–5/2012

- Planned daily practice schedules and drills for team of 15 children ages 5 and 6.
- Taught children fundamentals of soccer with assistance from parents.
- Organized and implemented strategies to incorporate all children into game situations equally.

NORTH FLORIDA TITANS (SEMI-PROFESSIONAL FOOTBALL)
Assistant Defensive Coordinator

Jacksonville, FL
7/2010–2/2011

- Developed, organized, and utilized practice and game plans.
- Worked with and coordinated training of assistant coaches with the system.
- Established and developed a variety of defensive schemes in conjunction with head defensive coordinator.
- Guided team to conference championship.

ST. CHRISTOPHER'S ACADEMY
Junior Varsity Assistant Basketball Coach

Orange Park, FL
7/2008–6/2009

- Implemented a variety of offensive and defensive plays.
- Monitored and communicated with players regarding daily school activities and occurrences.
- Planned daily practice schedules and drills.
- Established positive relationships with school administrators, teachers, and other school personnel.
- Provided quality leadership and sensible discipline for the players.
- Assisted head coach with transporting players and preparing for games.
- Helped turn the school into a winning program in one year with a record of 15–0 and a league championship.

ORANGE PARK HIGH SCHOOL
Junior Varsity Assistant Basketball Coach

Orange Park, FL
9/2007–6/2008

- Assisted head coach with statistics and strategy development during games.
- Implemented offensive and defensive plays.
- Taught basketball fundamentals to freshman and sophomore students.

Junior Varsity Summer League Assistant Coach, Batavia High School

6/2006–8/2007

- Instructed players on techniques, execution, and the principles of the game.
- Organized practices and transportation to and from the game.
- Created specialized offensive and defensive plays as situations arose.

SPORTS PARTICIPATION
Intercollegiate Basketball, Florida Community College at Jacksonville   2009

AWARDS RECEIVED
Peer Recognition Award for dedication to coaching—St. Christopher's Academy
Assistant Coach of the Year—Orange Park High School

EMPLOYMENT HISTORY
MERIDIAN BEHAVIORAL HEALTHCARE INC., *Children's Case Manager,* Jacksonville, FL *(2008)*
ST. CHRISTOPHER'S ACADEMY, *Senior Residential Counselor,* Orange Park, FL *(2007–2008)*
CITY OF JACKSONVILLE PARKS AND RECREATION, *Recreation Leader,* Jacksonville, FL *(2005)*

Example: Targeted: Community Health

LAWRENCE M. JONES   **6321 Oak Drive**
                                            Jacksonville, Florida 32082
                                                    (904) 862-4253
                                                   lmjones0@unf.edu

---

OBJECTIVE	A position in community health that will strengthen my academic and personal skills.

SKILLS

Computer	**Personal**
Windows	Work well in groups
Microsoft Word	Work well alone
Microsoft Excel	Very flexible
Internet	Dependable

EDUCATION

University of North Florida, Jacksonville, FL   May 2010
College of Health
Major: Community Health
Class Standing: Junior

Polk Community College, Winter Haven, FL   August 2010
Associate Degree in Liberal Arts

RELEVANT COURSES

Dimensions of Health: Older Adults	Health Trends and Issues	Epidemiology
Human Anatomy Physiology I	Medical Terminology	Microbiology
Human Anatomy Physiology II	Human Development	Ethics & Law
Substance Abuse Prevention	General Chemistry I	Nutrition
Intro to Health Professions	Wellness Concepts	

AWARDS   Full Scholarship to Polk Community College

WORK EXPERIENCE

Regency Women's Center, Winter Haven, FL   1/11–present
Neonatal Department Volunteer
• Assist nurses in daily duties
• Responsible for daily care of infants

Summit Consulting/Vincam, Lakeland, FL   8/09–4/10
Repricing Assistant
• Assisted registered nurses
• Repriced medical bills

Heritage Consultants, Auburndale, FL   6/08–8/09
Claims Prelogger and Repricing
• Served as liaison to hospitals in State of Florida
• Analyzed medical claims pricing/adjust to contract

SKILLS   Knowledgeable of WordPerfect, Excel, Lotus, Microsoft Word
Effective team player
Demonstrated leadership skills
Excellent oral and written communication skills

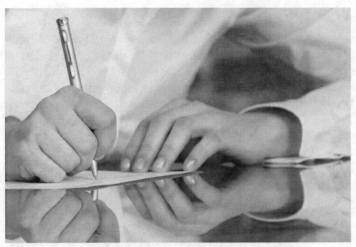

© dean sanderson, 2009. Used under license from Shutterstock, Inc.

Professional Correspondence: Beyond the Resume

With the rising popularity of e-mail, internet resume referral systems, and other computerized job posting networks, letter writing has become a "lost art." Even though resumes are zipping across the internet, these letters still play an important part of any job search, and knowing how to write an effective letter is a must for any job seeker. Since most hiring managers refuse to take phone calls from candidates, your written correspondence will have to do the talking for you; therefore, every effort should be made to present yourself in the best possible light. Remember, you do not get a second chance to make a great first impression. Your cover letter speaks volumes about your ability to communicate and will often help the hiring manager decide whether to continue on to review your resume. You have about 30 seconds to keep the reader's attention in your cover letter, so be a person of interest. Research the organization and address the needs of the organization. Give the reader a reason to review your resume and to interview you. Think from the reader's perspective and most importantly, personalize the letters. You may be writing several letters a day to different employers, but nothing will ensure your resume getting thrown in the trash than a letter with the wrong company name or position on it. Every position is different and you must tailor each letter to take this into account. Always remember to end your letter on a "proactive" note by telling them how and when you will follow-up with them.

Types of Professional Correspondence

Cover Letter (Letter of Application)

Even if a cover letter is not specifically requested in a job ad, employers always expect to receive one. Though job seekers will spend hours developing their resumes, they often spend little or no time creating their cover letters. This can be a critical mistake. This highly significant letter can be the deciding factor in whether or not you get an interview, so take the time to make it notable. A cover letter should contain information that your resume does not, such as your work style, resourcefulness, and personality. This letter will allow the reader to decide if he or she wants to take the time to read your resume and ultimately invite you to interview for the position.

Thank You Letter

A thank you letter should always be sent immediately following an employment or informational interview. Thank you letters help to reiterate your interest in the position and organization as well as reinforce why you feel you are qualified for the position. It also illustrates that you have the ability to follow-up and be proactive.

Sending a thank you letter may be the deciding factor in who is offered the position. Make your letter interesting and detailed. Mention something about the interview, such as a staff member you met, or something you failed to bring up in the interview that you feel will be beneficial to the organization.

Acceptance Letter

Even if you don't enjoy writing letters, you will enjoy writing an acceptance letter. The company will send you a written job offer that outlines the offer, including compensation, benefits, and start date. This offer letter is the company's way of completing the legal agreement between you and the company, but it is your responsibility to verify the details of the offer. The acceptance letter can be used to clarify details of the offer that may have been vague or unclear and state explicitly what you are agreeing to. This acceptance letter is particularly important if critical items are not mentioned in the offer letter or remain vague, which is common when an offer is made verbally. **Don't forget to:**

- Thank the employer for the offer.
- Accept the position.
- Restate the terms of your contract. These may include salary, benefits, location, or others.
- Restate any instructions given to you by the company. These might include your start date or the hours you will be working.
- State your happiness at joining the company.

Decline of Offer Letter

With today's unemployment rates, many job seekers feel fortunate to receive any job offer. But often it is necessary to turn down an offer. Whether it is because the compensation is too low, the location is inconvenient, or it just isn't the right fit, you may just need to say, "No thank you." During these often long and stressful job searches, it is tempting to simply turn down the offer over the phone and ignore writing a letter. This can be a mistake. You never know if or when you will work with this organization again, so end the interview process on a professional note. Also, remember to keep this letter prompt, courteous, diplomatic, and concise.

Letter Requesting Informational Interview

As you explore careers and potential employers, meeting with professionals from various career fields and conducting "informational interviews" to gather information will be an important part of your research. To set up an informational interview, it is proper to send a letter of introduction asking for the interview. Attaching your resume to give them an idea of your background information is also helpful.

© Petro Feketa, 2009. Used under license from Shutterstock, Inc.

Important Tips for Effective Letters

Following these correspondence letter tips can take time, but the reward is worth it. You'll receive more calls for interviews and a greater chance of securing a new position.

Keep it Professional but Friendly

While a resume is generally a formal document, a cover letter gives you a chance to reveal your personality. Not only do you want to show that you are a good fit for the position, but you also want the reader to feel good about you. Your letter should have a friendly and professional tone. Keeping your letter professional and friendly can help endear you to the hiring manager.

Make It Personal

If at all possible, address your letter to the hiring manager. If you cannot get this information, at least get the name of the HR representative in charge of recruiting for the position. You can usually get a name from the company website, an employer directory, or by phoning the organization directly. If you do this research, it will enhance the chances of your resume and cover letter getting "ahead" of the rest of the candidates. Keep the salutation professional by using "Dear Mr. Jones," not "Dear Jim." Using "Dear Hiring Manager" is always a last resort, but is acceptable if you truly cannot get a contact name.

Focus on the Employer's Needs

Before writing a cover letter, research the employer and find out what types of problems hiring managers are facing, qualities they look for in employees, and their future goals. An effective letter illustrates to the employer that you understand and can meet the company's needs. Most importantly, do not focus on your needs; focus on theirs. Use the words "I" and "me" sparingly. If every other sentence of your letter begins with "I" or "my," you need to consider changing the focus. Use this letter to prove that you are the answer to their problems. The most persuasive letters explain what you can do for the employer, not what the employer can do for you.

Be Creative

Creative cover letters will stand out to employers and to make yours unique, you could include a brief summary of your most challenging project or toughest sale. You could also include excerpts from past performance reviews to highlight your record of success.

Proofread, Proofread, and Proofread!

Companies value excellent written and verbal communication skills. Careless writing gives a poor impression of your abilities and can seriously damage your chances of getting an interview. If you cannot spell a word, look it up in the dictionary or use the spell checker on your computer.

Caution: Spell checkers can make errors too, so when in doubt, use a dictionary! Review your letter several times and then have another person proofread it as well. Often, another "pair of eyes" will pick out an error that you will not recognize as an error, no matter how many times you review it. Also take the time to identify and eliminate all unnecessary words and sentences—even entire paragraphs. Most importantly, spell the hiring manager's name correctly! You can usually get this information from a company website or call the company directly to ask for the correct spelling.

Be Concise

Limit your letter(s) to a single page with 3–4 paragraphs. Busy hiring managers don't have time to wade through letters that could pass for dissertations. Get to the point as expeditiously as possible, and break any paragraphs seven lines or longer into short, easily digestible ones.

When emailing your cover letter, don't fall prey to the one-line cover letter that some job seekers try to pass off, such as "Please see attached resume, and thank you for your time and consideration." You can either cut and paste your 3–4-paragraph letter into the email or simply attach it along with your resume.

Include Supporting Documentation and Signature

If you mentioned any supporting documentation such as writing samples, list of references, or proof of certifications, don't forget to enclose them. Failure to do so will show a lack of attention to detail. Do not forget to sign your letter. A letter without a signature leaves the reader feeling like something is not finished.

Plan the Arrival of Your Letter

Try to time the arrival of your letter so that it is received sometime in the middle of the week. On Monday, the employer is usually inundated with paperwork. On Friday, employers may frequently be away at meetings or on business trips. You can inquire with the U.S. Post Office and receive good information on when your letter should arrive.

Typing the Envelope

Below is an example of a typical business envelope

Samantha Jobseeker
5442 Apple Lane
Jacksonville, FL 32256

Mr. Will Receiveit
Director of Human Resources
The All American Company
1234 Bless America Drive
Jacksonville, Florida 32224

Sample Letter of Application

Your Street Address
City, State, Zip
Date of Letter

Contact name
Contact's Title
Contact's Department
Name of Organization
Street Address
City, State, Zip

Dear Mr./Ms./Dr. Contact's Last Name:

First Paragraph: State why you are writing, name the position or type of work for which you are applying, and mention how you heard of the opening.

Second Paragraph: Explain why you are interested in working for the employer, and specify your reasons for desiring this type of work. If you have had experience, be sure to point out your particular achievements or other qualifications in this field or type of work.

Third Paragraph: Refer the reader to the attached application, resume, or to whatever media you are using to illustrate your training, interests, and experience.

Fourth Paragraph: Have an appropriate closing to pave the way for the interview by asking for an appointment, by giving your phone number, or by offering some similar suggestion to facilitate an immediate and favorable reply.

Sincerely,

(sign your name here)

Type Your Full Name

Enclosure (indicates what is enclosed with letter; i.e., resume; transcript etc)

Sample Letter of Application—Semi-Block Format

25 Always Avenue
Jacksonville, FL 32224
April 25, 2012

Dr. Hiriam Firem
Superintendent of Schools
East Side Public School District
123 Learning Lane
Jacksonville, FL 12444

Dear Dr. Firem:

I would like to be considered as a candidate for the position in the English Department at the East Side Senior High School. I learned about the opening through the job vacancy listing which appeared in the Florida Times Union.

In May 2012, I will be graduating from the University of North Florida with a Bachelor of Arts Degree in Education with a specialization in English. As you will note on the enclosed resume, I am currently student teaching at West Side High School in Jacksonville. I am working with juniors and seniors in required English courses and in an elective writing class. As cosponsor of the student Golden Key Club, I have had an opportunity to work with students outside the classroom as well. I believe I have the skills and qualifications needed to work effectively with the students, faculty, and administration of East Side Senior High.

My transcripts are being forwarded to you by the registrar's office. I have also enclosed the names and addresses of three references. Please let me know if any additional information is required. I would welcome the opportunity to discuss this position and my qualifications in more detail in a personal interview. I will contact you within the next two weeks to arrange a time to meet. If you need to contact me, I can be reached after 6:00 p.m. at 904-123-2555.

Thank you for your consideration; I look forward to speaking with you soon.

Sincerely,

Jonathan Doe

Jonathan Doe

Enclosure: Resume

Sample Letter of Application—Block Format

14 East Cherry Lake Rd.
Jacksonville, FL 32245
August 19, 2012

Millhouse Vanhauten
Director of Recruiting
College Relations
Xerox Corporation
1132 Copier Hwy.
Orlando, FL 30456

Dear Mr. Vanhauten:

From your webpage on the internet, I noted your advertisement for marketing representatives. This is the type of position that I am seeking upon my graduation from the University of North Florida (UNF) in December.

Last summer, I had the opportunity to work at your Jacksonville office as a file clerk. The summer was most rewarding and educational. The insight gained into the sales industry and the competitive role Xerox plays in the copier services market is invaluable to me.

My major of psychology at UNF, complemented with courses in marketing and sociology, provides an understanding of the behavior patterns of people. This knowledge would be beneficial in the marketing representative position. Furthermore, I feel that my interests in consumer satisfaction could be of assistance in your consumer products area. Please see the enclosed resume which provides additional information.

Would you please consider my request for a personal interview to discuss my qualifications and to learn more about this opportunity? I will call you next week to see if a meeting can be arranged. Should you need to contact me before then, I can be reached between noon and 5:00 p.m. at (904) 555-6889. I look forward to speaking with you and appreciate your consideration.

Sincerely,

Lisa Andrews

Lisa Andrews

Enclosure

Sample Letter of Application—Block Format

123 Maple Lane
Jacksonville, FL 32225
April 20, 2009

Mr. Hassa Jobopening
Recruiting Coordinator
Campbell, Inc.
P.O. Box 987
Jacksonville, FL 32224

Dear Mr. Jobopening:

This letter is in reference to the Financial Analyst position (Job ID#7564), as posted in the *Florida Times-Union* on April 18, 2012. With a background in economics, a relevant personal portfolio, and a strong interest in international trade, I believe I would be a strong candidate for this position. The combination of my skills and educational background will enable me to make a significant contribution to your organization.

I will graduate from the University of North Florida in May 2012 with a Bachelor of Arts degree in Economics. I have taken a variety of courses and developed a clear understanding of economic principles and concepts. Due to my particular interest in international trade, a portion of my focus has been on Japanese economics and import/export regulations. In addition to a solid theoretical base, I have developed the strong research and analytical abilities critical in making business decisions.

During the past few years, while developing a financial portfolio of my own, I learned the importance of carefully assessing information before making decisions. By working on my personal portfolio, and through my role as treasurer for the Finance Club, I gained the ability to hone my business skills and acumen. Additionally, during my internship at the Sterling Financial Company, I acquired valuable experience in developing a business and marketing plan. These skills provide a solid foundation upon which I hope to build.

Since your merger with Abbott and Company this spring, your dynamic organization has made some critical and successful decisions. I am interested in joining your team and wish to personally discuss my qualifications in an interview. I will contact you the week of April 27th to arrange a time that is mutually convenient to meet. I have enclosed a copy of my resume for your review. If you need to contact me, I can be reached at (904) 555-3456 after 6:00 p.m. Thank you for your consideration, and I look forward to speaking with you soon.

Sincerely,

Pat Brown

Pat Brown

Enclosure: Resume

Thank You Letter (Post-Interview)—Semi-Block Format

134 Apple Lane
Jacksonville, FL 32245
April 20, 2012

Dr. Sarah Newman
Principal
All American School
1234 School Drive
Jacksonville, FL 32225

Dear Dr. Newman:

Thank you for the opportunity to speak with you earlier today regarding the Ninth Grade Mathematics position. The discussion we had was particularly informative, and I found myself even more enthusiastic about this position. I was very impressed with the philosophy of your school and the support for teachers from the community.

To reiterate my qualifications, I believe that the research and writing skills I have acquired here at the University of North Florida combined with my teaching experiences at East High School and Ribault High School make me a strong candidate for your position. I work well independently, am able to manage my time efficiently, and communicate easily with all types of people. To clarify my present situation, I will be graduating the week of May 6th and will be available for employment beginning August 16th.

Again, I appreciate your time and consideration. Should you have further questions, please do not hesitate to contact me at home (904) 324-7777. I look forward to hearing from you soon.

Sincerely,

Shelley Smith

Shelley Smith

Acceptance Letter—Block format

123 Camp Drive
Box 3000
Jacksonville, FL 32234
April 28, 2012

Dr. Bill Danders
Senior Engineer
NCR Microelectronics
4435 Northpark Blvd.
Jacksonville, FL 32225

Dear Dr. Danders:

I was very pleased to receive your phone call on April 27, 2012, in which you invited me to become a member of your organization as a Systems Analyst. I enthusiastically accept your offer of employment at an annual salary of $41,000, beginning May 1, 2012.

I am enclosing the completed personnel form and official transcripts you requested from me. I am certain that my educational background and previous work experience will permit me to be a contributing member of NCR.

The opportunities with your organization appear to offer a real challenge, and I shall make every attempt to meet your expectations. I look forward to seeing you on May 1st, but please feel free to contact me via phone at (904) 273-5555 or email at sdavis@email.com should you need to reach me prior to my start date.

Sincerely,

Susan Davis

Susan Davis

Enclosures: Personnel Form; Official Transcripts

Decline Offer Letter—Semi-Block Format

123 Camp Drive
Box 3000
Jacksonville, FL 32234
April 30, 2012

Dr. Bill Danders
Senior Engineer
NCR Micro Electronics
4435 Northpark Blvd.
Jacksonville, FL 32225

Dear Dr. Danders:

Thank you very much for your letter offering me employment as a Systems Analyst within your organization. Your confidence in me is very much appreciated.

After considerable thought, I have decided to accept another position which seems to fit my needs and qualifications more closely. This has been a very difficult decision for me and only time will tell whether or not my decision is correct.

Thank you again for your time and patience with my decision-making process. I will remember your company favorably throughout my career.

Sincerely,

Susan Davis

Susan Davis

Letter Requesting an Informational Interview—Block Format

1234 Peartree Lane
Jacksonville, FL 32224
May 3, 2012

Mr. Randall T. Winston
Partner
Edwards, Winston, and Smith
Attorneys at Law
20050 Lincoln Rd.
Jacksonville, FL 32226

Dear Mr. Edwards:

I am writing on the recommendation of Professor Marty Edwards, Pre-Law Advisor at the University of North Florida (UNF). Dr. Edwards and I have discussed my interest in the field of law, and he suggested that since you are an alumnus of UNF who practices law, you might be willing to offer some advice and provide me with information about the best way to prepare for a career in law. I have enclosed a copy of my resume to familiarize you with my background.

At present, I am looking for a position as a paralegal or legal assistant. It is my intention to gain some exposure to legal work and learn some of the fundamental skills required of a lawyer before applying to law school. I would be interested in your thoughts concerning this strategy.

I would like to arrange a meeting with you in the next 2 weeks to discuss specific questions about the legal profession. I will call your office the week of June 8th in order to arrange an appointment at your convenience.

Thank you for your consideration.

Sincerely,

Ellen Patterson

Ellen Patterson

Enclosure
Cc: Dr. Marty Edwards

Filling Out Applications

Having an "award winning" resume and cover letter will not always give you a lock on that great job you are going for. Remember, the purpose of the letter and resume is to get a job interview. Most employers require candidates to complete an application as part of their hiring process. They look to see if you can follow instructions, how neatly you complete the application, how you respond to questions, and if you provide all the required information. Oftentimes, candidates are screened out for not filling out the application correctly, or simply writing "see resume" on the application.

Here are some tips for completing applications:

- Answer all relevant questions.
- Respond to each question or fill in each section (put N/A if it is Not Applicable). This shows you didn't just skip that question or section.
- Fill in the sections neatly and with blue or black ink.
- Use a "cheat sheet" which has all the information asked for in any application so you can fill in all sections of the application completely and quickly. It comes in handy when you are trying to remember dates of past education or employment and information on your references.
- Check your spelling; typos and misspellings are a "no-no" on applications.
- If they ask for the job title or position you are seeking, provide a position title that interests you. Don't write "Any Job." This approach doesn't go over well with hiring officials.
- Complete the application neatly and completely. You will most likely be judged on how you complete the application. Take the time to do it correctly and neatly.

 Key Discoveries

- The targeted resume is the most effective style of resume. Tailor your qualifications to meet the needs of the employer.
- Your resume should be able to pass the "30 second test." This means it looks professional and is easy to read quickly with key words highlighted.
- Use action verbs to highlight your skills and accomplishments.
- Proofread your resume and cover letters. Typos are the quickest way to the waste basket.
- Personalize your cover letters and don't use form letters.
- Be sure to fill out applications neatly and completely!
- The S.T.A.R. Program helps you develop important job search skills.

Career Connections: Internet Links

- http://careerplanning.about.com/od/resumewriting/Resume_Writing.htm (*About.com—resume writing tips and samples*)
- http://bestcoverletters.com (*Best cover Letters—includes sample letters in all categories and fields*)
- http://jobsearch.about.com/od/jobapplications/Job.Applications.htm (*About.com—tips on filling out job applications*)

RESUME VERB LIST

Leadership/Management
Assigned
Chaired meetings
Coordinated
Delegated
Developed
Directed
Evaluated
Hired
Improved
Initiated
Interviewed
Led
Managed
Motivated
Oversaw
Planned
Promoted change
Reviewed
Sold
Supervised
Trained

Administration/Organization
Allocated resources
Audited
Budgeted
Calculated
Categorized
Classified
Compiled information
Designed
Developed programs
Established procedures
Estimated
Forecasted
Implemented
Maintained records
Made decisions
Managed budget
Managed time
Marketed
Organized
Prioritized
Recommended
Sorted Data
Systematized

Communication: Human Relations/Teaching
Adapted
Advised
Aided
Assisted
Coached
Communicated
Conversed
Counseled
Defined

Educated
Empathized
Empowered
Encouraged
Explained
Facilitated
Guided
Influenced
Informed
Instructed
Listened
Mediated
Mentored
Negotiated
Nursed
Presented
Taught
Trained
Translated
Treated
Tutored
Understood

Communication: Written and Verbal
Addressed
Advocated
Collaborated
Corresponded
Debated
Demonstrated
Edited
Informed
Integrated information
Interpreted
Persuaded
Proofread
Publicized
Reported
Sold
Spoke
Summarized
Synthesized
Translated

Artistic/Creative
Acted
Composed
Created
Designed
Developed
Directed
Drew
Entertained
Fashioned
Generated Ideas
Illustrated
Initiated
Performed
Portrayed Images

Sang
Sketched
Visualized
Wrote

Research/Investigative
Assessed
Collected
Critiqued
Diagnosed
Disproved
Evaluated
Examined
Extracted
Identified
Inspected
Interviewed
Monitored
Observed
Researched
Reviewed
Solved problems
Studied
Summarized
Surveyed
Synthesized
Tested

Physical/Mechanical/Clerical/Technical
Arranged
Assembled
Built
Calculated
Catalogued
Classified
Computed
Constructed
Cooked
Counted
Designed
Devised
Engineered
Entered data
Fabricated
Filed
Inspected
Installed
Lifted
Operated
Processed
Program computers
Recorded
Repaired
Sorted
Transported
Word processed

When you approach your job search, it is helpful to look at the process from the employer's perspective. *You are now a member of the Search Committee for the World Wide Widgets Corporation screening applicants for a customer service position. There are four applicants, and your job is to screen the resumes and rank them in the order (1–4) that you would recommend them for a one-on-one interview. Below is the description that was listed for the position:*

WorldWide Widgets, Inc.

123 Sprocket St.
Jacksonville, FL 32223
(904) 345-3456

"We Make the World Go Round"

Founded by Wilbur Widget in November, 1989, World Wide Widgets is one of the top 10 manufacturers of widgets in the world, with offices located in Jacksonville, New York, London, and Tokyo. WWW delivers three types of widgets (large, medium, and small) to watch and clock manufacturing companies all over the world. (Widgets are the little sprockets found in all watches and clocks.)

Position Description

Position Title: Customer Service Representative

Brief Description of Duties:
1. Handle incoming calls from clients
2. Provide information about company and products
3. Process customer orders
       a. Maintain tracking system of types and numbers of widgets processed
4. Enter order information and client profiles into database
5. Process all confirmation correspondence
6. Send order information to manufacturing and shipping departments
7. Handle customer complaints and questions regarding orders

Job Qualifications:
·Must be proficient in Microsoft Office, email, and databases
·1-2 years of previous customer service experience preferred
·Must possess excellent written and verbal communication skills
·Must have marketing or business degree
·Leadership skills
·Must have minimum 3.0 GPA

Salary:
Commensurate with employee's qualifications

To Apply:
       Send resume to: Ms. Alice Ledbetter, Director of Customer Service Division
                             WorldWide Widgets, Inc.
                             123 Sprocket Street, Jacksonville, Florida, 32223

Candidate #1

Eric Cartman
2719 Applewood Lane
Jacksonville, FL 32211
(904) 555-9121

OBJECTIVE

Seeking a challenging position in a growth-oriented business environment with opportunity to utilize skills.

EDUCATION

UNIVERSITY OF NORTH FLORIDA, Jacksonville, FL
Master of Business Administration 12/2011

UNIVERSITY OF FLORIDA, Gainesville, FL
Bachelor of Science
Business Management, Minor: Applied Mathematics 4/2005

WORK EXPERIENCE

SHARP WIDGETS, Central City, FL

2004–2008

Territory Manager
• Sales and promotion of multi-item line of corporate accounts

2001–2004

APPLETON, INC.   Springfield, FL
• Responsible for creating and maintaining sales in three county territory

2000–2001

COMPUTER TEK   Tallahassee, FL
• Responsible for installing and training customer to use computerized information systems

SKILLS

Computer skills:
• Microsoft Office Suite; Lotus 1-2-3; Microsoft Word; HTML; Pascal; D-base

REFERENCES

Available upon request

Candidate #2

MARY QUITE CONTRARY
123 Appledumpling Avenue
Jacksonville, Florida
(904) 555-5555

EDUCATION

UNIVERSITY OF NORTH FLORIDA
Bachelor of Business Administration
Major: Marketing

Jacksonville, Florida
August 2011

FLORIDA COMMUNITY COLLEGE
Associate of Arts

Jacksonville, Florida
May 2009

RELATED EXPERIENCE

ABC ORGANIZATION
Intern

Atlanta, Georgia
August 2010–Present

• Assisted with the design and research of several marketing projects
• Created a survey for the general public to be used for a marketing research study
• Attended a two-week advertising seminar
• Effectively worked as a team player while also maintaining top performance on individual projects

UNIVERSITY OF NORTH FLORIDA
Strategic Management and Business Policy Class Project

Jacksonville, Florida
Spring 2010

• Worked in a group setting on the marketing and promotion of the Maytag Corporation
• Collected data via a survey on the marketing methods currently used by the Maytag Company
• Researched the history of their marketing strategies and conferred with other professionals in the field
• Received a grade of A, individually and as part of the team, on the project

OTHER WORK EXPERIENCE

UNIVERSITY OF NORTH FLORIDA
OPS Student Assistant/Career Development Center

Jacksonville, Florida
May 2006–Present

• Greet students, answer phones, and file
• Maintain the career library and assist students in the computer lab
• Assist staff with running errands, typing, and scheduling student appointments

SKILLS

Proficient in Lotus, WordPerfect, Microsoft Office, and ACCESS
Excellent oral and written communication skills
Receive and carry out instructions and tasks in a timely manner
Organized, with attention to detail
Ability to adapt to a changing work environment and deal with pressure comfortably

ACTIVITIES

Student Government Association, Member, 1999–2000
American Marketing Association, Member, present
United Way Student Fund Raising Committee, 1999
Humane Society, Volunteer, present

Candidate #3

Jack B. Nimble

1 San Marco Boulevard
St. Augustine, Florida 32084
(904)824-0000
jnimble@unf.edu

Education

University of North Florida
Jacksonville, Florida
Bachelor of Business Administration, Management
August 1997

Related Experience

Belk Hudson Department Stores
St. Augustine, Florida
Intern January-May 2011
Operated in all facets of store working with employees and management. Assisted misses and women's department buyer in selecting merchandise. Provided customer service and ran cash register
during busy times. Assisted human resources manager in training
new employees.

The Bookstore
St. Augustine, Florida
Customer Service/Cashier September 1998-January 2011
Assisted customers with textbook selection. Assisted faculty
with ordering textbooks for classes they taught. Oversaw store
when owner was not present. Trained new employees.
Worked with owner on creating new ideas for clothing and
other items to be sold in store. Balanced cash register
and prepared deposits.

Skills

Computer
• Lotus and Freelance Graphics
• WordPerfect
• Pagemaker

Organizational
• Excellent oral communication skills
• Extremely organized with attention to detail
• Capable of working in a fast-paced environment
• Punctual, dependable, and efficient

Other Work Experience

McDonalds
St. Augustine, Florida
Cashier May 1999-September 1999
• Provide customer service
• Take orders and operate cash register

References

Available upon request

234

Candidate #4

LISA SIMPSON
1234 Row Avenue
Jacksonville, Florida 32206
(904) 555-5555

Objective	An auditor position that will utilize excellent organizational and analytical skills with a company offering opportunities for advancement.
Education	**Master of Accountancy** University of North Florida Jacksonville, Florida **GPA 3.8/4.0** August 2011 Have passed three parts of the CPA exam. Registered to take the fourth part January, 1998. **Bachelor of Business Administration** May 1999 Accounting **GPA 3.5/4.0**

Education

Master of Accountancy
University of North Florida   Jacksonville, Florida
GPA 3.8/4.0   August 2011
Have passed three parts of the CPA exam. Registered to take
the fourth part January, 1998.

Bachelor of Business Administration   May 1999
Accounting
GPA 3.5/4.0

**Work
Experience**

William & Associates   Jacksonville, Florida
Customer Service Representative   2000–Present
· Process customer billing statements
· Handle customer inquiries and resolve existing problems
· Use computer system to provide customer service regarding current and new program

Coopers & Lybrand   Jacksonville, Florida
Intern   1999
· Conducted audit testing on balance sheet accounts
· Mailed bank confirmation statements
· Verified receipt of client checks

Jacksonville Insurance Company   Jacksonville, Florida
Office Assistant   1997–1999
· Provided information to clients regarding insurance policies
· Improved office administration through reorganizing file system

**Honors and
Activities**

Alpha Sigma Pi—Vice President and Public Relations Officer—Successfully
raised funds for children's charity, arranged guest speakers for meetings
InRoads of Jacksonville—Took part in leadership and job search training workshops
Eartha M. M. White Scholarship
Dean's List

References   Available upon request

Name _____   Date _____

Now that you have some basic information about resumes and *before* you head to your computer, it is important to take an inventory of the information and skills you have. Take your time and organize your thoughts. Below is a guide to get you started.

CONTACT INFORMATION

Name: _____

Present Address: _____

Phone: (   ) _____   E-mail Address: _____

Permanent Address: _____

Phone: (   ) _____

OBJECTIVE

_____

_____

_____

EDUCATION

1. College/University/Study Abroad _____

    City/State: _____

    Type of Degree, Major/Minor: _____

    Month/Year of Graduation: _____

    GPA (optional, only include if 3.0 or over): _____

    Thesis Topic: _____

    Relevant Coursework: _____

2. College/University/Study Abroad _____

    City/State: _____

    Type of Degree, Major/Minor: _____

    Month/Year of Graduation: _____

    GPA (optional, only include if 3.0 or over): _____

    Thesis Topic: _____

    Relevant Coursework: _____

EXPERIENCE

1. Organization: _____

   City/State: _____

   Dates of Services: _____

   Job Title: _____

   Duties/Responsibilities: _____

2. Organization: _____

   City/State: _____

   Dates of Services: _____

   Job Title: _____

   Duties/Responsibilities: _____

3. Organization: _____

   City/State: _____

   Dates of Services: _____

   Job Title: _____

   Duties/Responsibilities: _____

SKILLS

_____

_____

HONORS/AWARDS

Name of Scholarship/Award: _____

_____

LANGUAGES

_____

MEMBERSHIPS

Name of Organization: _____

Offices Held/Title: _____

Dates: _____

INTERESTS/ACTIVITIES

_____

REFERENCES_____

AVAILABILITY _____

OTHER HEADINGS

    Certifications:_____

    Licenses: _____

    Travel: _____

    Professional Development: _____

    Military: _____

Name _____   Date _____

_____   Your Street Address
_____   City, State, Zip
_____   Date of Letter
_____   Contact Name
_____   Contact's Title
_____   Contact's Department
_____   Name of Organization
_____   Street Address
_____   City, State, Zip
Dear _____   Mr./Ms./Dr. Contact's Last Name:

_____
_____
_____

_____
_____
_____
_____
_____

_____
_____
_____
_____

_____
_____

Sincerely,

_____   Sign Here
Type (Print) Your Full Name

Name _____ Date _____

Criteria

RATING SCALE: 0–5 Points Per Section
0 = No Basic Content
1 = Needs Improvement 2 = Fair
3 = Average   4 = Very Good
5 = Excellent

Overall Appearance/Layout   _____Points
- Is it visually appealing (i.e., easy to read, uncluttered)?
- Does it maintain a consistent format?
- Does it appropriately use margins and spacing?
- Does it appropriately use highlight features (i.e., bold, italics)?
- Has full contact information been provided?
- Is the email address appropriate?
- Were an appropriate font size and style used?

Error Free   _____Points
- Does it avoid errors in spelling, grammar, and punctuation?

Targeted
- If an objective is included, is it targeted and clearly stated?
- Does it include relevant education, experience, and/or skills?
- Overall, does it target a particular job, field, or purpose?

Effective Language/Communication   _____Points
- Does it avoid introductory phrases (i.e., "responsibilities included")?
- Do sentences begin with action words?
- Are phrases, sentences, and paragraphs concise?
- Does it avoid listing controversial information?
- Has extraneous material been eliminated?
- Are sentences worded in terms of skills or accomplishments?
- Do key selling points stand out?

Content   _____Points
- Are key elements included (i.e., honors, activities, skills)?
- Were the city and state provided for organizations?
- Were dates included?

_____OVERALL RATING

Name _____   Date _____

Criteria

Overall Appearance/Layout

_____Points

- Is it visually appealing (i.e., easy to read, uncluttered)?
- Does it maintain a consistent format?
- Does it appropriately use margins and spacing?
- Does it appropriately use highlight features (i.e., bold, italics)?
- Has full contact information been provided?
- Were an appropriate font size and style used?

Error Free

_____Points

- Does it avoid errors in spelling, grammar, and punctuation?

Targeted

_____Points

- Is the objective of the letter targeted and clearly stated?
- Does it include relevant education, experience, and/or skills?
- Overall, does it target a particular job, field, or purpose?

Effective Language/Communication

_____Points

- Are sentences and paragraphs concise?
- Are sentences worded in terms of skills or accomplishments?
- Do key selling points stand out?

Content

_____Points

- Are key elements included (i.e., honors, activities, training, skills)?

_____OVERALL RATING

CHAPTER QUEST

At the end of this chapter you should be able to:

- Understand the different types of interviews you might have

- Know how to "dress for success"

- Know how to effectively prepare for your interviews

- Understand how you will be evaluated by employers

- Answer interview questions effectively

- Use the STAR technique to answer behavioral questions

- Know how to follow up after the interview

© Andrejs Pidjass, 2009. Used under license from Shutterstock, Inc.

You Don't Get a Second Chance to Make a Good First Impression: Interviewing

From the moment you walk into view, shake hands, and greet an employer for a job interview, he/she has already made a quick evaluation of you and within the next few minutes will have made a tentative hiring decision on you. Your goal for every job interview should be to present your skills and qualifications in such a way that you will receive a job offer. You can then decide if you want to accept the offer. Interviewing relies on a set of skills that can be developed and improved, and you can increase the number of job offers you receive simply by preparing and practicing for your interviews.

What to Expect

The interview enables the employer to evaluate a candidate's personality, strengths, and educational and work experiences. It has been described as a mutual "exchange of information" because it also affords the candidate an opportunity to gain information about the organization and the position, and to evaluate how these match his/her own skills, interests, and career goals.

CANDIDATE	← Information →	EMPLOYER
Skills	Exchange	Duties/responsibilities of job
Accomplishments		Organizational structure
Values		Advancement opportunities
Goals		Training
Interests		Salary/fringe benefits
Experience		Supervision
Education		

Types of Interviews

The type of interview and the selection process will vary from organization to organization. The style used by the interviewer will also vary according to the amount of experience and the personality of the person conducting the interview. Here are some of the types of interviews:

1. **General interview**—One half-hour to one hour in duration; a general interview provides for an exchange of enough general information to enable both employer and candidate to determine if further contact is warranted. This interview may be conducted by a personnel representative or one member of a selection team or committee.
2. **Screening interview**—A short-term interview designed basically to eliminate unqualified candidates (i.e., college recruiters use screening interviews to decide which applicants are best qualified to meet their organization's needs). Based on these brief interviews, a determination is made to invite the candidate in for a second interview (selection interview).
3. **Second or selection interview**—One hour to an entire day in duration; both employer and candidate engage in a more in-depth discussion of qualifications, responsibilities and other aspects of the position and the organization. The candidate is seriously being considered for the position, and the interviewer must gain as much information as possible to make a final decision. Often other members of the staff or selection committee will participate in this interview session.
4. **An interview with a panel or committee**—A committee will often meet and agree upon the questions to be asked and their sequence. Each committee member may be asking a question for the entire group or out of personal interest. When answering questions, try to make eye contact with each member and include him/

her in your response. You can often lose the support of a committee member by excluding him/her with a lack of eye contact. This is an important skill to master and may require a lot of practice.

5. **An interview during lunch, dinner, or cocktails**—Trying to discuss your qualifications while eating is not an easy task. It is hard to look professional with sauce dripping down your chin. Order food that is bite-sized and can be eaten quickly without fear of spilling on your clothing. Do not order alcohol even if your host has done so. They may be testing you to see how you handle certain situations. Do not become so relaxed that you disclose compromising information.

6. **Group interview** (more than one candidate is interviewed)—Although this is not common, you might be interviewed in a group with other candidates for the same position. Often employers use this type of interview to disseminate information about the position and to make initial assessments about the candidates. This might make you feel like you are in a wolf pack fighting to be the dominant leader, but you should try to keep your cool, listen to what is said, ask questions when appropriate, and look for opportunities to discuss your qualifications.

7. **You are asked to give a presentation**—To determine your communication and public speaking skills, often you will be asked to give a presentation as part of your interview process. It could be on an assigned topic or your thoughts about how you would handle the job if you were to get it. Usually you will be given advance notice for such a presentation. How well you do on such a presentation will be a very important factor in the hiring process. Presentations are asked for when you are applying for a position that requires similar presentations (e.g., conducting workshops, teaching, training, giving sales presentations, etc.).

8. **Role-play**—To give you an opportunity to demonstrate specific skills (e.g., counseling, advising, etc.), you may be asked to take part in a role-play where one of the interviewers assumes the role of a client and you are asked to counsel or advise that individual. It is difficult to prepare for such a role-play, since it is a demonstration of your abilities.

Before the Interview

Setting the Interview

Normally, the employer will contact you by telephone to arrange an interview. It is important that you obtain the following information:

- What is (are) the name(s) and title(s) of the interviewer(s)? Ask for the correct pronunciation.
- How will the interview be structured?
- What is the name of the organization?
- What is the address (location) of the interview? Ask for directions to get there.
- What is the phone number?
- What are the time and date of the interview?

Be Knowledgeable about Yourself

Know yourself and be prepared to talk about your skills and qualifications as they relate to the position and the organization. Display confidence and enthusiasm. Conduct yourself with professionalism at all times. Be prepared and turn nervousness into positive energy. Be yourself and let your personality shine.

Be Knowledgeable about the Organization

Interviewers are continually amazed at the large number of candidates who come into job interviews without any apparent preparation and a very vague understanding of the organization or field. This lack of preparation guarantees that the interview will go poorly and decreases the likelihood of receiving a job offer. Remember that the needs of the organization and not the needs of the candidate are the most important factor. The interviewer is trying to determine if you can become part of their organization and do a specific job. Do your homework and find out as much as you can about their organization. Most organizations maintain websites with information about their organization. You can also try to obtain their annual report, newsletters, etc., which provide information about them.

How Will You Be Evaluated in Your Interview?

As you prepare for your interview, it is important to understand the perspective of the interviewer. How are you going to be evaluated? Below are many of the traits on which you will be judged in the interview evaluation process:

Punctuality	Appearance	Oral Communication	Personality
Assertiveness	Energy	Enthusiasm	Leadership
Maturity	Motivation	Loyalty	Initiative
Career goals	Education	Experience	Confidence

© iofoto, 2009. Used under license from Shutterstock, Inc.

Nonverbal Communication and Body Language

You will also be judged on the basis of your body language during an interview. Your actions communicate a great deal of information about you to the interviewer. Before interviewing, assess your interview body language and work at getting rid of or incorporating gestures and movements. Here's what to look for:

Handshake: Begin and end with a good firm handshake (women too!). This projects self-confidence.

Avoid: The limp, wet washcloth type of handshake. Don't crush the interviewer's hand, either!

Eye movement: How often and for how long does your gaze meet the interviewer's? Good eye contact is critical to being viewed as a candidate who is self-confident and interested in the organization and the job. Staring at the interviewer for too long can make the person feel uncomfortable. What is desirable is making sure you are looking at the interviewer when he or she is asking you a question. When you are answering the question, try to maintain eye contact, too, although it's fine to momentarily shift your gaze elsewhere if you are pausing to look for the right words.

Avoid: Rolling your eyes, squinting, rapid or too frequent blinking.

Facial movements: The best one, of course, is the smile. From the moment you shake hands until you say goodbye, it's smart to smile often—at appropriate moments. Smiling sends the message that you are relaxed and enjoying the conversation. It's also interpreted as a sign of self-confidence. Keep toothy smiles and ear-to-ear grins to a minimum.

Avoid: Twitching your nose or mouth; licking, chewing on, or pursing your lips.

Head movement: With the exception of the occasional nod (to show you are following the interviewer's train of thought), it's best to keep your head erect and turned in the direction of the interviewer.

Avoid: Tilting or rotating your head; tucking your chin.

Hand and foot movements: Generally, the less movement the better.

Avoid: Pointing your finger at the interviewer, drumming your fingers, gripping the arms or seat of your chair, wringing or clenching your hands, cracking your knuckles, pulling at your chin, nose, or hair, jingling keys or pocket change, or folding your hands behind your head.

Posture: An upright but relaxed position is your best bet, something that you can usually achieve by sitting all the way back in a chair and leaning slightly forward (from the waist).

Avoid: Slouching, slumping, or hunching your shoulders.

Tone of voice/inflections: Use the tone of your voice to draw attention to key points, show enthusiasm toward the job and organization, and keep the interest of the interviewer.

Avoid: The dreaded monotone.

Dress for Success!

First impressions are lasting impressions, and you don't get a second chance to make a first impression. Appearance should reflect maturity and self-confidence. Be neat and clean, and dress in good taste. No extremes! Leave large bags outside the interview room. Some points to remember:

Attire and Grooming for Women

A professional wardrobe should always include a suit, with either a skirt or pants. The suit is the best bet in an interview. However, you should dress according to the job or field in which you are working. For example, if you are interviewing for a first-grade teaching position, a suit may seem rather cold and staunch and not convey the warm and caring feeling the teaching environment brings. In this case, a tailored dress, slacks and shirt, pantsuit, or skirt, blouse, and jacket would be appropriate.

© Kurhan, 2009. Used under license from Shutterstock, Inc.

General Tips for Women:

- Maintain an attractive, controlled hairstyle with hair pulled away from your face.
- Wear pantyhose without runs.
- Wear comfortable shoes with medium or low heels that match your interview outfit.
- Skirts should be no shorter than an inch above the knee.
- Blouses should not have plunging necklines; white, ivory, and other neutral colors are safe.

- Keep makeup and perfume to a minimum.
- Remember, no gum, food, or cigarettes.
- When it comes to jewelry, less is always best; keep it simple.
- Keep your fingernails clean and trimmed. If you wear polish, avoid bright colors and be sure it is not chipped.
- Choose colors that complement you and are not especially bright. When in question, navy and black are always good bets.
- Bring a portfolio, purse, and briefcase. You may want to invest in a portfolio or briefcase that can neatly hold all of your necessary items (i.e., pens, paper, resumes, reference sheet, etc.) and any other needed items from your purse. The less you have to carry, the better.

© Stephen Coburn, 2009. Used under license from Shutterstock, Inc.

Attire and Grooming for Men

In a corporate setting, it is recommended that men wear dark or gray suits (solid or subtle pinstripes). In organizations that are less formal (possibly nonprofit or education), one might consider a blazer, shirt, and tie rather than a full suit.

General Tips for Men:

- Keep your hair trimmed and out of your face.
- If you have a beard, goatee, or sideburns, be sure they are neatly trimmed.
- Make sure your shoes are clean and polished.
- Be sure your socks match your suit and each other.
- Keep aftershave or cologne to a minimum.
- Remember, no gum, food, or cigarettes.
- When it comes to jewelry, less is always best. Keep it simple.
- Keep your fingernails clean and trimmed.
- Dress shirts should be solid, preferably white. Be sure the shirt and suit are pressed/ironed. Avoid short-sleeved shirts.
- Bring a portfolio or briefcase. You may want to invest in a portfolio or briefcase that can neatly hold all of your necessary items (i.e., pens, paper, resumes, reference sheet, etc.). The less you have to carry, the better.

Be On Time!

Arrive at least 15 minutes early for the interview in order to acclimate yourself. You don't get a second chance to make a good first impression. Being late is the "kiss of death" for interviews, and it is extremely difficult to overcome this negative impression.

What to Bring

You may want to bring the following (carried in a small portfolio or binder):

- Extra copies of your resume.
- A listing of the names, titles, organizations, addresses and phone numbers of your references.

- A "cheat sheet" that contains information to assist you in filling out an application neatly and completely. (Employers often use the application as a screening device.)
- Paper and pen/pencil.
- A portfolio containing samples of your work (if appropriate).

Note: You may never be asked for any of these items, but when the occasion does arise, having them will show that you are prepared and professional.

The Interview
Helpful Tips

1. Be energetic and full of life. In brief, be a person of interest. Never be just an applicant or just another job seeker.
2. Be pleasant, friendly, courteous, and tactful.
3. Be relaxed, cool, and calm.
4. Always maintain good eye contact. Follow the interviewer's eyes. (If there is more than one interviewer, include each person by moving from one to another.)
5. Listen carefully and answer the questions asked. Don't go off on tangents.
6. Keep your answers concise and to the point, unless you're asked to elaborate.
7. Use facial expressions and gestures to help communicate your thoughts and convey your personality.
8. Be truthful but positive.
9. Don't be defensive, hostile, apologetic, desperate, or critical.
10. Let your sense of humor show through.
11. Create a positive feeling toward yourself.
12. Restate your interest in the position at the close of an interview.

The Interview: Tips for Answering Questions:

1. **Make a clear connection between you and the position.**
   Use past experience and background to prove your strengths required for the position.

© ArrowStudio, LLC, 2009. Used under license from Shutterstock, Inc.

2. **Use specific examples whenever possible!**

   Describe a specific situation in which you were required to utilize a certain strength or skill. Examples support your statements and show that you understand what they are looking for and how you can meet their needs. Examples are the "secret ingredient" necessary to proving your strengths to the employer!!

3. **Don't take a defensive attitude or make excuses when handling liabilities!**

   An apologetic approach and sob stories turn recruiters off. Accentuate the positive by identifying what you have learned from your mistakes and take responsibility for them. Don't make excuses!

4. **Don't be afraid to ask for clarification.**

   Make sure you know exactly what you're being asked before you respond.

Answering Interview Questions

Close to 70% of an interview will be devoted to you talking about *you*. No matter how personable you are or how well you communicate, you cannot anticipate some of the intricate, probing questions that may be asked. Experienced interviewers can spot an unprepared interviewee very quickly. It is critical to prepare and practice for your interviews. In just about every interview you will have, you will be asked something about your education, your experience, your skills and abilities, your short-term and long-term goals, and your knowledge of the organization. Here are examples of commonly asked interview questions:

Sample Questions

Self-Awareness

1. How would you describe yourself?
2. Tell me about yourself.
3. How do you think a friend or a professor who knows you well would describe you?
4. What motivates you to put forth your greatest effort?
5. How do you determine or evaluate success?
6. What academic subjects did you like best? Least?
7. What led you to choose the career for which you are preparing?
8. What personal characteristics are necessary for success in your chosen field?
9. What is your philosophy of life?
10. Why have you switched career fields?

Weaknesses/Negatives

1. What major problems have you encountered and how did you deal with them?
2. What have you learned from your mistakes?
3. What do you consider to be your greatest weakness?
4. Did you ever have problems with your supervisor?

Skills/Abilities/Qualifications

1. What do you consider to be your greatest strengths?
2. Are you creative? Give an example.
3. What qualifications do you have that make you think you will be successful?
4. In what ways do you think you can make a contribution to our organization?
5. Why should I hire you?
6. Why do you feel qualified for this job?
7. What are your own special abilities?
8. Why should we hire you over another candidate?
9. What is your managing style?
10. Why do you want this job?

Knowledge of the Organization

1. Why do you want to work for us?
2. Why did you decide to seek a position with this organization?
3. What do you know about our organization?
4. What job in our organization do you want to work toward?

Values Clarification

1. What is your attitude toward working on weekends?
2. What part does your family play in your life?
3. What are the most important rewards you expect in your career?
4. Which is more important to you: the money or the type of job?
5. Do you enjoy independent research?
6. In what kind of work environment are you most comfortable?
7. How do you work under pressure?
8. How would you describe the ideal job for you?
9. What two or three things are most important to you in your job?
10. Are you seeking employment in an organization of a certain size?
11. What criteria are you using to evaluate the company for which you hope to work?
12. Do you have a geographical preference?
13. Will you relocate?
14. Are you willing to travel?
15. Are you willing to spend six months as a trainee?
16. Describe your idea of an ideal job.
17. Do you prefer working with others or by yourself?
18. How do you like to work?
19. Under what conditions do you work best?
20. What is the highest form of praise?

Experience

1. In what part-time or summer jobs have you been most interested?
2. Tell me about your experience.
3. What jobs have you held?
4. How did your previous employer treat you?
5. What have you learned from some jobs you have held?
6. What jobs have you enjoyed most? Least? Why?
7. What have you done that shows initiative and willingness to work?
8. Describe your current job.
9. What did you like least about your last job?
10. What did you like most about your last job?

Goals/Objectives

1. What are your short-range and long-range goals and objectives?
2. What specific goals other than those related to your occupation have you established for yourself for the next 10 years?
3. What do you see yourself doing in five years?
4. What do you really want to do in life?
5. How do you plan to achieve your career goals?

Education

1. How has your education prepared you for a career?
2. Describe your most rewarding college experience.
3. Why did you select your college or university?
4. If you could, would you plan your academic study differently?

5. Do you think your grades are a good indication of your academic achievement?
6. What have you learned from participation in extracurricular activities?
7. Do you have plans for continued study?
8. Why did you pick your program or concentration?
9. What courses did you like best and why?
10. What courses did you like least and why?
11. How has your college experience prepared you for this job?
12. How did you pick your dissertation?
13. Describe your dissertation process.

Salary

1. What do you expect to earn in five years?
2. What are your salary demands?
3. What did you earn in your last job?

Interests

1. What are your outside interests?
2. What do you do with your free time?
3. What are your hobbies?
4. What types of books do you read?
5. How interested are you in sports?
6. How did you spend your vacations in school?

General

1. What do you think it takes to be successful in a company like ours?
2. What qualities should a successful manager possess?
3. Describe the relationship that should exist between a supervisor and subordinates.
4. What two or three accomplishments have given you the most satisfaction?
5. If you were hiring a graduate for this position, what qualities would you look for?
6. What can I do for you?
7. Tell me a story.
8. Define cooperation.

Stress Questions

1. What causes you to lose your temper?
2. How often have you been absent from work, school, or training?
3. Have you ever had trouble with other people on the job?
4. Can you take instructions without getting upset?
5. Don't you feel you're a little too old/young for this job?
6. How does your family like you being away on business trips?
7. With your background, we believe that you are overqualified for this position. Why have you applied for this job?
8. You haven't had sufficient experience in this field. Can you elaborate on related experiences?
9. Our experience with women on this job has not been good. Why do you think you would be better suited?
10. What would irritate you most if I as a manager did it?

Behavioral-Based Questions

More and more interviewers are using behavioral-based questions or situational questions to predict future behavior based on past behavior. Here are some examples:

1. Tell me about the time you were most persuasive in overcoming resistance to your ideas or point of view.

2. Tell me about the last time you had a disagreement or clash with someone in your work/school/internship.
3. Tell me about the most difficult or frustrating person with whom you have worked.
4. Tell me about a time when you felt most pressured and stressed in your work/school/internship.
5. Describe a time when you were most frustrated or discouraged in reaching your objectives or goals.
6. What do you feel has been your most significant work/school/internship-related accomplishment within the past year or so?
7. Describe the last time you did something which went well beyond the expected in your work/school/internship.
8. Tell me how you go about organizing your work and scheduling your own time.
9. Tell me about the most difficult problem or decision which you faced in your work/internship/school assignment.
10. Tell me about the last time you made a decision which backfired.
11. Tell me about the time you most regretted not getting advice before going ahead.
12. Tell me about the last significant crisis situation you faced in your work.
13. Tell me about a time when you were most persuasive in overcoming resistance to your ideas.
14. Describe your most disappointing and frustrating experience in gaining the support of others for an idea or proposal.
15. Tell me about the last time you were criticized by a supervisor/professor.

The "STAR" Technique

One strategy that will help you respond to behavioral-based interview questions and styles is the STAR technique. The steps involved are to describe a

SITUATION (S) or TASK (T) encountered,
to identify the ACTIONS (A) taken to address the SITUATION or TASK,
and to discuss the RESULTS (R) achieved by the ACTIONS.

An easy way of remembering is to think **S T A R.**

Another example of a question you might be asked is: "Thinking back over your college experience, describe a situation in which you were challenged in using your communication skills. Tell me all about it in detail."

Your response might be: *"Last semester, I participated with four other students on a research project for a biology course. One of the members was difficult to work with, as she had a tendency to not want to listen to our ideas on how to complete the research project. In fact, she had appointed herself 'group leader.'"* **(SITUATION/TASK)**

"The other members of the group and I recognized that she was impacting our efforts to complete this project. I decided to approach her and discuss with her our thoughts and feelings on her being in charge and not listening to our ideas. When I sat down with her one-on-one and communicated our concerns to her, she was surprised." **(ACTION)**

"As a result of our conversation, she admitted that she had a hard time trusting other individuals to do quality work and would take charge of a group to ensure that quality work would get done. When we discussed further with her what her concerns were and more specifically the project and what we were

trying to accomplish, she began to understand the different ways we could all contribute to the project. She realized that she would not have to singlehandedly deal with everything and would have less stress if she shared the workload of the project with the rest of us. We all worked well together through the rest of the project and received an A for our efforts." **(RESULTS)**

Illegal Questions

There are several questions that employers may not legally ask applicants. These include questions about race, religion, national origin, marital status, children, relatives, age, birthplace of applicant or relatives, prior record, sex/gender, and handicaps. Anything that is not a "bona fide occupational qualification (BFOQ)" may not be covered directly, though the interviewer may seek the information indirectly.

Note of caution: Employers are perfectly in bounds in asking questions about prior work experience, academic background, GPA, and how you financed your education. They can even ask about unemployment and having been fired. There are weaknesses in almost everyone's background. In job interviewing, the best thing to do is to be honest about major problems and present your case in a positive manner. For any sensitive area, you must honestly explain the circumstances and avoid blaming others (e.g., if you blame a professor for failure, an interviewer will assume you'll also blame a boss for failure).

Employers are required to make all employment decisions in a manner which ensures that discrimination does not occur. It is improper to ask handicapped applicants about their disabling conditions. In order to determine whether a handicap will affect a person's performance, questions should be asked in regard to the person's ability to do activities that are job-related. Therefore, it would not be appropriate to ask a job applicant if he has impaired vision, but it would be permitted to ask if he has a valid driver's license (if such is required on the job). Make sure you know whether a question is illegal before you question the interviewer about its appropriateness.

Be sure you know the law—what questions are legal and which ones are not.

Request clarification if you need it.

Know how you feel about different issues and prepare for possible questions in advance.

Here are some approaches—none is better than others, but some may be more appropriate in a given situation:

1. Answer truthfully, if the truth is positive, but keep your answer concise.
2. Refer to the illegality of a question, and say that you'd rather not answer.
3. Address the issue rather than the facts: "If you're concerned about staff turnover, I can assure you . . ."
4. Ignore the question, and ask your own question in return: "Are you concerned about staff turnover?"
5. Move the question on to something else quickly.
6. Agree. "Yes, it does seem I'm overqualified, doesn't it?"
7. Use humor.

Remember to "keep your cool" and be as positive and confident as possible. You need to evaluate the situation and decide how much the interview is a real reflection of attitudes within the organization.

Some Examples of Illegal Questions and How to Respond:

SEX:

Question: (Asked of women) **"Do you have plans for having a family?"**

Suggested response: *"I don't know at present. I plan on a career and believe my career will be successful with or without a family."*

AGE

Question: **How old are you? Or, what is your date of birth?**

Responses: *"I wish to be evaluated on my skills, competence, and experience. Age is irrelevant."*

"I feel my age is an advantage at work in terms of the broad-based experiences it has afforded me."

NATIONAL ORIGIN

Question: **Where were you born? Or, where were your parents born? What country are you from?**

Responses: *"I am a permanent resident of the United States and have legal permission to work here."*

"Actually, I am American to the core, and America consists of people from many national origins. I feel like I was born here since it has been my home for so long."

"I am quite proud that my background is _____. My heritage has helped me deal effectively with people of various ethnic backgrounds."

DISABILITIES

Question: **Do you have any disability?**

Response: *"Any disabilities I may possess would in no way interfere with my ability to perform all aspects of this position."*

RELIGION

Question: **What is your religion? Or, what church do you attend?**

Response: *"My religious preference should have no relationship to my job performance."*

RACE OR COLOR

Question: **Do you feel that your race/color will be a problem in your performing the job?**

Response: *"I've had extensive experience working with people from a variety of backgrounds. A person's race, whatever it may be, should not interfere in the work environment."*

Adapted from: Journal of College Placement, Winter 1982

Questions You Might Ask

Remember that you have as much right to evaluate an employer as an employer has to evaluate you. One way to ensure that you have adequate information to make a sound judgment is to ask questions. You may do so at any point in the interview: at the beginning, to clarify the job description so that you can relate your experience and skills adequately; in the middle, to clarify a question you do not understand; or at the end, to show your interest in the organization and to fill in points which are as yet unanswered. Below are some possible questions for you to ask:

*   Where does this job fit into the organizational structure?
*   How will the work be evaluated?
*   What kind of supervision will there be?
*   Whom would I be working for and with?
*   What opportunities for advancement are there?
*   What kind of orientation and training are available to new employees?
*   Are there any long-range plans for the office or department?
*   If someone had this position before, why did he/she leave?
*   What are the major issues that this organization will be facing in the near future? What role do you see my department (my job) playing in these issues?
*   What do you see as the biggest challenge for the person taking this job?
*   How often will I be evaluated?
*   What happens next? (Before leaving the interview, be sure to know what the timetable for the selection process will be and how soon you can expect to hear from them. Find out what your next steps should be and who should initiate them.)

Closing the Interview

If you sense the interviewer is trying to close the interview and you are interested in the position, briefly highlight your relevant skills and, if you have any pertinent questions, ask them at this time. However, questions about benefits or information that can be found in company literature should be avoided. Before you leave, ask what the final selection process will be.

Negative Interview Factors

1. Poor personal appearance
2. Late for interview
3. Limp handshake
4. Sloppy application blank
5. Discourtesy
6. Tactlessness
7. Immaturity
8. Passive or indifferent manner
9. Poor verbal communication, grammatical errors
10. Overbearing, conceited tone
11. Vague responses to questions
12. Lack of confidence and poise
13. Lack of career focus/goals
14. Lack of vitality
15. Indecisiveness
16. Low moral standards
17. Never heard of company
18. Defensive response to criticism
19. Narrow interests
20. Strong prejudices
21. Cynical attitude
22. Lack of participation or interest in outside activities
23. High-pressure type
24. Wanting job for a short period of time
25. Just shopping around
26. Unwilling to start at bottom
27. Unwilling to relocate
28. Condemnation of past employers
29. Overemphasis on money
30. Little or no interest in organization
31. Failure to express thanks for interviewer's time
32. Poor eye contact
33. Little sense of humor
34. Lack of initiative
35. Asks no questions about job

© scion, 2009. Used under license from Shutterstock, Inc.

After the Interview

Follow up your interview with a thank-you note. In this note, you may refer to specific issues that were discussed, express your thanks, and restate your interest in the position. Also, provide whatever credentials, references, or employment applications may have been requested by the employer. If you do not hear from the employer in the specified period of time, you may wish to contact the employer with a phone call.

Discussing/Negotiating Salary

Before the Interview

Prior to the interview stage, research the job market and learn the salary range for the types of jobs for which you will be interviewing. There are salary surveys which are produced annually by various professional associations (e.g., the National Association of Colleges and Employers (NACE) publishes a salary survey newsletter which is published on a quarterly basis, and the U.S. government often provides salary survey information). Check the professional publications in your field for salary information.

Determine Your "Bottom Line"

Spend some time reviewing your current or most recent salary and benefit package in relation to your budget. It is important to establish a minimum salary figure that you are willing to accept. The low end of the salary range you give to an employer should

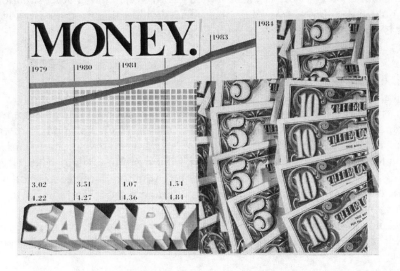

be a little higher than your bottom line: for example, if you determine that with your budget you need to make $25,000 to survive, you could give a range of $25,000–$30,000 as your range, but a recommended range would be $26,500 to $32,000. At some point your bottom line will be tested. An employer will offer you a salary that is below this amount. You need to know "how low you can go."

Salary Is Often Based upon Value and Your Ability To Produce

You will need to know your market value. There are no clear-cut guidelines for assessing one's value. Based on salary ranges, your education and experience, and your skills and capabilities, you need to personally assess what you are worth. If, for example, your research indicates that the average salary for this position is $37,000 (above your bottom line), you might give the employer a salary range of $37,000–$42,000. Many people make the mistake of naming a figure in the middle of a salary range. Ask yourself why you don't deserve the top. It's easy to be impressed by a higher salary than you've been earning, only to resent two months later that you didn't ask for more. Negotiate on the basis of your qualifications—your education, experience, skills, and capabilities in relation to their worth in the job market—*not* on the basis of your wants or needs.

Do Not Negotiate Salary Until a Job Offer Has Been Made

Once the job offer is on the table, salary negotiation takes place to determine a salary and benefit package that both sides will be able to live with. It does not have to be an adversarial relation and should be a cordial discussion. The job offer will remain on the table regardless of what you express in the negotiation. Negotiation involves compromise. It is a "win/win" situation. Some salary scales are non-negotiable, especially in the nonprofit and public sectors.

Other Options

If you cannot get the salary you want, ask when you can be reviewed again, or try for other non-fixed benefits (memberships, a few extra days off).

Making Your Decision

Once the final figure has been reached, you will need time to make your decision. In all negotiations, the time will come for the "final offer" to be made and for you to make a decision to accept or decline. Ask them how much time you have for your decision. Sometimes you can ask for as much as two weeks, and in other situations you might only have a day or two. The "final offer" should come from the employer, not you. It is your role to find areas of mutual agreement.

Accepting or Declining a Job Offer

Do not accept a job offer with the idea that if a better job offer comes along, you will just "back out" on the first offer. It is very risky to give your word to an employer and then cancel out at the last minute. "What goes around, comes around" is often true, and this action could come back to haunt you later down the road. Your word should be good for something, and your reputation in the community is at stake. Decide on each job offer for what it is and has to offer. Once you have accepted a job offer, write to those employers who are still considering your application and inform them that you are withdrawing. This action is a matter of courtesy and is a way of protecting your reputation with the community. At a future point, you might be considering employment with these organizations. You don't want any burned bridges to get in your way.

How Did Your Interview Go?

Interviewing is a skill that is developed through experience and evaluation. After each interview, sit down and assess your performance "under fire." Examine both the strong points and the weak points of your interview and develop strategies for improvement.

PRACTICE, PRACTICE, PRACTICE

Role-playing with a friend or counselor, practicing in front of a mirror, or utilizing the Career Services videotaped mock interview service are good methods of preparing for an interview. By practicing, you may be able to change or reduce distracting mannerisms, such as fiddling with your hair, staring at the floor or ceiling, or punctuating your remarks with "uh." A critical point to remember while practicing is to avoid memorizing. Let the words flow naturally, whether you are discussing the company or yourself. If you come across like you've prepared a speech, your interview will be less effective.

Key Discoveries

- Preparation is the key to effective interviews.
- Practice makes perfect. Practice interviews help you develop advanced interview skills.
- The first 30 seconds of the interview is critical. Be sure you are dressed professionally and well groomed.
- "Winging" an interview is the quickest way to rejection. Be prepared.
- Be prepared to ask questions. It shows you are interested in the position and the organization.
- Always evaluate your interviews and improve your interview skills for the next interview.
- Be sure to send a thank-you note to the interviewer after your interview.

Career Connections: Internet Links

- http://jobsearch.about.com/od/interviewsnetworking/a/interviewguide.htm (*About.com*)
- http://www.collegegrad.com/intv (*College Grad.com*)
- http://www.jobinterviewquestions.org

Name _____ Date _____

Answer the interview questions below, using the STAR technique.

Q: Tell me about a time when you were able to successfully resolve a conflict with a co-worker, fellow student, or professor.

S or T _____

_____

A _____

_____

_____

R _____

_____

_____

_____

Q: Give me an example of a time when you set long-range goals. Tell me what your goal was, how you decided on the goal and the outcome.

S or T _____

_____

A _____

_____

_____

R _____

_____

_____

Q: What is the most difficult decision you have had to make that involved other people who did not agree with your decision? Tell me about the process of making that decision and the results.

S or T _____

_____

A _____

_____

_____

_____

R _____

_____

_____

_____

Exercise 10.2: Practice Interview #1

Name _____   Date _____

Please start by telling me about yourself.

How has your college experience prepared you for this job?

Why do you feel you are qualified for this job?

Tell me about your previous experience.

What have you done that shows initiative and a willingness to work?

What criteria are you using to evaluate the company for which you hope to work?

What are your short-range goals? Long-range goals?

What are your strengths? What are your weaknesses?

Why do you want to work for us?

Describe your working style. How do you like to be supervised?

Please describe a situation where you demonstrated leadership abilities.

In what extracurricular activities are you involved?

Describe a problem you encountered and how you solved it.

Why should I hire you?

Do you have any questions?

Name _____   Date _____

What five adjectives would your closest friends use to describe you?

What do you consider to be your greatest strengths? Weaknesses?

Tell me about a bad decision you made. What was the result and what did you learn?

What is the best advice your parents have given you?

Tell me about a time when you failed to meet a deadline. Why did this happen? What happened as a result? What did you learn from this?

In what school activities have you participated? Why? Which did you enjoy the most?

How has your college experience prepared you for this job?

In your opinion, are grades important?

Tell me about your previous experience.

What kinds of people rub you the wrong way?

Give me an example of a specific event that helped to shape your approach to dealing with diverse groups of individuals. How has your approach changed over the years?

What are your short-term and long-term goals?

How does this position fit into your career plans?

Why do you want to work for us? What do you know about us?

Any questions?

Exercise 10.3: Interview Self-Evaluation Sheet

Employer _____   Date _____

CRITERIA	Yes	Needs Improvement	Comments
1. Was I on time?			
2. Was I dressed appropriately?			
3. Did I speak clearly and distinctly?			
4. Did I use complete sentences and not speech mannerisms (like um, you know, etc.)?			
5. Was my manner appropriate? Were my nonverbal messages on target?			
6. Did I make points that seemed to interest the employer? (If yes, which ones?)			
7. Did I use cues which gave me openings to sell myself?			
8. Was I too aggressive or not aggressive enough?			
9. Did I respond promptly, and were my answers clear and concise?			
10. Did I talk too much or too little?			
11. Did I maintain good eye contact?			
12. Was I relaxed?			
13. Did I avoid criticizing former employers?			
14. Did I ask questions which were pertinent and showed I was interested in employment with this organization?			
15. Did I close with a statement that would allow me to call back?			
16. Did I avoid discussing personal problems?			
17. Did I thank the employer for the interview?			
18. What was my overall performance on the interview? a. What did I do well? b. What could I do better next time?			

_____   _____
(Your Name)   Date

Name _____   Date _____

In virtually every interview you will have, you will be asked a question about your strengths, your skills, your abilities, or your qualifications. The interview is not the time to think of a great answer. Prepare and practice. This packet is designed to help you identify your key skills as they relate to the job or position you are interviewing for.

Personal Strengths: Self-Management Skills

Self-management skills include not only how you get along with others, but also how you relate to authority, to time and space, to the control of impulses, to the material world, to clothes and dress, etc. We usually describe them as "personality traits" or character traits. To understand your self-management skills, complete the checklist below.

Go through the checklist and place a check in the space before each self-management skill that best applies to you.

___ able	___ accurate	___ adaptable	___ adventurous	___ agreeable	___ alert	___ ambitious
___ analytical	___ articulate	___ artistic	___ assertive	___ attentive	___ broad-minded	___ businesslike
___ calm	___ candid	___ capable	___ caring	___ cautious	___ compassionate	___ competent
___ competitive	___ concise	___ confident	___ congenial	___ conscientious	___ considerate	___ conservative
___ consistent	___ constructive	___ cooperative	___ creative	___ curious	___ daring	___ decisive
___ deliberate	___ democratic	___ dependable	___ determined	___ diplomatic	___ disciplined	___ discreet
___ dynamic	___ easygoing	___ effective	___ efficient	___ empathetic	___ encouraging	___ energetic
___ enterprising	___ enthusiastic	___ ethical	___ fair-minded	___ faithful	___ farsighted	___ firm
___ flexible	___ friendly	___ generous	___ goal-oriented	___ good-natured	___ helpful	___ honest
___ humorous	___ idealistic	___ imaginative	___ independent	___ individualistic	___ industrious	___ informal
___ inquisitive	___ insightful	___ intelligent	___ intuitive	___ inventive	___ kind	___ logical
___ loyal	___ mature	___ methodical	___ meticulous	___ modest	___ motivated	___ neat
___ objective	___ observant	___ open-minded	___ optimistic	___ organized	___ orderly	___ outgoing
___ patient	___ perceptive	___ persistent	___ personable	___ persuasive	___ pleasant	___ poised
___ polite	___ positive	___ practical	___ precise	___ productive	___ punctual	___ rational
___ realistic	___ reasonable	___ reflective	___ relaxed	___ reliable	___ reserved	___ resourceful
___ respectful	___ responsible	___ secure	___ self-assured	___ self-aware	___ self-directed	___ self-reliant
___ self-starting	___ sensible	___ sensitive	___ serious	___ sincere	___ spontaneous	___ stable
___ steady	___ strong-minded	___ sympathetic	___ systematic	___ tactful	___ teachable	___ tenacious
___ thorough	___ thoughtful	___ tolerant	___ trusting	___ trustworthy	___ understanding	___ unselfish
___ verbal	___ versatile					

Work Content Skills

Work content skills are those skills which deal with mastering a particular vocabulary, procedure, or subject matter. Thus, knowing a particular foreign language is a work content skill. These skills are acquired as one goes on in life, and they involve the use of one's memory.

In the spaces provided below, write down the technical abilities and/or specialized knowledge you have acquired through formal or informal means.

FROM ACADEMIC SETTINGS	FROM WORK SETTINGS	FROM RECREATION SETTINGS
Example: Speak a language Present in front of class Conduct research Write a term paper	*Example:* Conduct inventory Work cash register Train and supervise staff Customer service	*Example:* Singing Mountain climbing Sports team orientation Team leadership

Functional/Transferable Skills

(These are your "natural abilities" and can transfer from one setting to another.) Place an X in the space at the left for those skills you consider to be your "strengths."

____ **Writing Skills**: Writing reports, articles, ads, stories, or educational materials.

____ **Negotiating:** Ability to discuss with a view to reaching agreement; bargaining for rights or advantage.

____ **Selling/Persuading:** Promoting a person, company, goods, services, or ideas; convincing of merits.

____ **Public Speaking:** Ability to speak effectively to groups.

____ **Teaching/Coaching:** Ability to teach skills, concepts, or principles to others; creating a learning environment.

____ **Counseling:** Facilitating insight and personal growth of individuals.

____ **Listening:** Ability to draw out thoughts, feelings, and ideas of another; accept, express sensitivity, defuse anger, calm, appreciate, empathize.

____ **Designing/Developing Programs:** Coordinating, developing, or structuring new or innovative practices; handling logistics.

____ **Facilitating:** Ability to guide group discussion soliciting participation from all members.

____ **Treating/Nursing:** Healing and caring for patients or clients.

____ **Managing Time:** Ability to use time effectively; meet deadlines.

____ **Managing Budgets:** Economizing, saving, stretching money or resources.

____ **Attentive to Detail:** Ability to deal effectively with individual steps or components associated with an overall project/task.

____ **Organizing:** Grouping or categorizing data, people, or things to achieve specific goals.

____ **Planning:** Defining goals and objectives; scheduling and developing projects or programs.

____ **Motivating Others:** Ability to motivate and lead others.

____ **Directing:** Ability to oversee all aspects of a program or project.

____ **Evaluating:** Ability to assess the performance of individuals or programs.

____ **Managing/Supervising:** Ability to oversee or direct the work of others.

____ **Problem-Solving:** Ability to analyze, break down, and figure out problems logically.

____ **Analytical Thinking:** Ability to quickly and accurately identify the critical issues when solving a problem.

____ **Database Management:** Ability to create and maintain databases.

____ **Mechanical Ability:** Ability to assemble, tune, repair, or operate engines and other machines.

____ **Research:** Ability to design an experiment, plan, or model that systematically defines a problem.

11

CHAPTER QUEST

At the end of this chapter you should be able to:

- Understand the job search process

- Utilize a variety of job search strategies

- Identify and utilize a wide variety of job search resources

- Maintain and keep records of your job search activity

- Know how to set up and conduct an informational interview

- Create and develop your own job search network of contacts

© Stephen Coburn, 2009. Used under license from Shutterstock, Inc.

Finding Your Dream Job: Job Search Strategies

Introduction

The thought of conducting a job search creates a variety of feelings in people ranging from fear and trepidation to hope and excitement. These feelings can create energy that can and should be used to assist you in achieving your career goals. However, many people are confused as to how to use this energy effectively or where to begin. As is true in all goal setting, a job search requires an organized step-by-step approach to put you in the "driver's seat" and help you maintain control. Remember that job hunting is a process which, to be successful, must be pursued and evaluated regularly. The average job search can take anywhere from three to nine months depending on the type of job you are seeking.

Keep in mind that there are SEVEN main areas of consideration in job hunting that will help you to be successful:

1. Be knowledgeable about yourself
2. Be knowledgeable about the job market
3. Understand the employer's perspective
4. Keep and maintain records of your job search activities
5. Identify and utilize sources of potential openings
6. Go directly to the person who does the hiring
7. NETWORK, NETWORK, NETWORK!!!!

Be Knowledgeable about Yourself

Before starting your job search, ask yourself these questions:

*   What skills, abilities, interests, values, education, and experience do you possess that will enable you to do what you want?
*   What are your short-term and long-term goals?
*   What type(s) of job(s) do you want?

If you have not developed a career focus or identified some career goals, your job search will be more difficult. Employers are seeking individuals who are able to articulate their skills and goals. Your Career Services office offers workshops, career counseling and assessment, handouts, and other services to assist you with the self-assessment process.

Resumes and Correspondence

Your self-assessment will come into play as you begin developing your resume and writing cover letters. In targeting a specific job or career, you need to draft a resume that highlights the experience and skills you have that relate to a specific job or career. Time spent on developing a targeted resume is well worth the effort. Indeed, the resume and cover letter are powerful tools in the job search process. It is the first impression an employer will have of you as an individual and you want it to be a positive one.

Interviewing

The largest percentage of an interview will be spent with you talking about you—your skills, interests, values, goals, education, experience, accomplishments, etc. Preparation is the key to good interviewing. Make sure you have researched the company/

organization and position before going into your interview. Your research might include asking the company or organization for promotional literature and annual reports. You will be better able to relate your specific skills to the position and how you would contribute to the company or organization. Think about the types of questions you might be asked and how you would respond.

Be Knowledgeable about the Job Market

Ask yourself these questions:

- What type(s) of employer(s) do you want to work for?
- Can you identify the size and type of the organization? The type of people? Organizational structure?
- Have you identified the geographical location (city, state, or region)?
- Do you know what type of setting (urban, suburban, rural)?

The Career Services Office has an excellent Career Library loaded with books on thousands of jobs and careers and companies and organizations that recruit UNF students and graduates. Career Services' website (www.unf.edu/dept/cdc) also has numerous links that will help you research both careers and employer organizations. There are also links to relocation resources.

Understand the Employer's Perspective

Before starting a job search, think about how potential employers feel and what their expectations might be. How will they view your potential? What are their needs and expectations?

Employers are generally looking for competency and for someone who will fit into their organizational structure. Be aware of the process of employment that often exists within an organization:

1. A need is recognized (new services, or products, new problems, organizational expansion, employee resignation, or retirement).
2. Reorganization occurs (positions are shifted, employees are given additional responsibilities).
3. There is a need to hire additional people (job description is written).
4. The position is posted internally.
5. Inside referrals are sought (employees are asked to recommend candidates).
6. Interviews are conducted internally.
7. If position can not be filled from within, it is openly advertised.
8. Resumes are received and selection process takes place.

If you can establish contact before the position is advertised, you have a better chance of getting the job. Statistics show that over 80% of all jobs never reach the advertisement stage. When a position needs to be advertised, employers publicize their openings in a variety of ways. You should do enough research in your field of interest to find out how employers list their job vacancies.

Keep and Maintain Records of Your Job Search Activities

Organizing Your Job Search

Employers will expect you to conduct yourself professionally in all aspects of the job search. This includes your letters, resume, references, phone conversations, and personal contacts. It is important to keep accurate records of all activities and contacts including:

- Name of organization
- Contact name and job title
- Address and phone number
- Date of contact
- Referral source
- Summary of contact and recommended follow-up

Establish Your Job Search "Headquarters"

This is your work area from which your job search efforts can be coordinated. It should be equipped with the following items: copies of your resume, stationery, envelopes, stamps, paper clips or stapler, typewriter or word processor, telephone, calendar, appointment book, pens and pencils, paper punch, and your record-keeping system.

© Jorge Pedro Barradas de Casais, 2009. Used under license from Shutterstock, Inc.

Time Management

Managing your time is another important aspect of a job search. If you are currently in school, the amount of time available to job hunt may only be 10% of your week. However, can you increase this amount? And, when you've graduated, this amount should significantly increase. Look at your time realistically and set aside large blocks of time free from interruptions to work on your job search campaign. It should not be a 24-hour-a-day project, and you will need to set aside time for other activities. Establish a time schedule that fits your lifestyle.

Note: It can take anywhere from three to nine months to obtain employment. The more time you can devote to your search, the sooner you will find the job you want.

Record Keeping

In a job search, follow-up is critical and good record keeping is essential. Use a job-hunt notebook, file card system, diary, log or journal, or any other system that works for you so you can refer to important information quickly and accurately.

Sample Job Search Record Sheet

_____   _____

(Name of Organization)   (Date)

(place ad here)

DATE OF ACTION

_____   Cover Letter

_____   Resume

_____   3 Letters of Reference

_____   _____

_____   _____

FOLLOW-UP

_____   _____

_____   _____

_____   _____

_____   _____

NOTES:

Job Search Record—Index Card

NAME OF ORGANIZATION: _____

NAME OF CONTACT: _____

Title: _____

Street: _____ Phone #: _____

City/State: _____ Date of Contact: _____

NOTES:

Follow-up: _____

_____

_____

_____

_____

Credentials: _____ Resume   _____ Cover Letter   _____ Transcripts

_____ References   _____ Writing Sample

Identify and Utilize Sources of Potential Openings

When organizing and conducting an effective job search campaign, it is important to utilize a variety of resources which will help you identify potential openings. Start by asking yourself:

*   Who can help you learn about job opportunities?
*   What resources are available for your chosen career field?

© Tom Mc Nemar, 2009. Used under license from Shutterstock, Inc.

Here Are Some Sources of Openings To Consider:

The Internet and World Wide Web: Surfing the web is another great way to identify employers and employment opportunities. The Career Development Center has developed a webpage that organizes many of these job-search-related links and helps you to navigate through the wide range of webpages and links

Newspapers/Want-Ads: If you are moving to a specific city, consider subscribing to the local newspapers of that city. A three-month subscription for the Sunday edition costs very little. When you read newspapers, however, don't just read the help wanted ads. Review the local, regional, and business sections of the paper, and you will discover which companies and organizations are new, which are expanding, and who might be potential contacts for you in your search. Many newspaper ads can now be accessed through the internet.

Responding to Job Advertisements

Once you see a job posted, respond as quickly as possible. Make sure you have researched the position and you understand the qualifications they are seeking. You also want to know who you need to send your application/resume to and when the deadline is for applications. Know what is required for your application. Do you need to have written references or will the names and addresses of your references suffice? Always follow up with a phone call to the organization to ensure that they have received your application.

Sometimes, you may see a job posted where you have missed the deadline by a day or two. Don't let this stop you from applying. Contact the organization and ask to speak to the hiring authority. Ask him or her if a late application will be accepted. In many instances, the organization will accept your application and your efforts can be rewarded by an interview. If you want to be proactive and a risk-taker, don't wait to be invited for an interview, but contact the organization and try to arrange the interview yourself. This is an appropriate strategy to take. Hopefully, if all goes well, you will be scheduled for an interview.

National Publications/Journals: There are a number of resources published that list national and international career opportunities. Examples of these resources include *The Business Weekly, The Chronicle of Higher Education, ACCESS: Opportunities in Non-Profit Organizations, Art Search,* and *Environmental Job Opportunities.* Do your research to find out where jobs in your career field are generally listed.

Directories: Check the *Directories in Print,* an annotated guide to over 14,000 directories published worldwide, to see if there are any directories published that relate to your specific career choice. This directory of two volumes is available at most libraries. *Directories in Print, Volume 2* provides a subject index that is helpful. For example, if you are seeking a list of management consultants, there are 17 different publications that are found in the *Directories in Print, Volume 2* that would provide you with this information. *Directories in Print, Volume 1* provides a description of each of the 17 publications and how you can purchase these different directories.

Chamber of Commerce: Most cities have a Chamber of Commerce, which is an organization that supports businesses in the community. Directories and lists of employers are often available free or can be purchased for a small fee. You will receive other information from the Chamber such as housing and living costs, educational institutions, and other factors which you consider in deciding where you might want to work. Many Chambers publish a weekly or biweekly business magazine (e.g., *Jacksonville Business Journal*). These publications have a great deal of information on new businesses, who's expanding, who's being promoted, etc. Numerous contacts can be gained by simply reading this publication regularly.

Employer Directories: Directories are often published that list employers from a particular region (e.g., *The Florida Job Bank*) or for the entire country with geographical cross-indexes (e.g., *Peterson's Guide to Independent Schools*). Names, addresses, and phone numbers of potential employers are provided, and often you will find a paragraph description about the organizations and companies.

Job Vacancy Listings: In order to bypass the want-ad route, employers post job openings internally and will try to get applicants or referrals from within the organization. Many employers send vacancy listings directly to college and university Career Centers and faculty members. Most use an online Internet-based system to post job listings.

Professional Associations: Once you choose a particular career field, it is helpful to know what professional organizations you might wish to participate in that will allow you the opportunity to network with other professionals in your field. Most industries have one or more professional associations that are committed to advancing the special interests of the industry and their members; many have dedicated job search engines. Examples of such associations include the American Physical Therapy Association (APTA), the Public Relations Society of America (PRSA), and the Society of Human Resources (SHRM). Do a Google search for professional associations for the careers that interest you. To access thousands of associations online, visit http://www.ipl.org/ref/AON and http://www.asaenet.org.

Associations provide lots of in-depth information with regard to the industry such as facts, trends, and current events. Many post job opportunities!

Annual Conferences: Associations often hold conferences in various regions of the country. Workshops, forums, panels, and seminars are the main focus of conferences. Not only do conferences allow you to network with professionals in your field of interest, but many conferences will offer a placement service. Interviews that occur are usually short, screening interviews. Be prepared to make a positive first impression quickly!

Meetings: Most national professional associations have local and regional affiliations that conduct monthly, quarterly, or yearly meetings. Check with the national association office for information on its local and regional groups. These meetings are often held over lunch or dinner and provide an excellent opportunity for you to make contact with numerous professionals in your career field of interest.

Publications: Professional organizations often publish newsletters, journals, directories of members, etc., that contain not only job vacancy listings, but information about what is happening in a particular career field.

Note: Many professional associations offer student membership rates. Consider joining a professional group before you graduate from the University of North Florida. Membership includes receiving information on all of the above services. You also will obtain a list of members that can be prospective contacts for you in your job search.

Telephone Yellow Pages: The Thomas Carpenter Library and most public libraries will have telephone books for most major cities or regions of the country. Utilize the Yellow Pages as well as business sections of the phone book to identify companies or organizations that might be seeking an individual with your experience and skills. The Yellow Pages are an excellent way to identify smaller companies or businesses that are typically not listed in employer directories published by the Chamber. Many of these Yellow Pages can be found on the Internet.

On-Campus Recruiting: Career Services at UNF invites local and national recruiters to interview, screen, and select candidates for positions. Employers find this a cost-effective way of interviewing, as they can meet with a large number of candidates in one day. The types of organizations who recruit vary from companies like Deloitte and Prudential Insurance to nonprofit organizations like Teach for America and the Peace Corps. A recruiting schedule is available in Career Services and on our webpage.

Job Fairs: Companies and organizations will often participate in local, regional, or statewide job fairs. These fairs usually are large and can be somewhat impersonal. However, they provide an excellent opportunity for you to meet with many employers in a short amount of time. Interviews that occur are usually short and used for screening purposes. Career Services at UNF sponsors its Career Expos in September, January, and April of every year. Career Services also participates in the Statewide Job Fair held in May in central Florida. A list of participants is available in the Career Services office and on our webpage.

Employment Agencies: Agencies usually place individuals who are mid-to-executive level managers, etc. If you choose to register with a placement agency, be careful of the fine print on the contract that you sign. Try to work with an agency where the fee is paid by the employer.

Personal Contacts: When you think back to the summer jobs and internships that you have obtained over the past few years, you may realize that it was a personal contact that resulted in obtaining the specific job or internship. Many times it is "who you know" that assists you in obtaining an interview for a job. Thus, before you start your job search, make a list of those individuals who belong to your network. Don't just think of individuals who are in the career fields you are interested in—also identify those who are not in a related field, because chances are they know someone who is. You will also want to look at others you are connected to, such as faculty and alumni from your college, members of professional organizations you belong to, conference attendees and speakers, authors of articles you like, etc.

Go Directly to the Person Who Does the Hiring

Richard Bolles (*What Color Is Your Parachute?*) claims that for every 245 unsolicited letters received inquiring about employment, only one will result in an interview. Clearly, a big letter writing campaign will only have a payoff if you send out hundreds of letters and resumes.

In general, however, your letter is more likely to get noticed if it is directed to a specific person and shows the link you are making between yourself and the organization. Follow-up, initiated by you, is critical if you expect a response.

You might also have success if you have identified through reading your professional newspapers and journals, or even your daily paper, issues that might imply a need for new personnel in a particular organization. Jack Erdlen of Erdlen and Company, a human resources consulting firm, suggests that job hunters should be alert to:

1. Stories on products or services in great demand
2. Current developments in an industry or profession
3. Termination, resignation, and retirement notices
4. Reports of promotions and job changes
5. New patents and discoveries
6. Contract awards
7. Significant happenings and major events
8. Dedication of a new facility
9. Increased sales or earnings reports
10. Moving of a corporate headquarters
11. Acquisitions and mergers

While a number of these apply only to industry, those interested in schools, government, and nonprofit organizations should also watch for new legislation, new methods for meeting educational goals, and increased concern about particular issues or social concerns, among others.

© Konstantinos Kokkinis, 2009. Used under license from Shutterstock, Inc.

Network, Network, Network

Over 30% of job seekers, when surveyed, indicated they obtained their job through someone they knew—someone in their network. Even when an opening is clearly published, your network can make the difference in your probability of being interviewed. You know far more people than you think you do. The key to successful networking is not to restrict your contacts to those people who are in your target fields. Consider family members, friends, professors, former work supervisors, coworkers, etc.

Going on the supposition that everyone knows someone else, you can use your primary contacts to learn about people who may be more closely related to your goals; your best friend's parents may have acquaintances who could be helpful to you.

After your own acquaintances as mentioned above, you are connected with a large number of other people (including alumni from your college[s], members of organizations you join, conference attendees and speakers, authors of articles you like). You can reach out to this group through your common interests:

- "As an alumna of the same graduate school, I would like your help . . ."
- "I recently attended the conference on X, Y, Z, where I participated in your fascinating workshop on . . ."
- "I just read your interesting article in *Globe* magazine on . . ."

Contacting People in Your Network: Job Search Informational Interviewing

As the name implies, an informational interview is one you conduct with a person in your network to gather information, to learn about career options and job openings, and to build your professional network along the way. As we all know, in today's competitive and ever-changing job market, it's not what you know, but who you know. The more people who are familiar with you, your qualifications, and your career interests, the more doors will open for you when the time comes to land that job.

Contacts may be followed up either by phone or in writing, but the goal of both should be an appointment. A short letter of introduction is usually preferred where you do not know the person. Indicate the source of the referral. Since this is not a letter of application, you need merely state that you wish to set up a meeting time to discuss your agenda. Two or three background sentences about you will suffice. You may enclose a resume for additional information, if you wish. Assure the person that you do not expect him/her to know of specific openings. Indicate at the end how you plan to follow-up: "I will phone next week. . . "

Here Are Some Tips for Setting up an Informational Interview:

- When calling or writing for the interview, make sure to specify that you are only seeking information or advice (or both). Do not go into the interview under false pretense and violate the "rules" by asking for a job.
- Always request a short meeting (20–30 minutes). You will usually get more. Don't delay the end of the meeting; be prepared, be professional, and be businesslike. Don't waste his/her time.
- Prior to the interview, prepare yourself well. Know yourself and know as much about the employer and your career field as possible. Be prepared with relevant questions.
- Dress as you would for a regular job interview, even though you are not seeking employment at this time. Image is extremely important and you want to create a positive one.
- Bring copies of your resume, but don't show it unless the employer asks to see it. You want to create the impression you are prepared, but you don't want to violate the conditions under which the interview was arranged.
- Topics of conversation should revolve around the profession, the growth of the organization, and any particular points of interest you might have concerning the organization. Bring out your own qualities and abilities as a way of indicating why you have such a strong interest in that particular field.
- At the end of the interview, ask if there are any other people or organizations he/she would recommend that you contact. If yes, ask if you can use his/her name.
- Always send a thank you note. It may earn you more points than you can imagine. Remember that the purpose is not to get a job offer immediately but for the employer to remember you later, especially when a job opportunity may occur.

Many job seekers feel embarrassed about asking people to assist them. Advice is free and people love to give it. Everybody you know is a possible source who might lead you to a job in the "hidden job market." When you think you are bothering someone, keep in mind that most people love to talk about their jobs and what they do for a living. In fact, they are very flattered when someone asks for their advice. Just do not take their advice and favors for granted. Be sure to acknowledge their help and send thank you notes when appropriate.

Making Contact

Before you begin calling people to set up informational interviews, here are some tips:

- **When to Call:** The best time to phone an individual is before 11:30 a.m. on Tuesday, Wednesday, or Thursday.
- **Establish an Objective:** Determine why you are contacting this person. What are some of the things you want to learn?

- **Visit Them at Their Work Site:** Whenever possible, you want to meet them at work in order for you to gain exposure to various work environments.
- **Prepare a Script:** Develop a conversational script that you can loosely follow. The script can make sure you maximize your phone conversation with that person and get useful results.
- **Evaluate Your Approach:** As you make contacts, rework your script or approach and go with what seems to work.

Remember, the purpose of a networking contact is not to ask for a job but to gain information about the following:

- Facts about the organization
- Feedback on your resume and qualifications
- Tips for your job hunt
- Other departments or jobs you might wish to contact
- Additional names of individuals within or outside the organization that might be able to assist you in your job search
- Potential job openings

Follow-Up with Contacts

Follow-up is the key to an effective job search. Make sure you follow up with contacts on a regular basis. It is important to:

- Follow up each meeting with a thank you letter expressing gratitude for the specific help you received. If the interview went well and the individual agreed to keep you in mind regarding future opportunities, remind him/her that you appreciate the assistance.
- Keep detailed records concerning whom you have interviewed, date of the meeting, what transpired, and any additional contact names.
- Maintain copies of all correspondence.
- Maintain contact in the future. This step is the most neglected. Establish the ongoing nature of your acquaintance during their interview by mentioning that you would like to get back to this person to let him/her know the progress of your exploration. Future contact can be made by phone or letter.
- If the person directed you to call someone else, follow up and let them know what the result was. Many people have expressed frustration in never hearing back from an individual they have helped.

To follow up on every contact in your network takes a great deal of time. Therefore, it is important for you to set some daily and weekly goals in the beginning of your job search to help you manage your time effectively. The more organized you are, the less time it will take you to find the job of your choice.

Furthermore, you must be willing to take some risks. Be assertive and proactive in your job search. If you are reactive or passive, your search will be extremely frustrating. Examples of risk-taking include:

- Cold-calling a stranger to request an interview
- Writing a personal letter to potential employers
- Seeking out the person with power to hire you within a specific organization
- Dealing with the secretary screen

The more proactive you are, the more opportunities you will have to interview and the more offers you can choose from.

Job Search Informational Interviewing: Sample Letter of Approach

5425 Ute Road
Jacksonville, FL 32234
September 12, 2011

Mr. John Goodnight
Director of Sales
MCI Corporation
3003 Phillips Highway
Jacksonville, FL 32224

Dear Mr. Goodnight:

Last week, I spoke with Ms. Barbara Morning, and she recommended that I contact you concerning opportunities in the sales industry in Jacksonville.

By way of introduction, I have enclosed a copy of my resume, which highlights my education and experience. Both my degree in English and college leadership activities have prepared me for a career in sales. Thus, I am seeking information from you about the sales industry in Jacksonville.

Furthermore, your comments and suggestions of any people or situations I should pursue would be most welcome. If possible, I would like to arrange a brief meeting with you next week to hear your ideas about the local sales industry. I will contact you on Monday, September 26, to arrange a time that is convenient for you. Thank you for your assistance.

Sincerely,

Lisa Andrews

Lisa Andrews

Job Search Informational Interviewing: Sample Telephone Script

Charity:	Hello, my name is Charity Case. I would like to speak to Mr. Goodnight. He should be expecting my call.
Secretary:	May I ask what this is in reference to?
Charity:	Yes, I've been in contact with Mr. Goodnight about the sales industry in Jacksonville and wanted to follow up with him.
Secretary:	I'll see if he's available.

If the person you want is not available, ask for a better time to call back. Alternatively, leave your number with the message, "I'm following up on my letter of ____ (date)_____. I was referred by our mutual friend, Barbara Morning." If the secretary insists on screening you further, you may want to tell him/her that you are calling Mr. Goodnight because you have been referred by a friend of his. No matter how difficult it might be, always remain polite and cheerful! The last person you want to alienate is a front office person.

John:	Hello. John speaking.
Charity:	Hello, this is Charity Case. Our mutual acquaintance, Barbara Morning, had suggested I contact you about my interest concerning opportunities in the sales industry in Jacksonville. I sent you a letter last week, and I was wondering if you have had a chance to read it? I am hoping we can get together to discuss your ideas. (If he hasn't read it, give him a synopsis of your letter. Make it clear that you are not asking for a job.)
John:	Yes, I did. I would be willing to meet with you, although I'm very booked up for the next two weeks. (If he can't see you, ask, "Could you suggest a name or two of other people who may be able to help me?")
Charity:	I'm happy to fit in with your schedule. I only need 30 minutes of your time. First thing in the morning or late afternoons are best with me, but I'm sure I can arrange my time if neither of those are convenient.
John:	I could see you on October 8th, at 8:00 a.m.
Charity:	That would be fine. Where should I come?
John:	My office is located in the main building of our complex on Phillips Highway. When you come into the main lobby, the receptionist will direct you to my office.
Charity:	Thanks so much. I really appreciate your taking the time to see me. I'll look forward to meeting you. Goodbye.

Having an outline prepared for points you want to make will make telephone contacts much easier. Use the outline to direct your conversation but do not read your script. Be prepared for any situation you may encounter.

Job Search Informational Interviewing: Preparing

Research the professional's field and organization prior to your meeting to avoid wasting time with the basics. Information can be found in career and public libraries, professional journals, and by calling the specific organization for informational materials.

Develop a list of well-thought-out questions to be used as a guide during your informational interview. These questions should be open-ended to give the individual an opportunity to provide you with as much information as possible.

Before the Informational Interview

- Dress as you would for any interview.
- Arrive early.
- Keep track of the time.
- Listen to the language used.
- Take notes if you need to (but mention that you will be doing this).
- Make note of the environment and the way people interact.
- Thank the person for his/her time.
- Ask for additional referrals with permission to use his/her name.
- Share enough information about yourself to make your needs known, but do not let the meeting turn into a job interview.
- You may ask for feedback on your background and/or resume in relation to the career/job/field under discussion.

Job Search Informational Interviewing: Questions You Might Ask

To Find Out about the Company:

1. How does your company differ from your competitors, both in line operations and human resource management?
2. What would you say is your company's image and philosophy?
3. What type of management style is typically found in this company?
4. What types of problems is your company facing?
5. Do you feel there are some unique and innovative aspects to this organization?
6. Is your company planning on any future expansion, new direction, or projects?
7. What are the professional development opportunities available in your company? Does it include orientation and training in-house, tuition assistance, attendance at seminars/conferences, etc.?
8. What are the general policies or expectations (dress code, arrival times, is there flextime, etc.)

To Find Out about the Department:

1. How does your department relate to the company as a whole?
2. What would you say is the management style used in this department?
3. What are the department's current priorities, including programs and goals?
4. Are there current problems and issues your department is facing at this time?
5. What type of budget does this department have and how is it handled?

6. How is this department currently staffed?
7. Do you anticipate any turnover in the next six months?
8. Will the department be needing additional staff due to expansion or new business in the next six months?
9. What do you consider to be the ideal staffing pattern in this department?

To Find Out about a Particular Position:

1. Is this position newly created, or has it been held by someone in the past?
2. To whom does this position report?
3. Is there support staff available for someone in this position?
4. What are the expectations of the department for this position?
5. Whom do you see as being an ideal candidate for this position?
6. What is the promotional path of this position?
7. What can you tell me about the pay range for this position?

To Find Out How You Might Fit into This Organization and Department:
(You would first need to briefly discuss your background and skills.)

1. How do you see me fitting into this organization and department, given the needs and priorities of the organization and/or department? Where do you see my skills and background being utilized in this organization and/or department?
2. Would there be other individuals in this company who would be interested in the skills I have to offer and with decision-making power to hire? Would it be appropriate to contact them now?
3. I would truly appreciate any feedback on my resume and other suggestions you could make that would assist me with finding employment in my targeted area. Is there something I can improve on to help my application?

To Find Out about the Hiring Process:

1. What is the process the company uses to attract job applicants? Is it through ads, search firms, word-of-mouth referrals, other means?
2. What is the process once an applicant is being considered?
3. Are there any alternative ways of getting a job with this company? For example, do you hire interns or individuals to work on short-term projects?
4. What is the length of time for the selection process?
5. What do you feel are the special qualifications that would give a candidate on edge in the competition?

Making the Most of a Job Fair or Employer Showcase

Job fairs or employer showcases offer an excellent opportunity to develop and build your career network and to speak to employer representatives about internships and job opportunities. Some fairs can be quite large, with hundreds of employers staffing tables while thousands of job applicants or candidates mill about. It can be noisy and a bit overwhelming.

The Purpose of a Job Fair

Companies meet and screen large numbers of candidates. The fair provides an opportunity to increase the company's visibility and reputation. Recruiters collect resumes and make notes on the ones they want to follow-up with. Companies meet and screen large numbers of candidates to identify a select number of candidates for interview. The company's goal is to meet as many qualified candidates as possible. Your goal is to be one of those qualified candidates.

The Setup of a Job Fair

Typically, job fairs run three to four hours. Company representatives staff booths or tables, give out information, talk with candidates, and collect resumes. The reps talk about the company and screen potential candidates. Lists of participating employers are provided by the organizers of the event. Maps showing the location of each employer are also provided.

Tips for Working the Fair

- Know how the job fair is set up and how it works.
- Identify your career goals and objectives.
- Identify companies or organizations that interest you.

- Research the companies/organizations (mission, goals, product line, vision, etc.). Most companies have a website that provides a wealth of information about the company.
- Prepare your resume and have 50–100 copies ready to handout at the fair.
- Dress professionally.
- Be prepared to talk to the company rep about your interests, skills, and qualifications.
- Research the employers who will be participating.
- Make a target list of employers that you plan to talk with.
- Use the floor plan or map to locate your target companies.
- Systematically go and make contact with the reps.
- Display a positive attitude.
- Extend your hand (shake firmly).
- Collect their business card and ask if you can follow up.
- Give them a copy of your resume.
- Maintain eye contact.
- Listen.
- Speak clearly.
- Have a two to three minute opening.
- Ask for clarification.
- Demonstrate that you have done your research (knowledge of company).
- Demonstrate that you have thought out the question and know your story.
- Say thank you for their time.
- Be truthful.
- Follow-up.
- Write the company representative a thank you note, which should include:
  - A statement thanking him or her for their time and consideration.
  - A brief statement of how your goals, skills, and abilities will benefit the company.
  - Ask for an interview at their convenience
  - Attend career-related programs

Your 30-Second Highlight Clip

You are at a job fair and you see a company that you want to make contact with. Before you approach the employer representative at the table or booth, what are you going to say? Remember they are speaking with hundreds of other candidates or participants during the course of the fair. What can you say to be a person of interest? Your goal is to make a connection with the recruiter, get their business card, hand them your resume, and get them to agree to being contacted by you sometime after the fair. The trick is trying to give the recruiter a quick synopsis of your skills and qualifications and your interest in their organization. Before the fair, it is advisable to prepare and practice your highlight clip.

Your Personal Business Card

With the advancement of desktop publishing programs, it is easy to create your own professional business card to hand to employers and your network contacts. Don't overdo the card and load it up with too much information. It should be attractive and have your key selling points highlighted.

© Peter Jochems, 2009. Used under license from Shutterstock, Inc.

Sample Business Cards

Seeking an internship in business administration

William Efficient

345 Green Spring Drive
Jacksonville, FL 32256

Bachelor of Business Administration
Expected May 2012

(904) 555-7898   wefficient@aol.com

JESSICA JOBSEEKER
12345 Appletree Lane
Jacksonville, FL 32224
(904) 555-4354
jjobseek@mail.net

Bachelor of Science: Computer and Information
Science Expected May 2013

Seeking a position in computer programming

Key Discoveries

- The most effective way to get a job is through people you know (networking).
- Applying directly to organizations that interest you and following up is the second most effective job search method.
- Record keeping and follow-up activity are the keys to an effective job search.
- Want ads and Internet listing account for only about 14% of available jobs.
- Informational interviews are a great way to develop your network and to learn about various organizations and jobs.
- Job fairs are an excellent way to add hundreds of employers to your network and to have direct contact about jobs.
- Dressing professionally, being prepared, and having a 30-second highlight clip will help you make the most of a job fair.

Career Connections: Internet Links

Websites:
There are hundreds of online to job search resources. Here a few of the better ones:

www.onetcenter.org

www.acinet.org

www.employmentguide.com

www.employflorida.com

www.vault.com

www.careerbuilder.com

www.careersearch.com

www.monster.com

Jacksonville Job Websites:

www.myjaxchamber.com

www.worksourcefl.com

www.jaxjobs.com

Websites for Researching a Company:
Bloomberg: www.Bloomberg.com
Business.com: www.business.com
CEO Express: www.ceoexpress.com
Corporate Information: www.corporateinformation.com
CNN Money: http//money.cnn.com
Dunn and Bradstreet's Million Dollar Databases: www.dnbmdd.com/mddi
Forbes Lists: www.forbes.com/lists
Fortune 500: www.inc.com/500
Hoover's On-line: www.hoovers.com
Moody's: www.moodys.com
Standard & Poors: www.standardandpoors.com
The Corporate Library: www.thecorporatelibrary.com
The Street: www.thestreet.com
Thomas Register of American Manufacturers: www.thomasregister.com
Wall Street Journal Index: www.wsj.com

Using Social Networks in Your Job Search

The constant advances in technology have helped create ready-made networks of friends and contacts that can help you with your job search. There are a variety of social networks that can be used effectively.

On a **blog**, individuals can create and maintain a running commentary of their activities, thoughts, or happenings, including images and links to videos. Blogs allow readers or visitors to respond and post opinions or reactions. This interactive quality distinguishes this format from other media. The ability of readers to leave comments in an interactive format is an important part of many blogs.

LinkedIn was originally developed as a professional career networking tool. This site enables individuals to create and maintain lists of their network contacts. The network grows exponentially as other individuals add in and then include their contacts. This is a true networking site, bringing people together for the purpose of meeting their career goals. Individuals can post their photo and include a professional profile. LinkedIn sends out email updates to those individuals who are connected providing updates on networking activities.

Twitter is quickly becoming one of the more popular social network sites. Individuals can post messages on their Twitter page and either allow everyone to view them or restrict access to certain individuals. Individuals can subscribe to another individual's tweets and follow their daily activities.

Facebook is an interactive site that enables an individual to create their own Facebook page and allow full access to their page to selected friends and individuals or keep certain parts of their page open for all to see. Individuals can post photos and comments about their activities and interests. The system also allows individuals to post messages on the Facebook pages of friends in their network. The interactive nature of this site is very attractive to users.

MySpace is another interactive social site that enables individuals to create a profile page, post messages, and post photos. Access to the page can be controlled by the individual in terms of who can view information on the site. This site seems to have lost some of its star appeal as Facebook has quickly become the social site of choice.

Not all of the social networks will match up to your interests and your way of accessing and utilizing technology and applications. Check them out and choose the ones that you will enjoy working with; then start building your network of contacts and letting them know the types of jobs or internships you are seeking. Maintaining your network of contacts on these sites can be very time-consuming, so be prepared to schedule blocks of time for your social networks. More and more people, including employers and recruiters, are using these networks, so they are another resource you should consider using for your job search. It is estimated that over 80% of employers now use LinkedIn, Facebook, and Twitter to find new hires and to find out information about candidates.

Here Are Some Quick Tips for Using Social Media for Your Job Search:

1. **Identify the top companies that you want to work for.** This will allow you to target specific companies and make a professional presentation explaining why you are the right candidate. Avoid "spamming" people; the shotgun approach to job hunting has about a 3% response rate.

2. **Utilize search engines to identify employees of your target companies.** Search blogs, Facebook, Twitter, and other sites to find people who work for your target companies. Tailor a message to them and express your interest in the company. Try to establish communication with these people.

3. **Develop your "brand" and market yourself.** Launch a blog that focuses on your skills and interests. Coordinate the various social media that you are using—make sure all information is consistent and professional.

4. **Utilize Twitter to connect with employers.** Conduct Twitter searches, follow recruiters on your account, and then communicate with them. Be sure to have a completed profile and a link to more information (your LinkedIn account). Sites such as http://www.twiredjobs.com are designed to search Twitter feeds for job posts.

5. **Subscribe to blogs that also offer job listings.** Many of the larger blogs now have integrated job banks and job posting systems.

6. **Link your social media sites on your resume.** Be sure to include links to your blog and your accounts on LinkedIn, Facebook, etc. on your resume. Be sure your information (dates of employment, schools, employers, etc.) all matches on your resume and your social media sites.

7. **Be friendly and be willing to share information about yourself.** Get to know your online contacts and let them know about you. Always be courteous and professional.

8. **Be proactive.** Ask for help from your network of contacts. Let them know what you are looking for and ask them for leads on jobs in your field.

9. **Adjust your privacy settings to accept InMail on your LinkedIn account.** This enables recruiters to find you and communicate with you.

10. **Develop a Facebook page for your professional life.** Keep your personal Facebook page for "friends only" and not available for employers.

Name _____   Date _____

Use the following "test" to determine if you are ready to conduct a job search campaign.

__Yes   __No   1. Can you clearly state your career goals?

__Yes   __No   2. Can you identify specific job objectives?

__Yes   __No   3. Can you describe your greatest strengths?

__Yes   __No   4. Can you describe your greatest weakness?

__Yes   __No   5. Can you list five job skills relevant to your objective?

__Yes   __No   6. Reviewing your past experiences, can you identify five major accomplishments?

__Yes   __No   7. Have you identified your geographical target area for employment?

__Yes   __No   8. Have you joined any professional associations in your career field?

__Yes   __No   9. Can you name three career fields that would be a good match for you?

__Yes   __No   10. Can you name 10 types of organizations that might hire you?

__Yes   __No   11. Can you name 10 job titles that would be a good match for you?

__Yes   __No   12. Do you know five resources that can help you answer questions 10–11?

__Yes   __No   13. Can you name four resources that can help you identify employers?

__Yes   __No   14. Have you talked to at least three people who are employed in your field?

__Yes   __No   15. Can you name five employers to whom you have applied for work?

__Yes   __No   16. Have you developed a "network" of people who are familiar with your career?

__Yes   __No   17. Do you have more than advertised job ads as a source of job leads?

__Yes   __No   18. Is your resume targeted to the types of employers you are applying to?

__Yes   __No   19. Have you asked anyone for feedback on your resume?

__Yes   __No   20. Are your cover letters personalized and targeted to the employer?

__Yes   __No   21. When you apply, do you address your letter to a specific person?

__Yes   __No   22. Are you familiar with the organizational structure of employers?

__Yes   __No   23. Do you know what questions the employers are likely to ask?

__Yes   __No   24. Can you clearly state why you are interested in working for certain employers?

__Yes   __No   25. Have you developed a record keeping system to track your job search?

Add up your "Yes" answers for each question.

Total "Yes" responses: ____

SCORE: 20–25   You are on a roll! You will have that job in no time! Keep up the good work!

SCORE: 10–20   You are doing some things right, but you might want to meet with a job search counselor to discuss how to better organize your job search.

SCORE: 0–10   Uh, oh! You definitely could use some help. We suggest meeting with a job search counselor to help you get on track!

Name _____ Date _____

Develop a script for your highlight clip:

Hello, my name is _____

_____

_____

_____

_____

_____

_____

_____

_____

_____

_____

_____

Name _____   Date _____

Design your own personal business card (to be developed later with desktop publishing program).

Name _____   Date _____

Faculty Members:

1. _____

2. _____

3. _____

**Internship/Volunteer/Work Experience
Co-workers/Supervisor/Clients**

1. _____

2. _____

3. _____

| **Your Name:** |
| _____ |

Family Contacts

1. _____

2. _____

3. _____

4. _____

5. _____

Friends/Classmates

1. _____

2. _____

3. _____

4. _____

5. _____

Name _____   Date _____

Your Career Goal: _____

_____

_____

Name of Person Interviewed	Notes: How They Can Help Me	Phone Number/Email Address
1.		
2.		
3.		
4.		
5.		

Name _____   Date _____

Plans to enter the military or currently in the military	Had the same breakfast as you today	Is more likely to be honest with you than nice	Has been to jail	Has a medical doctor in their family (immediate or extended family)
Is an aunt/uncle	Never had a speeding ticket	Scored 1300 or higher on the SAT or 26 + on the ACT	Related to or friends with someone famous	Can sing better than contestants on *American Idol*
Wants a big family one day (4+ children)	Someone who left the country for spring break or summer	**BINGO (free square)**	Is an athlete at UNF	Has been on television
Plays a musical instrument	Has been on the radio	Related to a politician or worked for a politician	A female who is a sports fanatic	Wants to own their own business
Raised on a farm	Comes from a large family (5 or more children in family)	Favorite color is purple	Has an uncle named Bob	Owns property (land or a house)

CHAPTER
QUEST

At the end of this chapter
you should be able to:

- Understand the difference
  between the academic
  culture and the world of
  work

- Know what it means to be a
  professional

- Understand how to succeed
  in your new job

- Manage personal and
  professional relationships
  effectively

- Understand how you will be
  evaluated as a new
  employee

- Seek out professional
  development opportunities

- Research potential graduate
  and professional school
  programs

- Understand the graduate
  school admissions process

© Andresr, 2009. Used under license from Shutterstock, Inc.

Turning "Pro": From Academics to the World of Work

Congratulations! The time and energy spent on your job search has paid off, you've been offered a job, you've accepted, and now you are ready to start your career. The transition from academics to work is not always an easy one, and it really comes down to understanding what it takes to be successful in your new job and organization. The educational or campus culture is very different than the culture you will find in a work setting. As a new employee, you have yet to prove yourself, and you will need to pay attention to how you manage yourself in terms of getting established with your organization.

Usually, new employees are on probation for anywhere from 30 days to 6 months and are evaluated throughout that time period. A new employee whose work performance during the probation period has been rated as "unsatisfactory" can be terminated without much explanation or process. Extensive documentation is usually needed to terminate a long-term employee. Remember, first impressions are lasting impressions, and it is difficult to overcome a bad first impression. Your first year is the foundation for all subsequent years and the more solid that foundation is, the more likely you will have long-term success.

You probably had a varied and flexible schedule in school, but now you may be faced with a set schedule, such as a standard 8:00 a.m. to 5:00 p.m. work day. This can be a shock to one's system and can take a while to adjust to. Staying up until 2:00 or 3:00 a.m. or pulling an "all-nighter" before a work day probably won't work anymore.

In school, you probably made friends very quickly, but work settings are different and friendships take more time and more effort to develop. Although some companies encourage employees to socialize at employer-sponsored happy hours and social outings, others do little to foster a collegial environment.

Your Success as a New Professional

Being a professional is very different than being a student. It requires progressive, lifelong learning to continually and strategically better yourself and your situation. It includes the following:

- Specialized knowledge and extensive preparation
- High standards of performance and achievement
- High standards of ethics and integrity
- Strong commitment to work
- Ongoing training and study
- Acceptance of responsibility
- Sense of ownership of your work

Getting Started in Your New Job

The first impressions you make are very powerful and difficult to change. During the first few months on a job, you are creating an image of yourself. People will notice how you look, speak, act, and think. This is a time to put in the extra effort and create the image of someone who can produce.

How to Dress

Understand the dress code or culture of the organization and dress appropriately. Pay attention to what your coworkers and supervisors wear. You don't want to stand out as a nonconformist or nonteam player. As a "newbie," it is better to dress conservatively. After you are established, you can begin to make your own fashion statement.

© Philip Date, 2009. Used under license from Shutterstock, Inc.

Being a Team Player

Companies or organizations have rules so that all employees are treated fairly and equally. It is important to learn and abide by the rules. Know your organization's goals and purposes. In this way, you can help the organization achieve them and in so doing bring credit to yourself. Recognize the contributions of others. Look for ways to make new ideas work, not reasons they won't work. Know your organization's goals and purposes.

Working Relationships

Show you have potential. Make good impressions. Become a professional. Get to know your organization. Don't be a "know-it-all" or "college whiz kid." You need to earn the respect of your coworkers by what you do and accomplish. Managers/supervisors have different management styles. You need to adapt to their way of doing things not the other way around. Most problems encountered in a work setting revolve around working relationships and politics, not necessarily from insufficient skills. Listening is an important skill to develop when you are new. One of your strengths as a recent college graduate is your ability to learn. Be flexible, adaptable, and willing to jump in and help where needed. Never badmouth your organization, your supervisor, or your coworkers. Respect should be mutual and putting down others will usually come back to hurt you. Establish positive working relationships with those around you. It is up to you to take the initiative. Build a network of constructive, successful people in your workplace and communicate with them frequently. Build a solid working relationship with your boss. Don't be intimated by coworkers.

Demonstrate Your Abilities

Tackle your assignments with enthusiasm and make certain to check even the smallest details. Set realistic goals for yourself that show a pattern of success. Follow through on all assignments and even ask for more. Make certain that you have the skills and background to handle assignments. Ask for more direction if necessary. Get organized and have a daily to-do list. Learn your job and build professional respect and credibility. Convince them that they were right to hire you. Never present a problem without being able to present a viable solution. A strong work ethic is highly valued in any work setting.

Watch What You Say and Do

Learn the culture. How you used to do things in college or in different work settings is no longer relevant, and you need to understand how to get things done in your current situation. As in most social settings, avoid talking about religion, politics, etc. Speak positively about others and about your organization at every opportunity. Maintain a positive attitude no matter what the circumstances. Many of the jokes you heard and told in college might not be appropriate in a work setting. Be conservative, and do not use profanity. Avoid sexual comments or remarks and steer clear of sexual-oriented jokes.

Computer/Email Etiquette

Remember, your emails can become a written record. Always review your emails before sending them out to anyone. Check for typos, spelling, grammar, etc. Your emails reflect on you, and you want to maintain a positive reputation. Computer networks can be monitored, so save surfing the Internet, doing personal work, playing computer games, and sending jokes via email for after work on your home computer.

Respect Other People's Space

A conservative approach is always recommended when dealing with other people. Avoid touching, hugging, and other physical contact. Physical contact of any kind can often be misinterpreted by a coworker or colleague.

Punctuality/Time Management

Get to work early and stay late if necessary. Be visible to the people who have a say in your career growth. Return all calls promptly. Show up on time to meetings and other assignments. Be punctual. This means being on time for work, for meetings, for appointments, etc. Establish a reputation for reliability by completing assignments well and on time.

Accountability/Record Keeping

Record and communicate your contributions and achievements. They are the building blocks of your career. Your first six months will be critical to your success. Keep track of your work and productivity, including statistical data when possible. At evaluation time, producing a report on your accomplishments can ensure an outstanding rating.

Look for Professional Development Opportunities

Look for a mentor. Find a person in the organization who has had long-term success there and is well respected by others. You may already have a mentor in mind: a professor in your field of study or an older professional you're comfortable with. A mentor can help you focus and give you advice on how to stay on track. If you don't know anyone in your field, ask friends and acquaintances to recommend someone they think you'd get along with personally and professionally. Joining professional associations and using your alumni network are great ways to meet potential mentors. Your local Chamber of Commerce might offer networking opportunities and programs for young professionals.

© Dmitriy Shironosov, 2009. Used under license from Shutterstock, Inc.

Career Advancement: Managing Your Career

You should always keep your resume up-to-date, including any new professional development and training. You never know when a great new opportunity will present itself. Always evaluate your job and your career and look for future advancement. If going in to work puts a knot in your stomach, it might be time to look for a new job. If you are having problems with a supervisor or coworker, try to resolve the problem first, but if it persists, it might be time to move on. Use your company's resources to build skills, earn a degree, and generally make yourself more marketable. Use every experience as an opportunity to develop your skills and to develop important working relationships with people who can help advance your career. Look at the jobs other people are doing and network with them to position yourself for future career moves.

Being Evaluated

Many new employees are on "probation" when they first start and don't become permanent employees until they demonstrate that they can do the job, accomplish goals, and meet expectations. A probationary period can last anywhere from 30 to 90 days. Your work performance will be evaluated by your supervisor both formally and informally.

Your supervisor will be gathering information about your work performance from numerous sources including:

- Observation of how you work and your interaction with other employees.
- Statistical data and records that you keep and provide to your supervisor.
- Information you provide in one-on-one supervisory sessions and in staff meetings or group discussions.
- Verbal/written feedback from your coworkers, subordinates, colleagues, customers, etc. This could include letters, email, phone calls, and conversations.
- Written or formal evaluations for your work or programs. Depending on the nature of your work, you might be required to ask others to provide an evaluation: for example, if you conduct workshops, you would ask participants to complete an evaluation form.

The Supervisory Session

The evaluation session should always be approached as an opportunity to enhance performance. In conjunction with your supervisor, you should quantify goals, clearly stating how they will be measured with expected outcomes. Write goals to the level of "meets expectations" and then work towards the level of "exceeds" or "exceptional." Bring supporting information to your evaluation sessions. Discuss issues or concerns with your supervisor or supervisee as they arise so they may be resolved prior to an evaluation session. Learn how to receive constructive criticism. Listen, ask for clarification, and look for ways to improve your performance.

Evaluation Process and Guidelines

A typical evaluation process has several components:

1. Goal Setting
2. Review of Goals
3. Mid-Year Review
4. End-of-Year Evaluation (requires two sessions, allowing the supervisor and supervisee to review ratings and feedback and make revisions if necessary)

See Exercise 12.2: "Self-Evaluation: Rating Your Career" for a better understanding of evaluation criteria.

Going to Graduate or Professional School

Another aspect of managing your career might include working on an advanced degree. Before investing a lot of time, energy, and money in graduate school, you need to be fairly clear about whether or not graduate work is likely to help you meet your career goals. Here are some strategies for deciding on graduate school:

• Use your personal network to seek out names of recent alumni/ae who are attending or have recently attended graduate school and ask them about their experiences. How do they feel their choices about attending or not attending graduate school have affected their careers?
• Talk with faculty members in the discipline you are considering. What would they advise, and why? What kind of graduate work did they do, and how has it meshed with their goals?

© Andresr, 2009. Used under license from Shutterstock, Inc.

- Talk to members of professions that you are interested in potentially pursuing. Find out about their careers and their career preparation paths. Did they need a graduate degree to get where they are? How has having/not having a graduate degree helped/hurt them? What do they wish they had done differently, and why?

Graduate Schools versus Professional Schools

Typically, "professional schools" are considered to include schools of medicine, law, dentistry, veterinary medicine, engineering, architecture, and several other specialized fields. "Graduate school" is the term used to refer to most other types of postundergraduate programs—for example, programs in psychology, history, art, etc.

Graduate School Is Not Like Undergraduate School

Graduate studies are much more tightly focused around a specific academic discipline than undergraduate studies. It is important that you both deeply love your chosen field of study and are committed to working on it night and day for an extended period of time. Your day-to-day life in graduate school will probably be very different from your undergraduate years, and your energies will need to be focused almost entirely on your academic work. If you have or are anticipating having a family at the same time you will be in school, it is important to recognize how difficult it may be to negotiate all of your needs simultaneously.

How Do I Choose the School That's Right for Me?

It is important to know that not all schools will offer programs in the discipline you want to study, nor are all schools that do offer such programs equally "good." You need to know what those differences are and how they match your own learning style and preferences. Here are some questions to ask yourself:

- What are the key characteristics you hope to find in a graduate school, and why are these characteristics important to you?
- Are there any schools or programs that you have an interest in at this time? If not, do you need to do some more exploring, or should you consider options other than continuing on to graduate school at this point in time?
- How important to you are location and size in selecting an institution?
- What other kinds of institutional resources are important to you, and why?
- What kinds of students and faculty members do you wish to work with, and why? What kinds of characteristics are undesirable in fellow students and in faculty, and why?

© 2399, 2009. Used under license from Shutterstock, Inc.

Criteria for Choosing a Program

There are many factors to consider when selecting a school. It is extremely important to remember that you are selecting a program and a school, just as much as the program and school will be selecting you. Some important factors you should consider and weigh when selecting a program are listed below.

Reputation of the School

Probably the single most important criterion to consider is the quality of the overall program and of instruction. In addition to the general reputation of the school, you need to consider the reputation of the particular department or program in which you are interested. To find out about the prestige of particular departments, you should talk to faculty in the discipline you plan to pursue.

Reputation of the Faculty

It is very helpful to enter a program with highly respected scholars in their field. How do you find out how prestigious the faculty are? One way is to get a list of the faculty members' names in the department in which you are interested, then run a quick search through the literature in your field. Are these people actively publishing and presenting at conferences? Is their work cited by other scholars working in the same field? Are they names you've run across in your own studies?

Accessibility of Faculty

Equally important, you need to determine how accessible those faculty are to graduate students. A program may be filled with internationally known scholars who never meet or work with graduate students. You can often get valuable information about these issues from graduate students already in the department. Typically, if you call a department and explain that you are potentially interested in their program, they can provide the names of graduate students who would be willing to talk with you about it. Follow up, and call those students. They can often give you the "inside scoop" that isn't available from the department's or school's literature.

Admission Standards

Another important factor is the program's admission standards. Are they taking everyone who applies, or are they selective? If they are selective, what are the criteria they consider important in selecting their students? At what level, and by whom, are selections made?

Program Accreditation

It is essential to know by whom the program is accredited. You do *not* want to earn a degree from a program that is not properly accredited, for a variety of reasons. Perhaps the most important is that if you are in a professional program (e.g., in dentistry, in mental health) that is not accredited, you might be unable to gain certification or licensure to practice your profession after graduation. If you are unclear about what kinds of accreditation are important in your future career field, find out from faculty here, and/or by writing to state accreditation boards in your field of interest.

Program Requirements

You need to know what courses and other learning experiences (e.g., internships, field experiences, etc.) are required to complete the graduate degree you are contemplating. All of these requirements affect the amount of time required to complete the program, and may affect your choice of one program over another.

Time to Complete the Program

One very important thing to find out is the average length of time required to complete the program. It is pretty obvious that a master's degree should take less time to complete than a Ph.D. The time to complete a Ph.D. in a particular field might range as much as four years at one school to 12 years at another.

Number of Students Who Finish

You also need to know the number of students who complete the degree program in which you're interested each year. You want to enter a program where students do successfully complete their degrees. You do want a program that offers you a reasonable chance of success at finishing your degree in some reasonable length of time.

Size of the Institution and Size of the Department

Both small departments and large ones have their relative advantages and disadvantages. Small departments may offer a higher degree of collegiality, but fewer course selections and fewer opportunities to engage in research. Large departments may have more resources and more opportunities, but a greater likelihood of you as an individual getting "lost in the shuffle."

Resources

How good is the library? You want to ensure that the schools you are considering do have good library facilities. The lack of such facilities can make completing a thesis or dissertation incredibly difficult. If you are going into a program in science or medicine, how modern and complete are the laboratories and equipment? Given a choice, it is preferable to go to a school that has state-of-the-art resources, to ensure that you acquire the essential skills, and knowledge in that field.

Support Services

Do they have good health care facilities, or do you have to provide your own (often expensive) insurance and find your own doctor? Is health care available for both you and your partner or spouse, and/or for your other dependents? Do they provide counseling, or is that another resource you must locate on your own if you need it? If you have children, is there a good daycare or preschool program available for young children, and/or good local schools available for older children? Are there any programs to provide career services to your partner or spouse, if that is desirable?

How Much Does It Cost and How to Pay for It

Since it is fairly likely that you will personally be footing most of the bill for your graduate education, you will want to check very carefully on the costs associated with the program. You should know that graduate school costs more than undergraduate education, often imposes a heavy debt burden (possibly adding to the debt you are already carrying), and usually has less financial aid available than is available at undergraduate institutions. However, you shouldn't automatically assume that you won't be able to afford graduate school—there are a number of sources of aid that are available to help with costs, several of which are described below. What you do need to do is engage in a realistic evaluation of costs and of available resources.

Sources of Financial Support

There are three basic kinds of financial support available to support graduate education:

- Education-related salaries, typically in the form of teaching or research assistantships, but sometimes including administrative assistantships and dormitory or counseling assistantships
- Outright grants and fellowships
- Government or institutional loans or loans from private sources

Not all of these kinds of support are equally available in all schools or to all students, so you must again do some homework on what is available from the programs that interest you.

The Graduate Admissions Process

All graduate schools and departments have some kind of admissions requirements. Usually these will include a minimum GPA, particular scores or score ranges on one or more standardized tests (e.g., the GRE, MCAT, LSAT, GMAT, etc.), official transcripts from your undergraduate institution, letters of recommendation, a thoughtful application essay, and a nonrefundable application fee. Some schools will also ask for samples of previous academic work, some will require the completion of particular courses in an academic area or completion of a particular major (although this is becoming less common), and some will require a personal interview. Where an interview is required, applicants will typically have to pay for their travel and other expenses themselves.

Finding Out about a Program's Admissions Standards

Many students wonder how tough it is to get into a good graduate program. Realistically, competition is tough everywhere, and your qualifications will be carefully compared with those of other potential admits. Typically, students with high GPAs, excellent test scores, and wonderful letters of recommendation will be admitted to very good programs, although perhaps not to all of the programs to which they apply. The important thing is to carefully evaluate what the standards are for each program and how well you match them.

The Application Essay

You will also have to invest considerable time, energy, and effort in writing the best possible application essay (sometimes called a "candidate statement" or "statement of professional intent"). If the program to which you are applying does require such an essay, you may be sure that they consider it very seriously as a criterion for admission, and it is essential that you also consider it seriously. You should consult with faculty on how best to approach this task, and get their feedback on one or more drafts. These personal statements are used by the graduate schools not only to evaluate your writing ability, but to evaluate your commitment to (and to some degree, understanding of) the field you wish to pursue. They are typically not the place to be cute or creative, but to show careful thoughtfulness about who you are, what your goals are, and how those goals are connected to the graduate pursuits you are considering.

Required Tests

The most common standardized tests required for admission to various kinds of graduate programs in the U.S. are the Graduate Records Exam (GRE), the Graduate Management Admissions Test (GMAT), and the Miller Analogies Test (MAT). Professional schools more typically require the Law School Admission Test (LSAT), the Medical College Admissions Test (MCAT), and the Dental Admission Test (DAT). In case you don't already know this, the deadlines for registering to take these tests are far in advance (usually several months) of the actual test dates, and most are given only a few times a year. Based on your research, you should know exactly which tests are required by the various programs you plan to apply to. Check this carefully, then prepare for and make arrangements to take the tests that are required by the programs you plan to apply to.

Letters of Recommendation

Many representatives of graduate schools indicate that candidates' letters of recommendation are what make or break them in terms of admissions—yet many potential graduate students don't appear to understand the importance of these letters. While good letters alone won't get you into a program, without them you almost certainly will not gain admission.

How Many, and from Whom?

Different graduate schools will require different numbers of recommendations, with the standard range between three and five. Similarly, whether or not your recommenders should all be faculty members depends partly on the requirements of the particular schools to which you are applying, on whether you have engaged in other career-related work (e.g., internships or summer jobs) in which your supervisor could provide an appropriate recommendation, on whether you have completed research projects which a knowledgeable professional might comment upon, and on many other factors. As a very general rule, most (if not all) of your recommendations should come from faculty members, but it does depend on the requirements of the specific schools and on your own background.

How Do You Actually Get Them?

The groundwork for getting good recommendations actually needs to be laid throughout your undergraduate career. Hopefully, you have gotten to know several of your professors well enough that they are able to comment knowledgeably and positively on your abilities and your potential. If you have not developed such relationships, you need to work now and engage in a genuine conversation about your involvement in that person's class or research or both, and how that involvement is related to your goals and future plans. Talk to potential recommenders about what you want to do, and why you want to do it. Ask if they feel they know your work and abilities well enough to write a letter of recommendation for you, and if they would be willing to do so. If the professor agrees to write a letter for you, you should provide her or him with a statement of your goals, objectives, and purpose (related to your application), a curriculum vitae or resume, the recommendation forms provided by the graduate schools (if any), stamped envelopes, and a list of names and addresses of schools and their deadlines.

Deadlines

As you research each institution of potential interest to you, keep a file noting their admissions requirements and their deadlines for application. Although deadlines vary from school to school, most are in early January or slightly later. Some schools do, however, have deadlines as early as late November, so be sure to check carefully. Next to the absolute necessity that all application materials are filled out clearly, completely, and accurately, the most important piece of advice in terms of applying is to *get your materials in on time!* Check with the graduate school *at least* three weeks before their final deadline and ask whether your materials have been received; they'll be happy to check and tell you whether there is anything missing from your file.

A Final Word of Advice

What you need to do right now is collect information. That means talking with people, reading in the library, and finding out as much as possible to help you make the best-informed decision that is possible. Appendix A below will help you focus on specific questions that you need to find or develop answers for and suggests strategies for finding the answers to those questions. Talk to everyone, read everything, and enjoy the process—yes, it's stressful, but it can also be one of the most rewarding things you will ever do.

References

Green, H. & Minton, R. (1989). *Beyond the Ivy Wall: 10 Essential Steps to Graduate School Admission.* Boston: Little, Brown and Company.

Wallace, W., Wagner, C., & Siska, N. (1990). *For Your Action: A Practical Job Search Guide for the Liberal Arts Student.* Bloomington, IN: Arts & Sciences Career Planning and Placement Center, Indiana University.

Key Discoveries

- The world of work is very different from the world of academics and requires specific job skills.
- As a new employee, you are always being evaluated on a wide range of criteria.
- Managing relationships is one of the keys to success.
- Effective communication is also a critical aspect of success as a new employee.
- It is important to establish yourself as a productive and professional worker.
- You are responsible for your career, including seeking out new and better career opportunities.
- Graduate and Professional studies might be a necessary part of your career development.
- Before committing your time and resources, it is important to research and compare schools and programs.

Career Connections: Internet Links

- http://www.career-success-for-newbies.com/work-attitudes.html
- http://careerplanning.about.com/od/workplacesurvival/workplace_survival_and_success.htm
- http://www.petersons.com
- http://www.gradschools.com
- http://www.gradview.com
- http://colleges.usnews.rankingsandreviews.com/usnews/edu/college/rankings/rankindex_brief.php
- http://www.petersons.com/finaid/file.asp?id=780&path=ug.pfs.financial

Name _____ Date _____

Using your most recent job as your frame of reference, check all that apply:

Dependability/Attendance

- [ ] Meets commitments and achieves stated goals/objectives thoroughly and on time
- [ ] Reports to work, meetings, and programs on time
- [ ] Follows through on assignments, with exception of conflicting priorities
- [ ] Works beyond set working hours *as needed*
- [ ] Follows guidelines and procedures when requesting leave

Communication

- [ ] Listens effectively
- [ ] Responds clearly and directly
- [ ] Prepares clear and concise reports or records
- [ ] Gives or explains instructions and ideas to others including (students, alumni, administrators, faculty, staff, coworkers, and other constituents)
- [ ] Creates an environment for open communication

Job Knowledge

- [ ] Understands job duties and responsibilities
- [ ] Participates in professional development opportunities
- [ ] Understands and operates office equipment and software and technology
- [ ] Understands and aligns plans with divisional and departmental mission and values
- [ ] Keeps current with changes affecting individual job responsibilities

Accountability/Time Management/Productivity

- [ ] Communicates calendar/schedule changes promptly to supervisor
- [ ] Effectively manages job duties
- [ ] Handles all record keeping (logs) in a timely manner
- [ ] Knows, understands, follows, and enforces all University and Departmental policies and procedures
- [ ] Determines and manages unexpected priorities effectively

Name _____   Date _____

The following questions were designed to help you think about your job, career progress, and plans for future improvement. Answer the following questions:

1. What do I consider to be the important abilities which my job requires?

2. What are some aspects of my job that I like best? That I like least?

3. What are the ways in which my supervisor can help me do my job better?

4. In what aspects of my job do I feel I need more experience and training?

5. What are my major accomplishments for the past year?

6. What have I done for my personal and professional development?

7. Are there any changes I would like to see made in my job which would improve my effectiveness?

8. Are all of my capabilities being utilized in my present position? If not, how can they be better utilized?

9. What are specific things I need to do in the next year for my own development?

10. What are my long-range plans? What type of work do I see myself doing 5 years from now? How am I preparing myself for this work?

Exercise 12.3: Evaluating Your Job and Employer

Name _____   Date _____

You are in a new job and a new organization. Did you make the right decision to accept this job? Are you happy? Do you plan to stay in this job? Below is a checklist to help you evaluate your current work situation.

Job Satisfaction Checklist

Directions: Consider your job in terms of the work satisfaction it offers. Place a check or X to answer yes or no.

	YES	NO
Do I enjoy working with my future coworkers, supervisors, and/or supervisees?		
Do I have a good opportunity to express myself on the job?		
Is the working environment satisfactory?		
Am I fully using my primary skills?		
Is there sufficient diversity and challenge?		
Do I get the kind of feedback I require to actually see the results of my efforts?		
Is there an opportunity to learn and expand?		
Is the commute to and from work within satisfactory limits?		
Are there open avenues of communication?		
Am I able to dress comfortably?		
Am I able to get value from my work to the extent that I make contributions?		
Am I motivated and satisfied with the ultimate purpose of the organization?		
In terms of work pressure, is there opportunity close to any of my "dream jobs"?		
Do I really want to do this kind of work?		
Is the salary and benefit package satisfactory?		
Add total number of boxes checked		

If you checked fewer than eight boxes, you need to look for opportunities to increase your satisfaction level:
- Seek out professional development opportunities (workshops, training seminars, etc.)
- Utilize employee assistance programs (counseling, career advising, etc.)
- Serve on committees (develop team skills, take on leadership roles, work with other departments)
- Ask your supervisor to schedule regular supervisory meetings
- Look for opportunities for advancement or promotion to higher-level positions

Name _____   Date _____

Using the following scale: 5 = Excellent   4 = Very Good   3 = Good   2 = Fair   1 = Poor
to rate graduate or professional schools programs. Add your own criteria in spaces at bottom:

Criteria	Graduate School #1	Graduate School #2	Graduate School #3
Reputation of School			
Reputation of Faculty			
Accessibility of Faculty			
Admissions Standards			
Program Accreditation			
Program Requirements			
Time to Complete the Program			
Number of Students who Finish			
Size of Institution			
Size of Department			
Resources			
Support Services			
Financial Aid			